SORRY 'BOUT THAT

SORRY 'BOUT THAT

A TRIBUTE TO BURLESQUE

Hal Sisson

Llumina Press

To Jim Robertshaw, a good friend and a
fine actor of many talents,

and to all the Peace Players

ACKNOWLEDGEMENTS

This book does not pretend to cover all the shows and revues of a burlesque, vaudeville or music hall nature in Alberta and British Columbia since World War II. In the process, a lot of humour will undoubtedly be missed and a great many people who deserve mention will be left out. Finding the exact source or authorship of vintage comedic material is a daunting, if not impossible task. I've done my best to give credit where due, and bear sole responsibility for any omissions or errors.

Once again I want to express my heartfelt appreciation to editor Clare Thorbes (whose leg appears on the cover) and editor and photographer Bjorn Stavrum, both of Salal Press, for their support and advice; and to Wil Wong of Postcript Design for pulling together the cover. Thanks also to scriptwriter and filmmaker Diane Farnsworth for her informative submission on Fran Dowie; to Verna Smith (formerly Verna Moore) for her memories of Jerry Gosley; to Howard (Woody) Woodland of Butchart Gardens fame, and to Don Weaver, Julian Packer, Jill Cairns, Bill Pobuda, Lindy Sisson and Claude Campbell for sharing their *Sorry 'bout That* memories. Dwayne Rowe, my legal partner in Sisson & Rowe, appeared in the inaugural 1967-68 season of *Sorry 'bout That*. A standup entertainer par excellence, Dwayne came up with the name of the revue, which was derived from the expression commonly used by Don Adams in the television series *Get Smart*.

Sincere thanks to my wife Doreen for her support and understanding and to every other Peace Player who appeared in our many shows.

No revue can be successful without the dedicated, active and enthusiastic hard work of an entire complement of people. Not only the actors, directors and choreographers, but also the set designers and constructors, musical directors and pit musicians, the makeup artists, the costume designers and staff, the light and sound technicians, the rehearsal pianists, prop people, front-of-house, publicity and ticket sales personnel and, if you're operating a bar in conjunction with the show, the bartenders and servers. At the back of the book I've listed the more than five hundred people who contributed to the popularity of *Sorry 'bout That* over the years. The list includes many couples, like Mike and Anne Arnold, Brian and Jen Imray (both these couples met while performing in the show), Chet and Kathi Gilmore, Elaine and Ed Mills, Ernie and June Skip, Malcolm and Donna Sokoloski, Don and Margot Weaver, Jim and Karen Weaver and Mike and Wilma Watson. You guys know who you are and that you were indispensable and a joy to work with.

CONTENTS

INTRODUCTION

On the chest of a barmaid from Wales,
Was tattooed the prices of ales;
And on her behind, for the sake of the blind,
Was the same information in Braille!

This book is dedicated to the art of burlesque theatre, training ground for such comedic stars as Phil Silvers, Benny Hill, Red Buttons, Jackie Gleason, Fanny Brice, Bert Lahr, Red Skelton, Abbott and Costello, Groucho Marx, W.C. Fields, Rags Ragland and many others. Canadian talent that came out of vaudeville or burlesque included Johnny Wayne and Frank Shuster, Dave Broadfoot, Jerry Gosley, Charlie Farquharson, Fran Dowie and Woody Woodland. All were graduates of the baggy-pants, putty-nose college, where they learned their business thoroughly.

In the heyday of the art, burlesque theatres dotted North America from coast to coast: the Orpheums, the Gaietys and the Empires, with the most famous being Minsky's. Great Britain enjoyed an equivalent entertainment form called music hall, spawning such long-lived programs as the Benny Hill Show.

Strippers were a later addition to burlesque and stripping produced some illustrious ecdysiasts: Lily St. Cyr, Ann Corio, Margie Hart, Sherry Britton, Tempest Storm, bombshell Ann Sothern and Gypsy Rose Lee. There was also Rose La Rose, Venus De Lovely, Margie Kelly and Blue Sapphire, the Gem of Burlesque. Even ones called Ginger Snaps or Ole Galore, the Mexican Spitfire.

Burlesque is enjoying a resurgence, and will likely provide, once again, an invaluable training ground for future comedic talent in the entertainment industry.

Let's step back in time and relive the memories, the laughter and the pleasures of a visit to a burlesque show. Admittedly, burlesque skits do not read nearly as well as when played on stage by competent comedians. But they're forever funny and there's enough material here to more than supply a burlesque revue if anyone wishes to stage one. Just add a good-looking chorus line, *sans* strippers.

Burlesque had its earliest beginnings in Renaissance Italy with the *commedia dell'arte*, in which the players would improvise freely on a given theme. The tempo and spontaneity of this type of humour became the backbone of the burlesque sketch. Some of the sketches included in this book have become classics, like the delightful set piece intermission pitch with candy butchers and hucksters touting art studies in France, designed to appeal to broad-minded people.

Theatre is a group enterprise, even if you're performing a single, because you need to collaborate with producers, composers, directors, set designers and managers. This was certainly true of vaudeville, which consisted of broad, slapstick humour and was full of specialty acts, dialecticians and malapropians. The comics needed great self-assurance to pull off these performances, and many acts, particularly those featuring eccentric comedy, required a straight man.

In the 1940s, Benny Bell, a mysterious, elfin old vaudevillian, wrote and recorded a so-called dirty song called Shaving Cream. The song enjoyed a revival in 1975 and can still provide some good belly laughs in today's ever more permissive age. Laughs are an answer to the world's problems, to the continual war, the oil crisis, global warming, rule by corporations and other related shit. That's a word for which Benny Bell substituted the words "shaving cream".

According to promoter Bruce Morrow, Benny began his theatrical career in the 1920s, when New York movie houses sponsored amateur nights for neighbourhood talent. Since many theatres had little local talent, they hired professional amateurs furnished by small booking agents who paid the pros a few dollars and collected any prize money. Benny Bell was also a songwriter, devising pieces for the jukeboxes that had just been introduced.

The jukeboxes were placed in bars and cocktail lounges, which gave Benny the chance to write lyrics that were slightly risqué by the standards of the day. He penned naughty songs like Take a Ship for Yourself, A Goose for My Girl, Wading in the Water, Everybody Likes My Fanny, The Tattooed Lady and the aforementioned Shaving Cream, in 1946. Here's a sample verse of the latter, in the best tradition of traditional North American burlesque and music hall humour:

I have a sad story to tell you,
It may hurt your feelings a bit,
Last night when I walked into my bathroom,
I stepped in a big pile of—
SHAVING CREAM, be nice and clean,
Shave every day and you'll always look keen!

The setting for *Sorry 'bout That*, western Canada's longest-running burlesque revue, has been described, especially in winter, as:

Cold as a frog in an ice-bound pool
Cold as the end of an Eskimo's tool
Cold as a monkey with balls of brass
Cold as a man with an aluminum ass
Cold as the hair on a polar bear's bum
Colder than that, and that's going some!
Western Canada, my home!

The skits and comedy sketches in this book, along with many other tried and true traditional American burlesque and British music hall routines, were all performed by the Peace Players theatrical group of northern Alberta as musical revues, including the *de rigueur* chorus line and band. No strippers were involved, but the beautiful chorus line was retained.

Intrigued? Well, you will be!

THE BURLESQUE CAR SKIT

The bee is such a busy soul,
He has no time for birth control;
And that is why in times like these,
There are so many sons of bees.

Some comics can just step out on a stage and wing it, literally make up the humour as they chat with the audience. Zany guys like Jonathan Winters, Steve Martin and Robin Williams all have that rare and awesome kind of brain and talent. Woe betide the average comic who tries the same approach.

Still, most comedians know exactly what they're going to say and do, even if it's untried material. If the new stuff isn't working, they can fall back on the tried and true, which they've thoroughly rehearsed in advance.

It pays to calculate the risks and try to figure out whose butts are in the seats. Every audience is different and therefore unpredictable, so you can never be sure what will make them laugh. What may be funny one night might not work the next.

Physical conditions can also affect a performance. You might have to tell front-of-house to turn up the heat, because there's nothing worse than an audience that's chilly, when you're the guy who's supposed to warm them up.

For twenty years I produced and performed in *Sorry 'bout That* in Peace River, Alberta. If I wasn't a little nervous just before the band stopped and the spotlight hit the curtain break, I knew I was going to come out flat. Standing in the wings, I used to lick my lips as I waited. I'd wonder if that was sweat sliding down from my armpits. Was there hair growing on my tongue?

My right hand on the curtain break, I'd watch for stage manager Don Weaver to give me the heads-up, then I'd be on with whatever routine I was doing, maybe something like this:

"Ladies and gentlemen—I see there are a lot of celebrities here tonight *(pause)* and if you'll look around the room I'm sure you'll recognize each other. . . Now, it's not only a great honour for us to appear here tonight, it's a goddamned inconvenience. . . Just kidding. Speaking of honour, maybe we should talk a bit about that. There's only two types of honour: get honour and stay honour! Here's a poem on the subject:

She offered her honour, and he honoured her offer,
And all night long it was honour and offer!

"Perhaps you're wondering how I keep in such good physical shape. I used to drink some Orange Tang every day. Now, that has a lot of vitamin C in it, but now I make my own Tang and I make it out of prunes. Orange Tang is all right but I kinda go for a little Prunetang now and then. . .

"We're sincere in bringing you a show of burlesque-style humour—about as sincere, actually, as Elizabeth Taylor when she says 'Ouch!' on her honeymoon. . . but enough of the preamble, before you believe I'm as full of crap as a ninety-pound robin. . . "

I'd settled into a groove and stood waiting in the wings for a skit to end. I wanted to watch the chorus line do their next number on stage. Three of the girls were gathered in the same spot waiting to go on. The skit contained the line, "Where's Pandora's box?" Denise, standing next to me, whispered, "About six inches below her belly-button!" This broke me up, and I decided we should work that line into the skit.

The dance number the chorus was about to do was called T'ain't No Sin to Take off Your Skin and Dance Around in Your Bones.

The chorus girls were dressed in black hoods and body stockings. The outline of a skeleton was painted on the back of the costume in white fluorescent paint. We used black light or flashbulbs to enhance the skeletal effect. Several times during the dance, cued to the lyrics, the girls quickly turned to face the curtain and all the audience saw was a row of dancing skeletons. Great number, if the technicalities and choreography were handled correctly.

The painting of the skeleton on the body stockings couldn't be done properly until the chorus girl had wriggled into what originally looked like an impossible fit, but could be accomplished because of the stretchy material of the body stocking. The painting job was much coveted by the more enthusiastic among the stagehands, who pictured themselves lingering artistically over the black-clad female bodies on the dressing room floor.

During my time with the Peace Players, several marriages came about because of just such situations. Recruiting a chorus line in a smallish town and trading area was a fun challenge, but after a few shows it ceased to be a problem. The recruits were young housewives and single secretaries, many of whom had always wanted to dance in a chorus line. They didn't need much previous experience.

The real problem was finding an able choreographer who could work within the limits of the available talent. For nearly ten years the show benefited from the talent of Judy Calvert, a dance teacher who had experience at the CNE in Toronto. She had married a Mountie who was later stationed at High Prairie, and was only too pleased when the unexpected opportunity of a burlesque revue with a chorus line sprang up in the unlikely setting of Peace River, three hundred miles north of Edmonton in the northern boondocks of Alberta.

Later there was Laura Gunning, who had ballet experience, Kathi Gilmore, Andre Brodeur, my daughter Lindy Sisson—when she became old enough and dance-wise enough to choreograph—Sheila Phimester and Brenda Marean. At the age of fifteen, Lindy had the ability and diplomacy to teach women five to ten years older than herself to perform the dance routines and fit into the overall requirements of the show.

On a flight from Edmonton to Peace River one day, I was sitting next to a young lady, one of our best dancers. She told me she didn't think she could dance with the company any longer. She was engaged to marry a young Mountie from the Peace River detachment, and he had indicated that he didn't like her performing and showing off her feminine charms in a chorus line.

Well, I knew this chap had been squiring her about for a couple of years, and that he had in fact been first attracted to her beauty while attending the show. I also knew that he played for the Peace River Stampeders in the North Peace hockey league, and that at every game he demonstrated his manly body and hockey skills to the adoring fans in attendance.

I was a defence lawyer in private practice and had handled a good many divorces over the years. I didn't consider myself a marriage counsellor by any means, but the divorce act stipulated that a lawyer should at least make some attempt to establish that the dissolution of the marriage was really necessary.

"You really like to dance, don't you?" I asked the girl. "And it is your hobby?"

She replied in the affirmative.

"Then you'd better get it established right now," was my advice. "Otherwise he'll always be telling you what you can and can't do. And after a while that doesn't sit very well. You'll have to either shut up and put up with a dictatorial attitude or get out. Best to establish your own space to start with. May save you some heartache later. Or maybe tell him you'll give up dancing if he agrees to stop playing hockey and prancing around the rink for the benefit of the female fans. He'll get the point."

They got married and she stayed on in the chorus line. So I hope it worked out well for both of them.

At one point in the show, I had to change into baggy pants gear (loud tie and sports jacket, pork-pie fedora with narrow brim) and get out into a seat in the audience along the side wall, ready for my part in an act I picked up from an old-time comedian named Irving Benson, who was working in Las Vegas back in the 1950s and '60s.

Irving had come up through the vaudeville and burlesque circuits and was playing in large and small shows in Vegas. On one of my trips there, Benson was staying at the same Vegas motel complex. The Bali H'ai, I think, behind the Desert Inn. After I got to know him a bit, he sold me some old-time burlesque scripts.

The car skit was one of his favourites. I certainly enjoyed performing it with my long-time comic partner Bill Seaman, also a great actor, singer and straight man. The girls who played the female parts were my wife Doreen, Pearl Baldwin, Elaine Mills, Linda Pelchat and others. I've reproduced the script in the following pages.

A Place to Park the Car

CHARACTERS: MC; Comic; Girls A and B.
PROPS: A big, flat-sided cardboard painted mock-up of an old-fashioned touring car with one large or two smaller doors that open and shut, or just split the car prop in half to allow "entry" into the car by the actors.

MC: (*Comes out stage centre and announces that he's going to sing several songs for the edification of the audience, then starts into a song*)
Comic: (*From down in the audience seats, with mike hook-up if possible, after a few bars or an appropriate time lapse*) You don't think I'm going to stick around to hear you sing two or three hundred songs, do you?
MC: It might grab you!
Comic: If you do, you're out of your cotton-pickin', chicken-pluckin', money-grubbin', glue sniffin', mustang-bangin' mind, I'll tell you.
MC: Look, I've only got five minutes up here to make a fool of myself—you've got all night and a head start besides.
Comic: All right, you'd get more laughs if you invited everybody into the back room to watch you take a shower."
MC: I wish we had more lights. (*Light man moves spot off MC onto comic*) Oh, it's you, Hal. Look, if you've got something to tell the people, go ahead.
Comic: Well, incidentally, folks, I just finished a book about income tax, dedicated to the department of national revenue—so buy it. (*To MC*) Have you read it, Bill?
MC: No. What do you call it?
Comic: Up Your Bracket! (*To crowd*) "And if the laughs don't pick up, up yours, too… I'll tell you that right now."
MC: Hey, can't you see I'm trying to sing?
Comic: Awright, you're not bothering me."
MC: Hey! You're bothering everybody, don't you know your seat's in the back?
Comic: It sure as hell would look funny anyplace else. . . Say, Bill, I just made a killing in the market. . . I shot the manager of the IGA.
MC: Look, for a guy your size, you do make a lot of noise.
Comic: Oh?
MC: Yeah, you're not that big, you know, you could get clobbered.
Comic: You think I'm small now?

MC: Yeah.

Comic: Would you believe it, when I was born, I only weighed a pound and a half!

MC: A pound and a half? How did you live?

Comic: I sold newspapers. . . Folks, this is it. If you're waiting for us to get hot—we don't do anything else, hey?

MC: Yep!

Comic: You know, come to think of it, I've heard you sing a couple of times.

MC: Oh, you have?

Comic: You're not so bad.

MC: Thank you.

Comic: I only got one criticism.

MC: What's that?

Comic: You're standing too close to the microphone.

MC: Oh, I'm too close to the microphone?

Comic: Yeah.

MC: How far back would you like me to be?

Comic: Got a car?

MC: Do you know you're ignorant, miserable and exasperating?

Comic: No, but hum a few bars and I may get it. . .

MC: Say, where's your wife now?

Comic: She's not in this show, boy. My wife happens to be out of town for a while. Matter of fact, she's visiting her weirdo brother.

MC: What does he do?

Comic: He's a milkman.

MC: What's so weird about that?

Comic: You show me a milkman who wears high-heeled shoes and I'll show you a dairy queen. . .

MC: So your wife's out of town. And what do you do?

Comic: I manage to cheat a little. Last night I went to a dance with Linda, Dorothy and Fido.

MC: Linda, Dorothy and Fido? Fido's a dog!

Comic: If you think Fido's a dog, you shoulda seen Linda and Dorothy. . .

MC: What the hey! Why don't you come up here on stage? Come on Hal, come up here! (*Comic comes up on stage*)

MC: Say, you did say your wife was outta town?

Comic: Yeah.

MC: That's a coincidence, so's mine.

Comic: Well, what the hell are we doing here?

MC: I dunno.

Comic: Let's get a couple of broads and go someplace.

MC: That's a wonderful idea, but I've got no transportation.

Comic: There's no sweat there, I got a car.

MC: Where?

Comic: Right back here. (*A cardboard mock-up of a car is behind the first traveller curtain*)

MC: (*Turns*) Back here? Let's see it. (*Surprised as traveller curtain opens, revealing the car*)

Comic: Ain't my car beautiful?

MC: Wheee!

Comic: Tell you what, let's move it down front so everybody can see it. (*They move the mock-up forward on the stage*)

MC: What did you pay for it?

Comic: 5,000 dollars. . . A helluva buy.

MC: 5,000 dollars, for that?

Comic: You don't understand. See, when I bought the car, there was a beautiful girl sitting in it. I paid the man the 5,000 dollars and got behind the wheel. She was sitting in the front seat, so I kept my mouth shut, I figured I could get something going. I started the car and drove away, out in the country about fifteen miles, turned off the ignition and put my arm around her. She never said anything. I reached over and kissed her and she still didn't say anything, so then I leaned over and I whispered in her ear.

MC: What did she say?

Comic: She said, "Oh, you got that when you paid $5,000 for the car."

MC: Say, let's get downtown and find some girls!

Comic: Well, if we're going down there, we gotta remember one important thing.

MC: What?

Comic: We gotta find a place to park the car.

MC: Park the car, okay. . . (*fakes driving*) Go down this way. . .turn.

Comic: Whoa! (*Two girls have just appeared on stage, one gorgeous with a large set of mammary glands. The other is good-looking but looks and acts tough*)

MC: (*Stops the car, yells over to the girls*) Hello, girls. How are you? (*Turns to comic*) Hey, get a load of the build on that one!

Comic: Uh huh, if I had a belt and spiked shoes, I'd climb her, that's for sure. . . She's got red hair and bangs. Hey, I got an idea, let's make it a foursome.

MC: Whaddaya mean, foursome?

Comic: Let's get them in the car, and if they don't wanna, we'll force 'em."

MC: Naw, you gotta be diplomatic about these things. Why is it that whenever you see a girl, you get all unmoved?

Comic: I dunno.

MC: Get all excited. . . Listen, what's the trouble, a woman is only a rag, a bone and a hank of hair.

Comic: Shake hands with a junk dealer.

MC: Hello, girls. How are you?

Girls: *(In unison)* Hi. Fine.

MC: I'm Bill, he's Hal. We're out on the town. How would you like to take a little spin?

Girl A: Okay. *(Girl A walks toward the car, Girl B hangs back)*

MC: Hey, this is going to be fine. Hey, you're all right. . . Get right in. You're cute.

Girl A: Thank you.

MC: What's your name?

Girl A: I dunno, I meet so many men. *(MC and comic trade a puzzled glance at this remark)*

Comic: Say, this kid hasn't got much upstairs, but what a stairway, eh? *(To girl A)* I'm glad you decided to come along, cause I like you. *(When he says this he's staring from close in at one of her breasts, which just come up to his eyes. Switches his gaze and attention to her other breast)* And you, too!

MC: Well, I got mine, you get yours! *(Grabs girl A and escorts her into the car)*

Comic: *(Looking at girl B, who is still standing outside the car at one side of stage)* Were there any survivors? Give me a stick and I'll beat it to death. Get a load of the size of the feet on this dame. Hell, I could get her a job stamping out fires in the Northwest Territories.

MC: That's easily explained. It's quite evident that the young lady was raised on a farm. Farm girls walk around in their bare feet in the soft, red clay and this has a tendency to make the feet spread.

Comic: She walked around in the clay and this is the reason her feet spread?

MC: Yes.

Comic: *(Pause, looks at her seat).* She didn't have to sit in it, did she?

MC: Go talk to her.

Comic: Okay, hold the car. *(Gets out of car and over to girl B)* How do you do?

Girl B: How do I do what?

Comic: Up your Gigi! *(Leaves girl and returns to car in disgust)*

MC: Get back out there. I want you to give her everything you've got!

Comic: *(Pauses while he considers this)* Well, I might have to make two trips, but I'll try. *(Goes out again and says to the girl)* See that car?

Girl B: What car?

Comic: Why don't you go out and play in traffic? Well, why don't you just get in the car? Maybe you and me can go out to Bear Lake and kill bloodsuckers or something.

Girl B: Okay, I got nothing to lose.

Comic: *(Aside to audience)* I'll find that out after I get you in the car. *(MC and Girl A stand so they appear to be in the front seat and comic and Girl B stand in the backseat)*

MC: All right, all we gotta do now is find a place to park the car.

Comic: *(To MC)* Before we make a move, ask them.

MC: Ask them what?

Comic: Ask them, ask them. . . I'm going to have to have a talk with this kid. Ask them, do they or don't they?

MC: Oh, I see what you mean. Girls, what my friend is trying to say is that the economic system being what it is today, the cost of gasoline being what it is, oil is up, and we need new rubber. . .

Comic: *(Looks over side of the car)* We also need new tires, we're riding on cardboard.

MC: What we want to know is. . . is it yes or is it no?

Girls: *(Both yell)* It's NO!

Comic: Get out of the car!

Girls: UP YOURS! *(They get out of the car and go downstage)*

MC: I'll go talk to them and see what I can do. I'll take my best shot. *(Leaves, says to girls)* Girls, you'll have to excuse my friend, he's a bit eccentric. But you do like me, don't you?

Girls: You're all right.

MC: Shall we get back in the car?

Girl A: Okay. *(Girl A goes with Bill, girl B stays out front)*

Comic: This is where I came in. . . *(Staring at girl A's breasts again)*

MC: Well, I got mine, there's yours.

Comic: To hell with her, let's split this one. . . Besides, there's enough here for the three of us.

MC: What do you mean, the three of us?

Comic: Me. . . you. . . then me again.

Girl A: Hey, he's so cute. *(Hugs comic's head to her breasts)*

Comic: Help! Lemme out. It's too hot down here. Let me out of here. *(He protests but doesn't come up for air)*
MC: Well, why don't you try to get out?
Comic: *(Lifts his head)* Think I'm a fool? *(Lowers his head)*
MC: What are you doing down there?
Comic: I'm a hillbilly.
MC: Come on, go talk to the lady, will you? *(Nods toward girl B)*
Comic: *(Opens car door, goes over to girl B)* Get in that car!
Girl B: NO!
Comic: I won't bother you.
Girl B: Then why should I get in the car?
Comic: That's enough out of you, get in the car. *(They enter the car)* Now all we have to do is find a place to park the car, right?
MC: Right!
Girl B: Do you like riddles?
Comic: Hmm. What did you say?
Girl B: Do you like riddles?
Comic: *(Sarcastically)* Oh, I just love riddles.
Girl B: What's red and goes dingle, dangle?
Comic: Oh, I dunno. What *is* red and goes dingle, dangle?
Girl B: A red dingle-dangle! *(She laughs loudly)*
Comic: Eight'll get you five I knock her right in the teeth. . . You're just this far *(spreads fingers apart a little bit)* from this! *(Shows her his fist)*
Girl B: I got another one.
Comic: I'll bet you have.
Girl B: What's green and goes dingle, dangle?
Comic: *(Bites)* A green dingle-dangle!
Girl B: No. They only come in red!
Comic: That's what I figured. *(Pause)* Ha, ha, ha. Get the hell out of the car! *(Girl B exits the car)*
MC: *(Who has been necking with girl A during this conversation)* Aw, come on, we're not getting anywhere, go get her.
Comic: You wanna go with green dingle-dangle, be my guest, go on. *(They argue to beat hell, shove and push)*
MC: *(Chases after girl B, saying)* I'll give it my best shot. *(To girl B)* I'm not going to waste any time. Would you like to get back in the car?
Girl B: No.
MC: Okay. *(Gets back in car and puts his arm around girl A, then to comic)* Well, I got mine, there's yours.

Comic: That was your best shot? Oh, all right, I'll try again. *(Goes over to girl B)* Get in the car. I appeal to you as a woman.

Girl B: You don't even appeal to me as a man.

Comic: *(Gets mad, yells)* Get in the car, you cotton-pickin', chicken-pluckin', corn-poppin', glue-sniffin', money-grubbin' tart! *(Girl B gets back in car)* Now all we gotta do is find a place to park the car.

MC: Yessir, and we're all one big, happy family.

Comic: All righty, that appeals to me.

MC: *(To girl B)* How about a kiss?

Girl B: You bet.

MC: Kiss, kiss. *(Bill makes kissing motions and noises with his lips toward the comic, who tries to understand what all this is about, as MC is trying to indicate comic should kiss girl B)*

Comic: *(Finally says)* Well, okay, I guess you're better than nothing. *(Tries to kiss MC)*

MC: Not me, you dope! Her!

Comic: *(Grabs girl B and kisses her long and hard, then comes up for air)*

Girl B: GET THE HELL OUT OF THE CAR!

Comic: I'll do better later.

MC: Now, look girls, before we go any further—*(interrupted by girl B)*

Girl B: Hold it! Hold it! Everybody freeze!

MC: What's the matter?

Girl B: Somebody's foolin' with my leg.

Comic: That's me, honey, and I ain't foolin'.

Girl B: If my mother knew I was out with you two guys, she'd knock the hell out of me.

Comic: This kid's all right, she's got a lot of class, she's goin' places.

MC: Yeah?

Comic: And right now, too. Get the hell out of the car.

Girl B: Aw, you guys stink!

Comic : O-U-T! Out! Out!

Girl B: Why, I wouldn't go out with you two creeps if you were the last men on this Earth. *(Gets out of car and out front stage)* This for you. . . *(snaps fingers of one hand)* and this for you. . . *(snaps fingers of other hand)* and you can just take THAT. *(Whereupon she turns and throws her skirts up high and flounces her rear end at them, giving the audience a good look at her colourful underpants)*

Comic: Hey Bill, we've found a place to park the car!

HANK HENRY & BILL WILLARD

The floor of the death cell he paced,
He must pay the wages of sin;
The warden said, "You have one hour of grace."
He said, "Okay, send her in."

The Peace Players were organized in 1967 as a Canadian Centennial project. The theatre troupe's first effort, *Sorry 'Bout That*, quickly became the financial backbone of the club. Its programs were in a purple punchline, adults-only vein, reminiscent of old burlesque, vaudeville and music hall. Those who thought the straight and narrow path would be a lot wider if more people used it were warned not to attend—which didn't hurt sales. But if, on the other hand, you believed that old actors never die—their parts just grow smaller; or the difference between a stick-up and a hold-up is age, then you were likely to get an hour's laughter from the conglomeration of skits, one-liners and other humour provided by the Players. The popularity of adult comedy in a cabaret setting was, and still is, hard to beat.

I've mentioned my acting partner Bill Seaman. Young Bill had spent a couple of years in the British Army right after the Second World War. His sister René married Ernie Hokanson, who was a Canadian Army cook during the war. Bill came to Canada in the late Forties and was in Peace River when I arrived in 1953. We hit it off immediately and soon discovered our mutual interest in theatre, especially the comedic kind. We appeared as a team in a production called *Twelve Foot Davis Nites*, with Bill playing Robert Service and myself in the role of Twelve Foot Davis.

The Davis character was based on Henry Fuller Davis, a Yankee born about 1820 in Vermont. Davis was also a legendary fur trader and gold miner in northern BC and Alberta, who got his nickname from his discovery of an unclaimed plot of land, just twelve feet wide, in Barkerville, BC during the Cariboo gold rush of 1860-1868. Davis promptly registered the claim and became rich from the gold the plot yielded.

Once the Peace Players was formed by Don Weaver, Marlene Morrison, Bill Seaman and myself, the new theatre troupe staged many plays and musicals like *Guys and Dolls*, *Fiddler on the Roof* and *Oliver*. Bill played a consummate Fagan, rivalling anything I've seen on stage or screen. Seaman could play any role and was particularly good at melodrama, appearing in Edmonton in *The Drunkard*. Peace Players ran the first subscription series in rural Alberta, along the lines of Edmonton's Citadel Theatre, bringing many touring companies and performers into town.

A melodrama we included in one edition of *Sorry 'bout That* was a number written by Bill Willard and Hank Henry, a burlesque comedy duo well known in Las Vegas and on the old American burlesque circuit. It is recreated here and followed by a short biography of both authors, whom I met several times in Vegas and from whom I purchased this little gem.

Revenge of the Klondike

PROPS: Table, not too large; two chairs, rustic; rocking chair; knitting needles and wool; knitting bag; pistol loaded with blanks; confetti snow; snowballs; wrapped hamburger; paper plate; moneybag with $$ signs; rubber dagger; two large foam rubber falsies; capsule filled with green dye
CHARACTERS: The villain, Cadwallader Crumley: despicable, saturnine, egregious trickster with flowing moustaches, heavily accented eyebrows and cruel eyes, mouth in perpetual sneer; salivates while contemplating the flesh of females or an equally tempting mortgage. He wears black top hat, white shirt with black string tie, black vest under black swallow-tail coat, dark grey striped trousers tucked into shiny black boots. He carries a riding

crop and manipulates a cape with extravagant gestures. He must be peanut- and tomato-proof.

The heroine, Nell: a lovely flower of womanhood twice as pure as driven cocaine or snow, a virginal beauty whose eyes are limpid pools, completely guileless. A natural innocence shrouds her rather voluptuous figure, which is stuffed into a frilly white shirt-waist and long swirling skirt under which peep from time to time a trim ankle or two encased in high button shoes. Her hair is piled high atop her dear head over an angel's face of white, white skin with eyes framed in lavender. She is so much the ravishable creature that strong men pale and tremble at the sight of her, and the sound of her voice is as sweet as tinkling bells.

The hero, Clarence Braveblood: his manhood is not to be questioned, for he is of noble breed, tall and tempestuous, handsome as an Arrow shirt model. He's a poor but honest working man, wears homespun, serviceable clothing, including an open shirt, but he carries a muffler to protect his strong neck from the bitter Arctic cold. He wears a cap and heavy boots. He's always sincere and, of course, his honesty shines as a beacon of light through clouds of obfuscation.

Grandma: a mysterious old frump off in a corner, rocking away and knitting, mumbling to herself, her head and entire frame draped in shawls that pool on the floor around her feet. She wears a grey wig and of course, granny glasses, but does not afford the audience too much detail to look at.

MUSIC: Home Sweet Home, until opening dialogue. Fade under.

SCENE: Interior of a cabin, early rustic, with table and chairs, also rustic. Door upstage centre. At curtain, Grandma is revealed in rocking chair upstage right, rocking and knitting. Old-fashioned radio sits on small table next to Grandma. Nell and Clarence are downstage centre, embracing.

Nell: (*Breaks from embrace to face front and declaim*) Oh, Clarence, what will become of us? 'Tis bitter cold and the wind is whistling (*Sound effect of whistling wind*) around our little cabin. My poor pa is laying out there colder than a mackerel.

Clarence: And as usual, stiffer than a goat. But courage, my Nell, everything will be all right.

Nell: Oh, how can you say that, Clarence, with the mortgage due and Cadwallader Crumley on his way to demand his pound of flesh. It is I or the money he wants.

Clarence: His pound of flesh! With the price of meat nowadays, you should be getting a refund. *(Gropes her)*

Nell: Do not make light of the matter. *(Calmly pushes away hand)* Without a roof over our heads, what will become of poor Grandma?

Clarence: Ah yes, there she be. She has sat and knitted in her rocker for fifty years. Sits and knits, knits and sits. Hasn't spoken a word since the blizzard of '88.

Nell: Ever since she rot the government.

Clarence: She what?

Nell: She rot.

Clarence: You mean wrote.

Nell: It's a rotten government. . . Nary a word from Grandma ever since she rot the government for help from the blizzard—licked the postage stamp and got her tongue frostbitten.

Clarence: Fear not, I will save you and Grandma.

Nell: Yes, but how?

Clarence: I will accept that offer to go on the raddio as a hillbilly singer.

Nell: A hillbilly singer?

Clarence: Ah, yes. Just like Dolly Parton.

Nell: Dolly Parton? How could you ever come across like Dolly Parton?

Clarence: I'll put up a big front. *(Does a bump)*

Nell: Will you make enough money?

Clarence: Enough money? Why, I heard they get as high as ten dollars. Dolly Parton would make twice that much.

Nell: Twenty dollars—that's enough to pay the mortgage and get married.

Clarence: I must be off. *(They embrace)*

Nell: *(Sniffs)* Yes, you must be. *(Pushes Clarence away)*

Clarence: Good-bye. *(Gives Nell a peck on the mouth. Her eyes are closed and her mouth puckered for more, which she doesn't get. As he backs away she gives him a disgusted look)* This is no time for lolly-gagging. I brave the storm.

Nell: But you aren't dressed to brave the elements. *(Follows him)*

Clarence: 'Tis no matter, for I have my love to keep me warm. *(He pulls her to him and both hold positions in freeze frame as the tune I've Got My Love to Keep Me Warm is played)*

Nell: *(Unfreezes)* And you leave me alone with Grandma, without protection.

Clarence: Never fear, for Jim Dalton of the Northwest Mounted

Police is in the vicinity. Farewell. *(Gesture of throwing his muffler around the neck swings him around a couple of times and he loses direction. Nell steers him toward door)* Again, farewell! *(Clarence opens the door up centre and gets confetti snow in the face. Wild flinging of arms to ward off the flakes, slams door)*

Nell: I will turn on the raddio and listen for my sweetheart's voice. *(Goes over to small table by Grandma where the old radio is sitting and squats to turns it on)*

Cadwallader: *(On tape over loudspeakers)* Good evening, homeowners. The Cadwallader Crumley Finance Company sends you this important message. Are you pressed for funds? I will help you. I do not need your signature, I do not want any collateral. All I want is your Grandma's right arm.

Nell: Oh, Cadwallader, you cad. I hate you. *(Sound of horses' hooves, then squeal of brakes)* He comes by horseback—alack! *(Sound of car door slamming, then knock on door)*

Cadwallader: *(Stomps in after opening door and getting confetti snow in the back of the head)* Aha! There you are, my little vixen.

Nell: *(Shrinks back. She has come down left centre)*

Cadwallader: *(Aside)* Egad! She grows more beautiful by the moment. Were she mine to tame. *(Struts down to join Nell, twirling moustaches and tossing back his cape in a devilish gesture)*

Nell: *(Wrings her hands)* Cadwallader, we are destitute. Oh, do not take our home from Grandma and me. . . I. . . we.

Cadwallader: You remember our bargain. You must choose. I'll either take the money, or your fair flesh!

Nell: I have no money.

Cadwallader: Well then, I shall carry you off to my twenty-room mansion with genuine plumbing. *(Skulls Nell, who is a woman of some embonpoint. Aside)* Gadzooks. I guess I'll have to make two trips.

Nell: But you can't do this to me. I must keep myself untarnished for Clarence Braveblood.

Cadwallader: Braveblood! Surely you have better plans for your future than that hillbilly bleater?

Nell: Oh, but he is to be a great star. He has gone to the city to sing on the raddio. He is going to be another Dolly Parton.

Cadwallader: Then he's a double booby. . . sillier than I thought he was. He'll earn but a mere pittance. Can he adorn your pretty figure with satins and laces? I will give you ropes of pearls for your swan-like neck, diamond tiaras for your lovely tresses, jade bracelets from the Orient. . .

Nell: Well, if it's all the same to you, I'll have a Whopper.

Cadwallader: A Whopper, eh? *(Rolls his eyes, grins fiendishly)* As luck would have it, I happen to have a Whopper. *(Turns his back to audience, acts as if he were unzipping his fly. Swings around quickly and flashes a Whopper hamburger wrapped and on a paper plate)* Sorry, I forgot the french fries.

Nell: *(Takes the burger and starts to nibble. Turns away from him to audience)* He's not bad looking—and such a generous cad. Should I succumb to his charms? *(Waits for audience reaction)*

Cadwallader: *(Reacting to audience biz with Nell)* A desire overwhelms me to kiss your luscious lips, me proud beauty.

Nell: *(Acts coy for a second, then drops Whopper, seizes cad and bends him back and plants a juicy kiss)*

Cadwallader: *(Struggles to get out of Nell's hefty grip. Straightens up, wipes face elaborately with handkerchief. Aside)* Her kiss is like a wet mop.

Nell: *(Faces front, wringing her hands, emoting horribly)* What have I done? What have I done?

Cadwallader: *(Sniffs around Nell)* Yes, what have you done?

Nell: Oh, the shame of it all. I have given myself to this cad and I promised Clarence Braveblood I would be pure.

Cadwallader: My blood is on fire with passion. My face is still wet from her kiss and I must have more. More. *(Lunges toward Nell)*

Nell: *(Backs off, holding hands in front of her as a shield)* Oh no, no, a thousand times no. If only Clarence Braveblood were here.

Cadwallader: Flutter your wings, me pretty bird, it will avail you naught.

(Villain music swells. Cadwallader stalks Nell as she retreats upstage. Chases her around table and Grandma, who pays no attention, just sits and knits, knits and sits, rocks and rocks)

Nell: *(Backing away and stumbling, fleeing, running, gesturing wildly)* Clarence! Clarence! Save me!

(She and cad wind up down right, clutching, unclutching, etc. Music builds to furioso, then stops abruptly. Clarence bangs open the door. Snow confetti hits him, followed by a snowball on the head. He holds a moneybag in one hand. Strides straight down front centre. Music comes up, a ta-da fanfare)

Clarence: I rode a Camel real Kool through Marlboro country and sang on the Lucky Strike Hit Parade. I just got back in the nicotine, *(Holds it for a second as the boos roll in for the bum joke. He then waves the moneybag aloft)* Here is enough money to pay the mortgage and save Nell from a fate worse than death.

Nell: *(Holds for audience reaction)* Jeez, I was doin' pretty good until this bum came in. And now back to the script.

Cadwallader: *(Glaring and twirling moustaches furiously, wagging cape and stomping as he tells the audience)* I will have both—the money and the wench. *(Pulls a dagger, deliberately and elaborately shows it)*

Clarence: Here is your money *(Proffers the money bag)* Now give me the mortgage. *(Cadwallader just looks at him, ditto Nell)* Give it to me. *(Pause, stamps foot in a snit, hand on hip)* Give it to me, I say!

Cadwallader: I'll give you something and it won't be the mortgage. *(Dagger aloft)* Take this, you fool!

(Struggle theme music roils and boils as Clarence and Cadwallader work back and forth down front, gripping each other. Cadwallader drops the knife. Clarence picks it up and hands it back to Cadwallader. Cadwallader bends Clarence to his knees and starts slashing. Cadwallader flings Clarence away and Clarence falls on one elbow, clutching his breast. Two falsies fall out. Cadwallader picks them up and shows them to audience)

Clarence: You've ruined my Dolly Parton costume.

Nell: *(Screams)* Help! The only one who can save me now is Jim Dalton of the Mounted Police. *(Ta-da chord from orchestra. Cadwallader glares at orchestra. Starts to drag Nell to door up centre)*

Nell: Jim Dalton! Jim Dalton! Save me! *(Wild sob)*

Cadwallader: No one can save you now.

Grandma: *(Stands up, takes out pistol from her knitting bag, aims at Cadwallader and fires five shots)*

Cadwallader: *(Reacts, clutching a different part of his anatomy after each shot. Stumbles around in death scene, chewing up the scenery. Pulls out a capsule with green dye. Squeezes it on white shirt)* I feel my life's blood slowly ebbing away. *(Shows green blood)* Curses! Foiled by a doddering old Grandma!

Nell: Grandma!

Grandma: Grandma, hell! *(Off with shawls and wig, picks up hat and stands in full Mountie uniform)* Jim Dalton of the Northwest Mounted Police!

(Curtain)

The Authors

Bill Willard, the consummate straight man, was a Las Vegas resident and newspaperman for over three decades, with an equally lengthy career in the visual and performing arts. An active sculptor and designer, he also spent some years in the theatre at Pasadena Playhouse and in burlesque on the Las Vegas Strip. At the *Las Vegas Sun*, he wrote columns and was the art and music critic and show reviewer for the daily and weekly Variety sections. His background also included classical and jazz programs on radio as well as news reporting, commentary and commercial spot announcing on television.

Willard owned and operated an advertising and public relations firm for many years and was once executive director of the Nevada State Council of the Arts. He taught commercial art at the University of Nevada in Las Vegas. His own creations ranged from graphics to paintings, but his chief love was sculpture.

Hey, how's a guy like this connected to burlesque? Well, like I've been telling you, burlesque is an art form and Bill Willard was one of its greatest practitioners as both straight man and comic on the Strip, where he was long associated with the legendary Hank Henry of the Silver Slipper Stock Company.

Willard was one of burlesque's best friends, and when a troupe like the Peace Players approached him, he was only too glad to be of assistance.

In the summer of 1983, his original musical, *Slo-o-o-wly I Turned*, was presented at the Las Vegas Playhouse as a tribute to Hank Henry. It included some of the sketches he and Henry had combined on, plus blackouts. The works.

In the world of burlesque comedy, the best comedians were known as top bananas. Hank Henry, who died on March 31, 1982 at the age of 74, was the top banana in all of Las Vegas.

Henry described his on-stage persona as an affable oaf, and he filled the wee hours of Las Vegas nightlife on stage at the Silver Slipper Casino in the 1950s and early Sixties. His Silver Slipper Stock Company's two a.m. shows played to audiences packed with the biggest names in show business, who had already done their own shows and wanted to spend the rest of the night being entertained by someone else.

Born Henry Rosenthal in New York, Henry began his entertainment career in the Catskill Mountains, where he met and teamed up with vaudevillian Stanley House in the 1930s.

Henry was eventually discovered by famed showman H.K. Minsky, who brought him into burlesque. Henry's name soon appeared on the marquee with other famous vaudeville players, including Phil Silvers. Henry found a straight man for his act when he met a production singer named Robert Alda. The two worked as partners until World War II.

During the war years, Henry, who served as a corporal and later a sergeant in the army, appeared with Julie Oshins and Dick Bernie in an Irving Berlin production called *This is the Army*. The group took the show on tour throughout the European and Pacific theatres.

After his discharge, Henry looked up his old friend Alda, who had gone to Hollywood to make films, and the two appeared with Abbott and Costello in several film shorts and features.

Henry came to Las Vegas in 1950 with his wife Jo Ann Malone. Together with straight man/emcee Jimmy Cavanaugh, they opened a Gay '90s revue with burlesque sketches at the club then known as the Golden Slipper. After a tour of *Kiss Me Kate* with Sparky Kaye, Henry brough Kaye back to Las Vegas to appear in his shows at the renamed Silver Slipper club. Henry, his wife Jo Ann, Cavanaugh, Kaye and Bill Willard formed the nucleus of the Silver Slipper Stock Company, which performed mini-musical sketches in the burlesque style.

Henry's success in Las Vegas led to several movie offers. He appeared in *Pal Joey*, *The Joker's Wild*, *Robin Hood and the Seven Hoods*, *Sergeants 3* and *Ocean's Eleven*, all starring Frank Sinatra. In 1970, Henry had a role in *The Only Game in Town*, starring Elizabeth Taylor and Warren Beatty.

In the Sixties, Henry moved his show to the Castaways and later the Hacienda Hotel before retiring from regular appearances. In subsequent years, special awards were presented to the best burlesque acts in Las Vegas. Just as the annual Academy Awards have come to be known as Oscars, the annual Vegas awards became known as Hanks.

"I've lived a picturesque life," Henry would tell his friends. "Every day's a bonus." In classic burlesque style, he would continue, "I was born at a very early age. It was so long ago, I don't remember. When I was born I was a young child, so if I stutter and stammer, it's a throwback to when I was a kid."

LEAD US TO LAUGHTER

Roses are reddish,
Violets are bluish;
If it weren't for Christmas,
We'd all be Jewish!

A theatre critic once said that a comedian is the tightrope artist of laughter. Comedy is indeed a risky business. If they're not laughing it's flop sweat time.

Students of comedy and comedians come up with all manner of humour—ethnic jokes, absurdities, one-liners, mime, sight gags, sick humour, slapstick, godawful, blue, situational, sexual, anecdotal, you name it.

One theory of what makes you laugh is that a joke has to release an existing tension and, by changing or switching a situation, liberate the will and desire to laugh about whatever unsettles, disturbs or is worrisome to people. This may account for the wide popularity of sexual humour, or gibes at local stereotypes and rural, urban, regional, racial or national stereotypes.

That's one theory. Another is that a good comedian can lead an audience to laughter—but only in the direction they were ready to go anyway, and that direction is, quite simply, escape.

But whatever your philosophy of laughter, burlesque humour usually manages to strike a funny bone. Burlesque characters are most often ridiculous, and outlandish characters become hilarious only if they take themselves completely seriously. Then they release that tension, change that situation completely and go the way you're going, and you escape into laughter at the humour of the situation.

A subtle joke is like a nude woman rolling down a hill—sometimes you see it and sometimes you don't. On the other hand, burlesque humour, a North American art form, is not noted for its subtlety. This perhaps makes us laugh the more easily if we're in the mood. As an example, here's a short, little-known version of the most famous Bud Abbott and Lou Costello skit called *Who's on First?* This one's called:

What's in a Name?

CHARACTERS: Comic; straight man; girl
PROPS: Office desk and chair
SCENE: In one

Straight man: *(Seated at desk interviewing comic)* Now, before you start to work here, it's important that you remember the names of the people you gotta work with. First of all, Watt is your boss's name.
Comic: How should I know?
Straight man: Well, now you know. His name is Watt, Mr. Watt.
Comic: Don't ask me, I dunno.
Straight man: I'm not asking you. I'm telling you. The boss's name is Watt—Izzy Watt.
Comic: Okay, I give up. Is he what? What is he?
Straight man: Listen, stupid!
Comic: Yessir, I'm listening.
Straight man: His first name is Izzy.
Comic: Oh-h-h-h-h.
Straight man: And his last name is Watt. Get it? Now, he's a very smart man and he's the boss, the president! A very smart man, and the vice-president, he's Knott.
Comic: He isn't.
Straight man: The vice-president's last name is Knott.
Comic: Not what?
Straight man: That's right, it's not Watt. The president, he's Watt, the vice-president is Knott.

Comic: Is he?

Straight man: No, no. That's the boss, the president. He's Izzy.

Comic: Is he what?

Straight man: That's right, now you got it. And Howe is the doctor in case you're sick or hurt.

Comic: In case I get sick or hurt, how is the doctor?

Straight man: That's right, Howe is the doctor.

Comic: What's the matter, doesn't *he* know how he is?

Straight man: No! I said Howe is the doctor.

Comic: Well, if he's the doctor, he oughta know. Tell him to stick out his tongue and look in a mirror.

Straight man: Listen—this man went to medical school. Now he's a doctor—Howe.

Comic: How? I dunno how, maybe he graduated.

Straight man: Listen, you halfwit.

Comic: Who, *me*?

Straight man: Well, how many halfwits *are* there around here?

Comic: Just the two of us, I guess.

Straight man: Look, we got a boss! He's the president of the firm. Watt is his name.

Comic: *(To audience)* Oh brother, this is where I came in.

Straight man: Watt is our boss and the vice-president is Knott.

Comic: Certainly not.

Straight man: Yes, he's the vice president.

Comic: And how is the doctor?

Straight man: He's fine, thank you.

Comic: *You* don't know any more than I do.

Straight man: Oh, yes I do.

Comic: Who is he?

Straight man: No, Hoo is the janitor.

Comic: What's that?

Straight man: NO, NOT what's that—HOO. Watt, that's the boss. Hoo is the janitor. H-o-o—Hoo—he's the Chinese janitor. Charlie Hoo.

Comic: Is he?

Straight man: No, not Izzy, Hoo! Watt is the president, he's the boss. The vice-president is Knott. Howe is the doctor and Hoo is the janitor.

Girl: *(Runs onstage dressed in a negligee, screaming)* HELP! HELP!

Straight man: Hey, what goes on here? What's the matter?

Girl: (*Hysterical*) Some men out there tried to grab me and kiss me.
Straight man: What? How?
Comic: Watt is the boss, Howe is the doctor. Was it them?
Girl: No, it was not.
Comic: Knott? He's the vice-president.
Girl: Whoever did it will have to marry me. Who did it? WHO?
Comic: Oh, Hoo? Hoo, he's the Chinese janitor!!!

(*Curtain*)

The following burlesque skit pokes fun at the outlandish characters that are a staple in evangelical circles.

The Faith Healer

CHARACTERS: Faith healer Orville Robarts; Charlie, his helper; Oka Cheddar, the girl; John John the drunk
SCENE: Full stage
PROPS: Prayer screen and crutches

Orville: Friends, my name is Orville Robarts. I'm sure you've seen our ministry on TV, direct from the Chapel of K-Tel University. . . in Gospel City, Oklahoma.
Helper: Oklahoma!
Orville: There's only one word to describe the thrill it has been for us to come up here and visit with you good folks in this lovely city of Alberta. . . here in this beautiful State of Canada. . .
Helper: Canada!
Orville: Rejoice, ye Children of Light—everything that you have ever done in your whole lifetime in the physical vessel on this plane on this planet, has brought you to this instant. Come in and have your faith uplifted!
Helper: Have your faith uplifted!
Orville: Oh, joy to the world! Dearly beloved, I believe that if everybody excelled to the height of what they enjoyed doing the most (*pause*) then some of you would say we'd all be a bunch of. . . No, what I mean is. . . Life is like a tin of sardines—we're all looking for the KEY.

Helper: Looking for the key!

Orville: This is the time of healing, my friends, when we invite all those with a sick body or a sick mind, or a sick both. . . to come forward now and let the heavenly spirit of cleansing power pass down.

Helper: Deep down double-action cleansing power!

Orville: Let that cleansing power pass down through my perfect body and out into your sick mind. . .

Helper: Come and get it!

Orville: Don't hesitate, friends, don't hesitate. Yes, that's the way, honey, just come forward now, come right up through the audience here. Go get her, would you, Charlie?

Helper: You got it, Rev!

Orville: Here we have a lady coming forward now, with her leg in a cast and on crutches. What's your name, honey?

Oka: Oka.

Orville: And your last name?

Oka: Cheddar.

Orville: Oka Cheddar! Oh, praise be to glory! Oka Cheddar. Her parents named her after cheeses. . .

Helper: The Almighty Jesus!

Orville: No, Kraft cheeses. . .

Helper: All right now, and hallelujah! Tell it now, Reverend, tell it.

Orville: All right now, honey, you tell us what's buggin' you, sweetheart.

Oka: Well, one night a gang of bikers I belong to, you know, we was going out on a rumble, you know, so like, before we hit out on the rumble, you know, like, we always like to pray, right?

Helper: Amen and amen and like, I mean, A-a-a-men!

Orville: Cool it, Charlie! Cool it.

Oka: So there I am, you know, there I am, praying like, you know? And damned if my damn bike doesn't damn well fall over on the middle of my damn leg and bust the damn thing, right?

Helper: Praise be to DAMN GLORY!

Orville: Hold on now, hold on *(worried)* A broken leg! Honey that's a very serious injury you have there, very serious indeed. *(Aside but loud)* Charlie, where's the fellow with the warts?

Helper: Search me! A no-show. Praise be to glory!

Orville: Glory? *(Pause)* All right, Oka, you hobble your way back behind our prayer screen there, while we continue to pray for your sick ugly broken leg out here in the audience. *(Helper goes back with*

Oka behind the screen for a second. There is the sound of a squeal, then a slap, and the helper staggers out from behind the screen, holding his head) Friends, our time is running out.

Helper: Running out!

Orville: Oh, yes, yes. You're getting on my nerves, Charlie. . . Is there any other sickie out there who would like to come forward tonight? Oh here's someone. Yes, come forward, brother. There's a man out there trying to make his way onto the platform. *(A drunk is staggering forward)* Is this the fellow with the warts, Charlie?

Helper: Never. No way. A-wrongo.

Orville: Well, you better help him up on the stage. Here, brother. Charlie, will you go help him? Bring him right up onto the platform. Here he comes now. Could I have your name, brother?

John: The name's. . . John.

Orville: John. And your last name, John?

John: The name's. . . John.

Orville: John? John John. A wonderful Old Testament name. John. I can tell by the way your body is trembling and that half-consumed bottle of medicine in your hand that you are in serious trouble here today. You have a severe case of what we used to call scurvy, but what medical science now calls the wa-wa's. . . for which there is no known cure. *(Aside)* Charlie, where's the fellow with the warts?

Helper: Not here! No show! No! No!

Orville: John John, you take your sick body behind that prayer screen with our friend Oka with the broken leg. And you wait there now, while we continue to pray for you out here in our audience.

John: Shure, okay.

Orville: Hold him up there, Charlie. He's a little weak.

Helper: I got him, Rev. *(Charlie takes a run across stage at John John, misses, goes right out into the wings to the sound of a great crash. Comes staggering back)*

Orville: Hold him up *(pause)* oh, where's the fella with the warts? Friends, do you believe that girl Oka, who is back there with that broken leg, do you believe that she can walk away from here today without her crutches? *(Long pause and silence)* I'm going to ask you again, friends. Do you believe that Oka can stand here as a cured woman and without the need of those crutches?

Someone in audience: NO!

Orville: I think we have a typically Canadian audience here tonight. . .

Helper: I don't have your knowledge, Rev, and I'd like to know. What is an act of faith?

Orville: I'll explain. In the front row we have brother and sister Fudpucker, with the five little Fudpuckers. She knows they are her children. Now, that's knowledge. He believes they are his children. Now that's faith! Oka, Oka, I'm gonna ask you—do you believe?

Oka: *(From behind the screen)* I do! I do believe!

Orville: Yes, she believes and I believe too, friends.

Helper: A-a-a-men!

Orville: But what we need is more than just words today, what we need is an act of faith.

Helper: An act of faith!

Orville: An act of faith. The mind is beautiful and we can think about a whole lot more than we can get. And so I say, Oka, if you know in your heart that you don't need those crutches anymore, you go ahead now and you just throw those crutches away. Just throw them out here on the platform for all the world to see. You don't need an assist. Don't hold back now, Oka.

Oka: Here they come!

Orville: Just throw those crutches away. *(The crutches come sailing over the screen and hit Orville)* Ow! Oh, Holy Moley! Hallelujah! Oh, what a performance. That girl Oka has been cured, friends, right here on our platform. I feel the spirits moving now. Thank you, Oka, for that act of faith. Now, brother John John, your body too can be rid of those loathsome wa-wa's that you've carried with you all these years, just as Oka's done already. Brother John John, speak it out loud if you believe. Speak out—do you believe?

John: *(From behind the screen)* O-O-O-O-O-O.

Orville: Yes, John, speak it out, brother.

John: O-O-Oka just fell flat on her ass. . .

Orville: Oh, oh, where's that fella with the warts?

(Curtain)

BRITISH MUSIC HALL

With heaving breast the dean undressed,
The bishop's wife to lie on;
He felt it rude to do it nude,
So he left the old school tie on!

The British Music Hall Society publishes a periodical called *The Call Boy*. I joined the society by mail and placed an ad in their publication indicating my interest, and that of the Peace Players, in obtaining music hall scripts. Through my correspondence with the Society, I made at least one friend, Wal Scott, whom I met on two occasions on trips to London. Wal still lived in the East End of London. On my first visit, I went to his flat by taxi. After a pleasant afternoon of conversation, he walked me back to the nearest tube station and told me the history of his exceedingly tough neighbourhood. As we proceeded through the wreckage of this ancient district, he pointed out where several murders had recently occurred. He might have been pulling my chain, but I didn't think so at the time.

Wal was always very helpful, and prior to his death, he sent me several notebooks full of material he'd used during his long career.

Wal Scott was the Fred Astaire of English music hall. When you met him, he'd strike you as being forever young. In his heyday he was known as the one-man music hall, and when the art form died with the advent of radio and the tellie, he became a music hall historian, writing under the name of Paul Gray.

Calling the Thirties the Great Depression would probably make Scott laugh, because depressed times were what led him into the life of a music hall performer and clown. At the ripe old age of twelve he left home because of maltreatment and made his way to the drab streets of dear old London. He joined the motley throng of half-starved, bare-footed urchins who slept in the doorways of Covent Garden, its streets carpeted with the smelly garbage spilled from dustbins, and lived on rotten fruit and stale bread.

Then he became a "ragged-arsed ranger," selling programs to the second-house patrons of the music halls going in, which he had obtained from the first house going out. He joined a juvenile troupe, where he was roughed up and cuffed about by a brutal manager who didn't believe in the word wages. He bided his time until he could escape the clutches of this wily manager. He blossomed as a boy mimic, then as a black-faced comedian, light comedian and tap dancer. He ran his own colossal show called *Shine* and ended his illustrious career by writing four separate autobiographies.

Scott didn't get rich from music hall, but he obviously enjoyed the life, even though it was hard, and ended up living comfortably in the East End of London. The Peace Players were indebted to this top-line performer, who was a sincere friend of music hall and of anyone involved in anything similar to it.

The older English scripts, especially those written before the war, were more slowly paced than their burlesque counterparts, low on one-liners, and relied more on situation and characterization. They needed to be punched up with verbal gags to produce more and quicker laughs for a North American audience.

In those early days, stage scripts had to be censored in advance by the British Board of Theatrical Censorship, and many of the ones I received bore the stamp of approval of that organization. The writers were continually trying to get risqué lines past the eagle eyes of the censors, who emanated from the office of the Lord Chamberlain. One example was a line in which it was said of a character in a play, "She sits down in the garden in the lettuce and peas." This was censored, so when the play was presented on stage, the writers had changed the line to, "She sits down in the garden in the cabbages and leeks."

North America experienced its own print censorship in the same period, and newspaper writers were always trying to slip risqué stuff past puritanical editors in the stories they filed. A classic example was, 'He said he was going to see his brother Jack off on the train."

Back in the Twenties and Thirties, in *Anything Goes*, Cole Porter wrote that a glimpse of stocking was something shocking. Double-entendres were the salacious order of the day. But in this new era, literally no subject matter is taboo and is explicitly dealt with on stage or in stand-up comedy. A glimpse of ankle or stocking, or even a black garter-belt and panties, leaves some sexual mystery. But now we have the new Las Vegas style, in which the dancers' costumes consist of a stringless G-string.

All of which now makes the following sketch, which I likely got from Wal Scott, rather quaint, but possibly more humorous. I admit to inserting a few burlesque-style one-liners into the script.

Never Kick a Sleeping Dog in the Ass: It Might Get Up and Bite You

CHARACTERS: Mr. Brown; vicar; newlywed couple; resident; female voice behind bathroom door; Mrs. Donovan the landlady; maid; girl
SCENE: A boardinghouse vestibule or main room (maybe table or desk with two chairs, stage front). There are doors leading off, marked with hanging signs: BATHROOM, BRIDAL SUITE, TOP FLOOR FRONT, MIDDLE PARLOUR and UPSTAIRS ATTIC. Only the first two have actual doors, the others are just signs pointing offstage.

Resident: *(Enters and tries bathroom door. It's occupied. He registers annoyance. Maid enters)* Excuse me, have you seen my wife?
Maid: No, I'm sorry, sir, I can't say I have. She might be 'aving a bath. *(Exit maid)*
Resident: *(To bathroom door)* I say, in there, Irene, honey… Irene honey. . . Sweet. . . Are you taking a bath?
Female voice from bathroom: Why, is there one missing? Buzz off, you silly ass, I'm in a bathroom, not a beehive.
Resident: Look, will you be long?
Voice: Why?
Resident: Because I wanted a room with a bath but I didn't get one.

Voice: I can give you a room, but you have to take your own bath.
Resident: Come on, Irene, I gotta go. . . How long are you gonna be? Look, you know I love you—but will you love me when I'm old and bald?
Voice: It's tough enough now, when you're young and hairy. What do you really want?
Resident: Well, can I put the touch on you for a tenspot?
Voice: For ten you can knock me down. . . now get lost!
Resident: *(Exits angrily)* They don't teach donkeys to talk, because nobody likes a smart-ass. . .
Landlady: *(Enters, reading National Geographic magazine)* These National Geographic books are sure full of information. . . Well, I declare, it says here that octopuses are female. . . Well, they may be right. . . who ever heard of an octocock? *(Reads aloud)* "The hardest part about milking a snake is getting the pail between its legs. . . " *(Puts magazine down on little vestibule table and sits)* Well, I've still got a few rooms to get rid of, I hope business picks up. *(Doorbell rings)* Come in.
Brown: *(Enters, heavily laden with luggage)* Good afternoon, Mrs. Donovan. Remember me? Mr. Brown. I've come down here again for my holidays. Can I have my usual room? The top floor front room?
Landlady: Why certainly, Mr. Brown. Glad to see you again. You're just in time to get your pick of rooms.
Brown: Thank you. I'll take the top floor front room. By the way, what are your weekly rates this year?
Landlady: I don't know. . . nobody ever stayed that long.
Brown: Well, I think I'll go along up there and get my things unpacked. So long for now, Mrs. Donovan.
Landlady: Bye-bye, Mr. Brown. *(Doorbell rings)* Oh, come in.
Vicar: *(Enters)* Oh, excuse me, madam. I've come down for the Regatta, etc., and as I like a room with a good view, I want to know if you'll let me have the top floor front room.
Landlady: Very sorry, Vicar, but I have just let that room to a gentleman by the name of Mr. Brown.
Vicar: Well, madam, that's too bad. *(Turns to go, then stops)* Look here, do you think this Mr. Brown would let me have his room? Could I see him and talk to him about it?
Landlady: He may do. I'll call him. *(Yells)* Mr. Brown. . . *(Brown enters. Every time Mr. Brown is called, he comes in missing one article of*

clothing—shoes, trousers, shirt—until he's down to his funny-looking underwear, and each time he changes rooms, he's carrying a bunch of stuff with him) Oh. This gentleman would like to speak to you, Mr. Brown.

Brown: Oh, would he?

Landlady: Mr. Brown, this gentleman wants to know if you will let him have your top floor front room.

Brown: Do he? What am I going to do?

Landlady: Well, let's see, I could let you have the bridal suite, if you wouldn't mind that.

Brown: The bridal suite. That's sort of a waste.

Landlady: Are you married?

Brown: No, I was hit by a truck!

Landlady: Well, how about it? Why not? For the Vicar here, Mr. Brown.

Brown: *(Looks vicar over)* Well, he don't seem a bad old stick. All right, I'll change over. You can have the top floor front room and I'll take the bridal suite.

Vicar: That's very kind of you, Mr. Brown, I'm sure. And also thanks to you, Mrs. Donovan. Well, I know I shall be quite comfortable here.

(Slight pause in action to give Brown time to go back into the wings and come back lugging his stuff to the bridal suite. Vicar and landlady converse during this time lapse)

Landlady: Tell me, Vicar, are there many very poor and needy people in the diocese?

Vicar: Far too many, Mrs. Donovan. Take Mrs. Smith for a start. She's so deprived, she doesn't have a stitch of clothing to wear.

Landlady: In what way can you help?

Vicar: I visit her three times a week.

Landlady: Yes, but what about charity?

Vicar: I visit her three times a week as well. . .

Landlady: No, I mean charitable donations so she can buy clothes. She's a member of the parish; she has a divine right.

Vicar: She has a divine left too. . .

Landlady: Vicar, you mistake my meaning. I mean charitable contributions. Do you get money from collections?

Vicar: Oh, we get good collections. My system ensures that.

Landlady: What system would that be, Vicar?

Vicar: It's quite simple. I announce from the pulpit each Sunday that I am aware that one of the men in the congregation has been unfaithful to his wife, and unless he puts ten dollars into the plate, I shall denounce him forthwith.

Landlady: And that brings you ten dollars each Sunday?

Vicar: No, last week we made five hundred and thirty. Works like a charm. Ours is a very energetic parish. *(Brown re-enters near the end of the conversation between the vicar and Mrs. Donovan)* Well, bye-bye, I'm off to the top floor front room. I know I shall be comfortable there.

Landlady: I'm sure you will, bye. *(Vicar and Brown go off to respective rooms)* Well, that's another room let. *(Doorbell rings)* Oh, come in. *(Newlyweds enter)*

Groom: Good evening, madam. You see, we're just on our honeymoon. . . we nearly had to call it off.

Landlady: Why?

Bride: Couldn't find a babysitter for two weeks.

Groom: Mmmm, yes. . . and we'd like a room, you know, well out of the way. We'll take the bridal suite if you have it vacant.

Landlady: Well, I'm very sorry, sir, but I have just rented that room to Mr. Brown.

Groom: That's too bad, madam. *(Turns to go, then stops)* Look, do you think this Mr. Brown would let us have the bridal suite? Could we talk to him?

Landlady: He might, I'll call him. *(Yells)* Mr. Brown! *(Brown enters)* Would you care to let this couple have the bridal suite? You could have the middle parlour room if you don't mind, Mr. Brown.

Brown *(Looks the couple over)* Well, okay. *(To bride)* You look stunning, my dear. *(To groom)* You just look stunned! Okay, I'll take the middle parlour room.

Bride: Thank you very much, Mr. Brown, it's very kind of you. Well, we'll be getting along then, madam, as we're feeling rather tired. See you later. *(Exit Mr. Brown and landlady. Brown goes into bridal suite to get his stuff as couple wait and talk)*

Groom: You've still got some confetti on you, darling, may I brush it off?

Bride: Why?

Groom: A bride should be well-groomed on her honeymoon. *(Coy silence)* I say, darling?

Bride: Yes, darling?

Groom: Are you tired?

Bride: Yes, darling, VERY.

Groom: *(Despondently)* Oh, darling!

Bride: *(Hastily)* But not TOO tired.

Groom: *(Enthusiastically)* Oh, DARLING. And darling, I hope you didn't think I was being naughty when I said, "Get up them stairs." Only, there were a lot of them, weren't there?

Bride: Yes, darling.

Groom: Of course I was only joking.

Bride: *(Despondently)* Oh, darling.

Groom: Well, not only joking.

Bride: *(Enthusiastically)* Oh, darling.

(Brown comes out of bridal suite, loaded down with stuff, goes offstage to middle parlour room)

Groom: I do hope that wretched maid won't be long with our bags. I can hardly wait.

Bride: What for, darling?

Groom: Well, I used to love to pinch your soft cheeks, but it's all over now. . . *(Enter maid, puffing, with honeymooners' bags)* Oh, here you are.

Maid: Nice bit of baggage you've got here, haven't you?

Groom: Are you referring to my wife?

Maid: No, it was just a conversation piece.

Groom: Oh, I see. I say, is there any water in our room?

Maid: There was, but we had the roof fixed. . . *(Carries baggage into bridal suite, groom carries bride over threshold)*

Maid: *(Coming out of room, to couple)* There's a lovely view in that room, I'm sure you'll like it in there.

Groom: *(Tipping maid at the door)* I'm sure I shall. *(Door shuts)*

Maid: *(Looking down at her hand)* Blimey! Ten cents and carrying all them bags up those stairs. *(Registers obvious disgust)* Cheap is cheap! I'll fix them! *(Takes BATHROOM sign and switches it with BRIDAL SUITE sign, then exits scene)*

Resident: *(Enters, hesitates at first door, then passes to other door. Tries door now marked BATHROOM, bangs on door)* Still in there, eh? Dammit, that's a bit thick. *(Yells at door of bridal suite)* I say, have a heart, you've been in there three quarters of an hour now, why don't you come out and let somebody else have a turn? *(Stomps off in disgust, in manner suggesting he really has to go. Groom comes out of door, angry, looks around, sees sign now marked BATHROOM, changes signs back the way they were)*

Brown: *(Re-enters from middle parlour room)* Dammit, now I've left my athletic supporter in the bridal suite. It was my best jockstrap, too. I wonder how I could get it without disturbing them? *(Listens at door)*

Groom: *(From behind door)* Darling, you have the sweetest lips, tell me, are they all mine?

Bride: They're all yours, honey.

Groom: Darling, you have the loveliest arms. Tell me, are they all mine?

Bride: They're yours, my love.

Groom: Darling, you have the loveliest breasts. Tell me, are they all mine?

Bride: Yes, darling, they're all yours.

Groom: Darling, you–

Brown: When you get to a double-decker pecker-checker, that's mine. . . *(Exits)*

Groom: *(Comes out to vestibule, angry, with brassiere in hand, as landlady enters)* Did you see a guy looking for a jockstrap?

Landlady: No, but I see you've found an upper topper flopper stopper. *(Groom hastily goes back into bridal suite and landlady continues to speak)* Well, thanks to Mr. Brown, that's another room rented. I've only got one more room vacant. *(Doorbell rings again)* Come in!

Girl: *(Enters)* Oh, madam, I've come down here for a quiet weekend. Have you got such a thing as a middle parlour room you could let me have?

Landlady: I'm very sorry, my dear, but I have just rented that room to a gentleman by the name of Mr. Brown.

Girl: Well, that is too bad. *(Turns to go, then stops)* Look, do you think this Mr. Brown would let me have his room? Could I see him and talk to him about it?

Landlady: He may do. I'll call him. *(Yells)* Mr. Brown!

Brown: *(Enters. He's down to his coloured undershorts. The two women stare at him)* Well, what is it this time? Nice shorts, eh? But a little tight! A pair of tight shorts is like this cheap hotel—no ballroom!

Landlady: This lady would like to speak to you, Mr. Brown.

Brown: *(Looks girl over)* Hmm. Well, this is a horse's patoot of a different colour.

Landlady: Mr. Brown, she wants to know if you will let her have the middle parlour room.

Brown: Do she? What am I going to do?

Landlady: You could have the upstairs attic if you care to change, Mr. Brown.

Brown: Oh, well, she don't seem a bad bit of stuff, I suppose I'd better do her a favour and change with her. I'll take the upstairs attic room.

Girl: Oh, thank you, Mr. Brown. I hope I shall see more of you.

Brown: I'd like to see more of you, too. (*Brown goes offstage, ostensibly to middle parlour room while girl and landlady wait. Brown comes out with his stuff*)

Girl: Oh, Mrs. Donovan, you haven't any dogs about, I suppose? I meant to tell you, I walk in my sleep and I'm always attracted to the bark of a dog.

Landlady: That's quite all right, miss, we haven't any dogs at all.

Brown: (*To girl*) You like dogs, do you?

Girl: Oh, yes, I really like dogs. As I was saying, even when I'm sleepwalking, which I do regularly, I am always attracted to the barking of a dog.

Brown: I like dogs, too. A dog is cheaper than a wife. The licence costs less, and the dog already has a fur coat. . . Well, I suppose I'd better get down to it. Good night, Mrs. Donovan. Good night, you sweet young thing! (*Lights dim after a second or two, denoting slumbering hotel guests and the passage of time. Girl comes out of middle parlour room in a negligee and sleepwalks across stage. Mr. Brown enters in his undershorts, starts barking like a dog. Girl turns toward him and walks into his arms*)

(*Curtain*)

Have you ever thought about a yellow god's green eye? No? Well, J. Milton Hayes (1884-1940), an English versifier, schoolteacher, insurance salesman, music hall entertainer and First World War hero, wrote a poem about just that in 1911, in just five hours. Of eleven stanzas, the first and last run as follows:

There's a one-eyed yellow idol to the north of Kathmandu,
There's a little marble cross below the town;

There's a broken-hearted woman tends the grave of Mad Carew.
And the Yellow God forever gazes down.

The poem was first recited on February 26, 1912 in Manchester, England, at the end of a night of Dickens character readings, and was an immediate success. Many still believe it to be the work of Rudyard Kipling, and Kipling himself considered it a successful imitation.

Later on, between the world wars, the poem became a comic production in British music halls. One half of a comic team would start reciting, *There's a one-eyed yellow idol to the. . .* while the other half, sitting in the audience and usually pretending to be drunk, heckled: "Yellow? Green sir, green!" So the first would haltingly start again and get as far as *north of Kathmandu. . .* before the other said, "North, did you say? South, you old fool." And so on, to mounting uproar.

Here is a slightly different version using three actors, performed in Saskatoon back in about 1950, by the touring company of the Canadian Navy Show, featuring the comedy team of Pratt and Matheson. Pratt became famous for his rendition of the song *You'll Get Used To It*, originally sung by British music hall singer Gracie Fields. The Peace Players' Claude Campbell never failed to bring down the house when he sang, or rendered, this song, using complete deadpan immobility and a very slow delivery of the parodied version—The first act is worse but you'll get used to it—as a running gag.

The Green-Eyed Yellow Idol

Skit for three men. Two of them, B and C, are dressed as British subalterns or officers of the Raj in India. The other one, A, is the narrator who recites the poem.

A. Ladies and gentlemen, as a complete contrast, I'd like to give a reading of the Green Eye of the Little Yellow God, by Milton Hayes:

There's a green-eyed yellow idol to the north of Kathmandu,
There's a little marble cross below the town—

(Sudden interruption from rear of hall. There's a shouted command to halt and two British officers come striding down the aisle and onto the stage, where they come to a halt beside the narrator and confront him)

B: Have you been there lately?

A: I beg your pardon?

B: I said, have you been there lately?

A: Where?

B: Kathmandu.

A: Well, to be perfectly frank, I've never been there.

B: We thought not. Well, we were stationed there and knew Kathmandu when Mount Everest was nothing but a mole hill. We know every inch of the place. I was there only last year. The whole place has changed.

A: That's interesting, but why are you telling me all this?

C: So as to get the facts right! Things are very different now. They've moved the city hall and made extensive alterations to its construction. The main street has been moved to enable them to build a sewer. The idol is now south of the town and the marble cross is above the town. So the whole thing is quite simple—south, not north. Above, not below.

A: May I continue?

B: Do, please do.

A: *(Clearing throat)* There's a green-eyed yellow idol to the–

C: *(Loudly)* South!

A: Thank you. South of Kathmandu. There's a little marble cross–

B: *(Loudly)* Above!

A: *(Dully)* Above the town. There's a broken-hearted woman–

C: Did you know Fanny?

A: *(Irritably)* Fanny who?

C: Fanny Shannon. Colonel Shannon's daughter. The girl whom you so erroneously describe as broken-hearted.

A: *(Emphatically)* No.

C: I thought not. I knew her quite intimately.

A: Is that so?

C: Yes. I grabbed her knee once and she shouted, "Heavens above!"

A: She wasn't broken-hearted?

C: But there was love light in her eyes.

B: That was no love light—that was tail light!

C: She was quite upset for a while but she got over it. She married a rich American who was heir to the Grape Nuts fortune.

B: Grape Nuts. I thought that was a venereal disease.

C: No. He always walked that way. . .

A: Well, but, then how shall I describe her?

B: I'll say this for her, she was no coward—even if she did take it lying down.

C: Oh, I would say a comparatively broken-hearted woman.

A: *(Tiredly)* I'll start again. There's a green-eyed yellow idol to the south of Kathmandu, there's a little marble cross above the town. There's a comparatively broken-hearted woman tends the grave of Mad Carew, and the Yellow God forever gazes down–

B: *(Furiously)* Up, you fool, up!

A: *(Hastily)* Oh, of course, yes, UP. There's a comparatively broken-hearted woman tends the grave of Mad Carew–

B: That, of course, is quite ridiculous. The man was mentally deficient, but certainly not mad.

A: Oh, well, I thought–

B: Well, don't. I'm giving you the facts. Even an idiot wouldn't call the fellow mad.

A: *(Faintly)* He was known as mentally deficient Carew, to the chaps of Kathmandu. He was hotter than they felt inclined to tell–

C: Now, that has nothing to do with Fanny Shannon. That was entirely due to malaria, poor circulation and his refusal to take a bath regularly.

A: *(Miserably)* But for all his foolish pranks–

C: Foolish pranks be damned, sir. Do you call writing dirty words on the wall foolish pranks? He wrote, "Sign up now for the PTA trip to Sodom and Gomorrah" and "Lady Godiva's ride made her cheeks rosy" and "The no-bra look is a letdown".

A: I don't know. . .

C: *(Roaring)* Well, I'm telling you, he had some pretty filthy habits.

A: He was worshipped in the ranks–

C: That's because he was queer.

A: *(Ignoring C)* And the colonel's daughter smiled at him as well. She was nearly twenty-one–

B: *(Roaring with laughter)* That's priceless. Twenty-one be damned, sir. She was forty if she was a day. Mind you, she didn't look it—she'd had everything lifted.

C: She didn't have any trouble holding her shape—her trouble was keeping others from holding it. . .

A: *(Persistently)* She was forty if she was a day–

C: Don't interrupt, young man, I can't hear a word I'm saying.

A: You're not missing much!

C: *(Reminiscing)* I remember Fanny. She wore short skirts to make it easier for the man who can't remember faces. . . She weighed two hundred pounds. When she fainted, it took four strong men to carry her. . . Two abreast.

A: Look, I appeal for fair play. With all these interruptions, how can I ever finish my monologue?

B: I can't think why you ever started it.

A: Well, I never wanted to be a monologuist in a lousy British colonial skit, anyway. *(Exits)*

B: *(To C)* I say, old chap, if we can get back to Kathmandu, maybe Fanny could, too. Why don't we go and look for her?

C: Good idea. There must be a lot of old Fannies in Kathmandu—or right here in Peace River. *(B and C exit)*

This is where somebody like Jerry Gosley might have made his entrance as Fanny, to the music of *When You're Smiling*, and do a monologue.

(Curtain)

JERRY GOSLEY AND THE SMILE SHOW

Just as the dew gently kisses the grass,
Just as the wine gently kisses the glass,
As for you, my friends—cheerio!

Jerry Gosley was a precocious and talented young member of the Royal Air Force when he first came to Canada in 1941. He was stationed at Patricia Bay, just north of Victoria, BC. He started the Smile Show as a morale booster for the troops stationed at the base.

Returning to Canada as an immigrant in 1947, Jerry revived the show as a civilian troupe. In 1951, he launched the first summer show, which was officially opened by Victoria's mayor, Percy George. The following year, the troupe toured the battlefronts of Korea, and after that, the Smile Show ran continuously in Victoria for the next thirty years, to become Canada's longest-running comedy and musical revue.

National recognition came from performances on CBC radio and television, feature stories in national publications, a National Film Board sequence now in the National Archives, plus a command performance on Parliament Hill for Governor General Roland Mitchener. In addition, there was a biography, Nowhere Else To Go: The Life Story of Jerry Gosley, and a long-playing record, A Bit of a Bash.

Jerry either invented or greatly refined one of the greatest revue finales of all time, called If I Should Ever Lose My Job.

Various versions of this bit turn up in revues all over the world, on cruise ships and in amateur performances. The piece is an acrobatic, bat-swinging, frenetic act of near mayhem for five people that always brings down the house and makes a particularly hilarious, sure-fire ending to any burlesque, music hall or other perform-ance. Jerry was a guest artist for the Peace Players and taught them the routine.

I traded skits, sketches and materials with Jerry over the years, as he was always ready, willing and able to help out any group similar to the Smile Show. One of those sketches, the Fatal Quest, likely came from Jerry's long experience in British music hall. It's presented here in three parts, the middle one being a burlesque insertion ending in a chorus number, before continuing with the rest of the sketch.

The Fatal Quest

CHARACTERS: The king; the devoted queen; the duke; the princess; the narrator; Time; the cat; chorus line. The lines are as written, the characters giving their stage directions as part of their lines, while fitting their actions to the words. The costumes are exaggerated and bright coloured.

Narrator: Ladies and gentlemen, The Fatal Quest. The curtain rises for the first act of our little drama.
King: Enter the King from stage left.
Queen: Followed by the devoted queen, also from stage left.
King: He seats himself on his throne, sceptre in his hand.
Queen: The devoted queen stands gracefully beside him, gazing at him fondly. "My Lord," she says in gentle tones. "Why do we keep the princess hidden from the eyes of men?" Then seating herself on his left, she continues, "Will wedlock never be hers?"
King: The king waxes stern. "Fairy Queen", he says gruffly, "a thousand times have I repeated—the princess shall become the wife of no man."
Duke: Enter the handsome duke from stage left. "Oh, King," he says in manly tones, "I have this morning come many leagues from beyond the borders of your kingdom. I have a message of the greatest importance."

Princess: The beautiful princess enters from stage left. At the sight of the handsome duke, she is startled. Her embarrassment increases her loveliness.

Duke: At first glance the duke falls madly in love.

King: The king rises in excitement. "Speak," he shouts at the duke, "and begone."

Duke: The duke gazes at the princess, his message forgotten.

Princess: The lovely maiden blushes and drops her eyes.

Queen: "Beautiful daughter," says the gentle queen. "Why do you intrude yourself here without permission?"

Princess: The beautiful princess opens her mouth to speak.

Duke: The duke holds his breath.

Princess: "Alas," says the maiden in tones melting with sweetness. "My angora kitten has strayed away and is lost."

Duke: "Beautiful princess", cries the manly duke in tones choked with feeling. "Any girl who owns an angora cat has a nice pussy. Service for you is a sheer joy. I swear to find your pussy. After all, I am an expert—I have been looking for pussy all my life and when I go looking for it, I usually find it. Yours will be no exception." With high courage, he strides away stage right.

King: "Stop him! Stop him," shouts the king furiously. "I am told my servants have no trouble finding the pussy of the beautiful princess."

Queen: "Well, I hope the duke has more success in finding hers than you do in finding mine." Exit the queen, stage left, in high dudgeon.

Princess: The dutiful princess dutifully follows in the footsteps of the queen mother, leaving the king on the stage by himself.

Narrator: Time crosses from left to right, as the king exits right.

Time: Time passes. "You must remember this, a kiss is still a kiss, a sigh is still a sigh, etc., as time goes by."

Narrator: Time passes again, the scene shifts and the curtain closes. The handsome duke is still out looking for pussy and in the turgid second act of this little drama, he finds it.

(Actual stage instruction—duke enters from one side of curtain and an actor in a catsuit from the other. They meet. The cat is sneezing)

Duke: From stage right the manly duke steps buoyantly, looks all around and suddenly spots the prettiest little pussy he ever did see.

Cat: Aha, aha, at last you have found me, you lucky devil. I hope you are not a wolf in cheap clothing."

Duke: "Is there anything wrong with being a wolf?"

Cat: "No, but if your wife finds out, she'll cut off your tail. . . I hope you're not with the vice squad."

Duke: "Vice squad, what's that?'

Cat: "That's sort of a pussy posse."

Duke: "Look, I'm a duke and" Pauses and incredulously turns to the audience while cat looks around and reacts. "Ladies and gentlemen, tonight I'm pleased to introduce the only talking cat in the world."

Cat: Cat makes facial gestures, eyes raised in disgust.

Duke: "This cat has been trained, not only to speak words, but to carry on conversations and answer any questions put to her."

Cat: "HIM, you fool. Now, belt up and let's get on with the act. I've got a date tonight."

Duke: "Very well, Felix. I must say, you seem a bit disgruntled today. You're being cheeky, too. What's upset you?"

Cat: "I had a bad night." Sneezes, wipes face.

Duke: "Have you caught a cold?"

Cat: "Yes, but that's not what's making me sneeze. Is that perfume … I smell?"

Duke: "It is, and you do… But don't be so rude. What gave you such a bad night?"

Cat: "I got picked up by the fuzz."

Duke: "I bet that hurt."

Cat: "It didn't tickle me that much!"

Duke: "You're a cat with a lot of vices. What others do you have?"

Cat: "Well, I used to play poker."

Duke: "Poker."

Cat: "Yes, but I gave it up."

Duke: "Why?"

Cat: "I put all I had into the kitty and she raised me four…"

Duke: "Kittens, no doubt…"

Cat: "I thought she really had something" pauses "and now I think I've got it. . . " Scratches himself.

Duke: "Well, are you the princess's pussy?"

Cat: "Do I look like a horny toad?"

Duke: "No, but you act like one…"

Cat: "No, I don't belong to the princess. But speaking of animals—do you know the difference between a tadpole and a mountain goat?"

Duke: "No."

Cat: "A tadpole mucks around the fountain, but a mountain goat. . . "

Duke: "Enough with the jokes, already. Look, I'm desperately in love with the princess and if I can find her pussy, I get to marry her. Can you help me?"

Cat: "Yes, the princess is very beautiful. But I must warn you of one thing. She is very different in the morning than she is in the evening."

Duke: "What's the difference between the princess in the morning and the princess in the evening?"

Cat: "In the morning the princess is fair and buxom! But in the evening she is" pauses, "Yes, I'll help you."

Duke: "How?"

Cat: "There's a cathouse just in here." Points behind curtains. "And I happen to know that the princess's pussy is in there right now. Let's go get her and bring her back to the princess."

Duke: "How will I recognize the princess's pussy? Is she young or old?" The curtain opens slowly as they talk.

Cat: "The difference between an old cat and a little kitty is that an old cat will bite and scratch, but a little pussy never hurt anybody."

Duke: "Do these cats ever get drunk?"

Cat: "Yes. Everybody likes a tight pussy".

(Actual stage direction. Curtain opens to full stage, revealing a group of dancers in cat costumes. The band strikes up Alley Cat and the cat and the duke join in the chorus number. Curtain closes at end of dance and narrator comes onstage)

Narrator: If the bowlegged girl who was having an argument with her waiter will come backstage, I'll straighten her out. . . Time passes again and re-crosses the stage *(Time does so while singing a few bars of As Time Goes By)* The duke has located the princess's pussy —about eight inches below the navel. . . station near the castle moat. . . and the scene shifts and the curtain rises on the final act of our drama.

Princess: The beautiful princess enters stage left and looks through the window. She hears the distinct sound of hooves. "It is he," she cries, placing her hand on her beating heart.

King: Enter the king, from stage left.

Queen: Followed by the devoted queen, also stage left.

Duke: From stage right the manly duke steps in buoyantly, pussy in his arms.

Princess: "My kitten, my kitten," cries the beautiful princess, joyously. She takes her pussy in her arms, but her eyes follow the stalwart form of the manly duke.

King: The king trembles with wrath. "Begone," he shouts furiously. "The hand of the princess shall be won by no pussy."

Duke: The duke departs stage left. As he passes the beautiful princess, he grasps her soft hand. "I will return," he whispers in her ear.

Princess: The beautiful princess does not speak, but her clear blue eyes reflect the secret of her soul.

King: The king stands morosely in the centre of the stage.

Queen: The devoted queen stands sadly beside him. "My Lord," she says in pleading tones, "Relent. The princess weeps day and night, nor will she be comforted."

King: The king turns his back, turns again, and says in relenting tone, "Hold your peace, I will relent. Call back the duke. I must not be selfish. I must think of my daughter's love and happiness. Let's do it."

Queen: The queen weeps with joy and cries: "Oh, duke, return— the king wants everyone to do their thing. So let's do it—let's all fall in love!"

Duke: Duke enters stage right, his sword at his side. "Oh, King," he says, overcome with passionate love, "May I have your daughter's mare in handage. . . I mean, mand in hairage. . . Oh, I mean— Let's Do It!"

(Actual stage direction. The king, the queen, the princess and the duke then finish the skit by singing a parody of the song Let's Do it, Let's Fall in Love)

(Curtain)

This next skit, a version of Cinderella, is another great piece from Jerry Gosley's repertoire, which requires stamina from the actors, because while onstage, they all continually hop up and down in time to the music as they deliver their dialogue in rhyme—which makes it more hilarious. This hopping action is difficult to sustain, so the skit is usually played front curtain so the actors don't have to hop any farther than absolutely necessary. The main curtain opens about three feet, and in front of this opening, a painted flat shortens the distance and facilitates the entrances and exits of the actors. The skit requires a good piano player and the adapted music with intro.

Cinderella

MUSIC: Phil the Fluter's Ball, adapted, with intro
CHARACTERS: Cinderella; Lord High Chancellor; Fairy Godmother; Buttons; Clarabelle; Hippolyta; Prince

(Enter Cinderella, hopping)

Cindy: My name is Cinderella and I have sisters two,
They're very, very ugly, they're not like me and you
They beat me and they treat me just like I was a slave.

(Enter Clarabelle, hopping, exit Cinderella, same)

Clarabelle: I am Cindy's sister, my name is Clarabelle
I'm looking for Hippolyta 'cause I must give her hell
She's stolen my tiara I'm wearing to the ball.

(Stays on, bouncing. Intro, enter Hippolyta)

Hippolyta: Now, Clarabelle you strumpet, you're wearing all my rouge,
And where is Cinderella, we need her as a stooge,
We really must get ready if we're going to the ball.

(Intro, enter Buttons, exit sisters, hopping)

Buttons: I am a bellhop, Buttons is my name,
I love Cinderella,

(Enter Cinderella, hopping)

Cindy: Now isn't that a shame.
Buttons: Oh, Cinderella, won't you come with me tonight?
(Both stay on stage, intro, enter fairy godmother)

F.G.M.: Stop that, you naughty man, you cannot have the wench,
She's going to the prince's ball, although she can't speak French.
Come on, Cinderella, I've got the goods for you.

(Cinders and F.G.M. exit left, Buttons right. Intro, enter Lord High Chancellor, left, and the ugly sisters right)

L.H.C.: I'm the Lord High Chancellor, welcome to the ball.
What are your names, please?
Pass right down the hall,
Cloaks on the right, the ballroom on the left.

(All stay bouncing on stage)

Hippolyta: I am Hippolyta, the youngest of the two.
Clarabelle: And I'm her sister Clarabelle—I rather go for you.
Both sisters in unison, speaking: Where is the prince?
Prince: *(rushes in)* He's here! *(rushes out)*
Both sisters in unison, speaking: He's where? *(Singing)* One of us he'll wed.

(Exit sisters, chasing Prince. L.H.C. left bouncing on stage. Enter prince, bouncing fast, knees up, fast music. He slows down, then sings)

Prince: Really, Lord High Chancellor, that Hippo is too much.

(Enter Buttons and Cinders)

Buttons: This is Cinderella, but you really mustn't touch.
Prince: Oh, you are the girl for me, come let us rock and roll. *(Both rock and roll to music. Others exit. Intro, enter fairy godmother)*
F.G.M.: Now, now Cinderella, this has got to stop. Come along, I've got to take this dress back to the shop.
Prince: You mustn't leave me, Cinders
F.G.M.: *(Speaking)* She must.
Prince: Then I am coming, too. *(Exit F.G.M. and Cinderella. Prince follows, ugly sisters enter right and pull him back)*
Hippolyta: Now, Prince Charming, where are you off to?
Clarabelle: You've mesmerized our Hippo, she wants to marry you.
Prince: Help, Lord High Chancellor. Where is that silly man?

(Intro, enter Lord High Chancellor)

L.H.C.: Did you call, Your Majesty? I happened on this shoe
The girl he wants to marry isn't one of you.
Prince: I'll marry the owner—where can she be?

(Intro, enter Buttons and Cinderella)

Prince: Here is the damsel I'll take unto my bed.
Cindy: *(Speaking)* You can't.
Prince: I can't. *(Speaking)* Why not?
Cindy: *(Singing)* I've married him instead.
L.H.C.: This is not traditional, you must have lost your head.

(Intro, enter F.G.M.)

F.G.M.: Ha, I have fooled you, it's I who made the switch. I'm not
a fairy, really, I'm a DIRTY ROTTEN BITCH!
All: So ends our story, and we are on our way.

(Curtain)

CINDERELLA

Piano

(PHIL THE FLUTER'S BALL)

HAVE A GOOD LAUGH

In the Garden of Eden lay Adam
Enjoying the charms of his madam;
And it filled him with mirth
To think that on Earth,
There were only two balls—and he had 'em!

Dr. Robert Leone, professor of psychology at the United States International University, once said laughter is the best way to relieve stress and put you in a fresh frame of mind. When you're down in the dumps, laughter can give you a little distance from the situation and help you feel better. Because when you're laughing, your attention is focused; you can't do anything else. Everything else, whether it's depression or stress, stops.

It's true that many people laugh to keep themselves from crying. Leone says laughter is a re-affirmation. When you hear yourself laugh, you think, "I must be feeling pretty good." Some people tend to settle for the middle of the road. They won't laugh and they won't cry, either; in reality, their emotions are blunted and it's a very tedious way to live. How you interpret life's events is what makes the difference, not the events themselves.

This next skit is for two people. One is a narrator/emcee, while the other is dressed as Mother Goose—fat, with a long floor-length skirt, but the main gimmick is a false arm which is stuffed and sewn to the costume around a basket. This is why the character has to be rather portly. Mother Goose's real arm and hand is in the form of a long goose's neck which comes out of the basket, and can hold a bottle of liquor and look around as if it's alive. This costume's the toughest part of making the act work. Mother Goose is played as a lush who keeps swigging from a bottle she carries in the basket. The fake goose in the basket also keeps making grabs for the bottle.

The announcer interviews Mother Goose, who is a terrible, drunken old bag and tells jokes based on Mother Goose characters.

Mother Goose Rides Again

MC: *(Sitting on high stool on stage)* Tonight we're going to interview Old Mother Goose. You'll remember her from your youth. . . she's always been a kid's bosom friend. Come on in, Mother Goose!

Mother: *(Enters, half corned with booze)* Shay, halloooo there. . . how are ya? In fact, who the hell are ya?

MC: Well, I'm by way of being a lay psychiatrist.

Mother: *(Makes as if to leave in mock fright)*

MC: *(Holds her back)* No, no, my dear, not that kind of lay psychiatrist. . . I merely mean that I'm studying psychiatry. I'm here tonight to introduce you.

Mother: Oh, I thought perhaps you wanted me to sing a song or something. Hey, that's a good idea *(sings)* Away, away, with fife and drum, Here we come, full of rum, lookin' for men who peddle their—

MC: Mother Goose!

Mother: *(Turns to band)* Just give me a ch-ord *(pronounces it with a soft ch. To audience)* Sure, it's ch-ord. . . Well, ain't it? Man, Webster must have known more than me. Then why did he put an *h* in it? Look, that's right. . . how about cocolate? Do you think cocolate is correct? Can you imagine going up to a girl and saying, "How about a piece of cocolate, honey?"

MC: Mother Goose, I think you're on the sauce.

Mother: Well, you know what they always say—what's sauce for the goose is sauce for the gander. *(Takes bottle out of her basket and takes a belt. When she puts it back, the goose in her basket grabs it and takes a slug, too. Mother Goose's other hand wrestles with the goose to get the bottle back. Corks it and stuffs the bottle and the goose back into the basket)*

MC: But you're supposed to be the symbol of purity. . . and here you show up half shot and—

Mother: (*Peering out into audience*) Whassa matter? This isn't a kid-die show, is it? You think I'm swacked. . . You should take a look at the mayor! And anyway, that's enough out of you, man. Shut up or I'll tell everybody you kept me awake for an hour and a half last night banging on my bedroom door.

MC: I had to, baby, you wouldn't let me out.

Mother: You think you're pretty smart, don't you?

MC: A brain!

Mother: Awright, you're so smart. Think you can answer this question?

MC: What is it?

Mother: What is over-sexed, under-loved and hums?

MC: I dunno. What is over-sexed, under-loved and hums?

Mother: Hmm. . . Shay, let's have another drink (*Catches the goose swigging from the bottle, belts the goose, grabs the bottle, hands it to MC*)

MC: Well, I dunno. . .

Mother: Ah, come on, let's live it up a little.

MC: Okay, if you'll tell me about some of your nursery rhyme characters. (*Takes a slug from the bottle*)

Mother: (*Takes a slug as well and lets the goose have one, too*) What do you want to know?

MC: How's Little Miss Muffet?

Mother: Oh, her trouble is that she's afraid of spiders.

MC: How did that happen?

Mother: Well, she was sitting on a tuffet one day, just eating her curds and whey, when along came this nasty spider. . .

MC: But why would a spider scare her?

Mother: Well, she wasn't the only one. The spider scared the living shit (*pause*) crap out of Little Bo Peep, too. I'm having a lot of trouble with those two girls, Little Miss Muffet and Little Bo Peep.

MC: Oh? Why?

Mother: They've even taken to wearing space panties!

MC: Space panties? What are they?

Mother: They're worn by girls who think their business is out of this world. . .

MC: Tell me about your own childhood. Do you ever wish you were just a barefoot kid again?

Mother: Not me—I used to live on a turkey farm.

MC: What about your own mother?

Mother: Oh, she was a big, mean woman. She had so many children she didn't know what to do.

MC: Well, behind every big woman there's a big woman's behind.

(Pauses as he reflects on this statement) Could that be right—she didn't know what to do?

Mother: Actually, she did do something.

MC: What was that?

Mother: She gave us some broth without any bread. She whipped us all soundly and put us to bed!

MC: No bread! Did you suffer from malnutrition?

Mother: We were so poor, we were made in Japan. At least I was!

MC: Where did you live? In a big house?

Mother: Would you believe in a big shoe? Looked like one, anyway.

MC: It must have been crowded.

Mother: I'll say! We were jammed in there, especially around the toes. . . there were little tots all over the place—tots upstairs, tots downstairs. The whole place was a mass of kids; you couldn't tell where they'd be next. Why, one day my mother was doing the washing and she got one of her tots caught in the wringer.

MC: *(Wincing)* I bet that smarts. But didn't I hear you say she put you to bed without any bread?

Mother: Yeah! That was before we got the bakery.

MC: Bakery?

Mother: At first my mother used to bake at home in the big shoe and then the iceman cometh every day and pinched her buns. He was a bad bun pincher.

MC: So that's why there was no bread?

Mother: When the iceman pinched my mother's buns, this made my father very cross. . . and my mother very hot. . . so they decided to go into business and they opened the first bakery to ever sell hot cross buns! *(The goose comes out of the basket, really drunk, and offers the bottle to Mother Goose, who takes a slug. Then she looks up at the guy handling the spotlight and shouts at him)* Hey Arliss, is it true your girlfriend just had a baby last week? *(Pause)* Well, why don't you call it Target? Everybody's had a shot at it. . .Well, did you hear about the guy who phoned the Salvation Army and said, "Hello there." *(Phone rings offstage)* Hey, Morty, would you mind answering the phone out there? I'm next girl up. . .You gotta make a living, you know, what with having trouble with the show, the band, the dingbats. And that's another thing. Show biz ain't what it's cracked up to be, anyway. My mother would die if she thought I was in show business—she thinks I'm a hooker in Toronto. . . *(To a woman in the front row of the audience who isn't laughing)* You know, you gotta get the laughs out, cause if you keep it inside it's going to cause gas and you'll offend everybody around you. Why don't you laugh it up like the guy behind you? He's got a big mouth—a nice laugh!

MC: *(Looks out into audience)* Yeah, that bald guy. . . You know, the way he was giving out, I'd swear he was sitting upside down *(Laughs at his own joke)*

Mother: I don't know about you, man, you laugh at comedy, you laugh at tragedy, you laugh at anything. . . Let's get back to my jokes. A guy calls up the Salvation Army and says, "Hello there. Is this where you save bad girls?" The lady says, "Yes sir, it is." He says, "Sssssswell, save three for me on Saturday night. . . " *(To non-laugher in crowd)* These are the jokes, Mother Superior. . . If you're waiting around for Billy Graham, forget it. The Catholic lady's sitting there waiting for the raffle. . . I came from a Catholic neighbourhood myself. I learned two words: rhythm and bingo. . . What's green and slithers from bed to bed? *(Pause)* Lizard Breath Taylor. . . Come on, gang, let's have a good time. Get in there. Say, man, looka there!

MC: Yeah, a genuine mink coat.

Mother: Is that a genuine mink coat, ma'am? Did you get that to keep you warm or to keep you quiet? Is that your husband you got there or just some guy you're planning to roll? Nice guy over here. . . *(Keeps up running gags with audience, ends on one calculated to segue into intro to next act while MC and Mother exit)*

(Curtain)

Laughter is the clinking of a couple of unexpected coins in the shabby pocket of life, which poetically seems to sum up the benefits of a good laugh in this often anxious age. Don't think badly of burlesque—it's a long-standing, legitimate form of entertainment in North America, and when we were staging *Sorry 'bout That*, we always presumed that if it wasn't your cup of tea, you wouldn't attend. One saying springs to mind: *Honi soit qui mal y pense* (Evil be to him who thinks evil). So here's a really old classic burlesque sketch that proves the point of that maxim.

Aunt Martha's New Maid

CHARACTERS: Husband and comic Irving Hyman; wife; straight man Stanislaus Montport; Shultzmeir as voice on phone; maid
SCENE: Living room.

Wife: That no-good husband of mine hasn't been home in three days. When he walks into this house I'm going to break every bone in his head.

(Enter husband)

Husband: Hello, honey. How are you?

Wife: Don't you "Hello, honey" me! Do you realize you've been gone three days? Where have you been?

Husband: I stepped out for a packet of cigarettes.

Wife: Cigarettes! Where did you go to get them?

Husband: I went to New Orleans.

Wife: New Orleans! What's the matter, don't they sell your brand here?

Husband: Yeah, but I save three cents on each pack.

Wife: And another thing, when you left this house you didn't leave me any money.

Husband: Oh, money. That's all I ever hear from you. What do you do with all that money I promise you?

Wife: Promises, promises, promises—that's all I ever hear from you.

Husband: Ohhh. . . just shut up!

Wife: Oh! You struck me.

Husband: (Surprised, as he has done no such thing) I struck you?

Wife: That's it, I'm leaving, I'm going home. I'm going home to mother.

Husband: Better than bringing the old walrus here.

Wife: Don't you dare call my mother no walrus. You'd better apologize right now.

Husband: I'll apologize to the first walrus I run into.

Wife: That does it. I'm leaving. Now I am leaving.

Husband: Oh, you're leaving, eh? So you're walking out on the Brain. Just when the going gets tough, you're pulling out. And why? Because I called your mother a walrus. You know I was kidding. A walrus has long whiskers. (Long pause) Hey, come to think of it, so has your mother! Very well then, walk out on me, after I've given you the best years of my life.

Wife: (Groans) Huh! Were those your best?

Husband: They were the best I had. I've worked and slaved for you. . . why, the very clothes you've got on your back I bought and paid for.

Wife: Huh! Now you're throwing that up to me.

Husband: Well, you haven't been throwing it up to me so well lately.
Wife: I can't stay home, I have to meet the girls at the bowling alley.
Husband: All right, all right. What's at the bowling alley. . . oh, the bowling alley!
Wife: And besides, Aunt Martha is sending over a new maid.
Husband: We're going to have another new maid?
Wife: Yes.
Husband: Good.
Wife: And Irving, when she comes, I want you to be very nice to her.
Husband: I certainly will, honey. Yes, I will.
Wife: And give her everything she wants.
Husband: I'll give her everything I've got.
Wife: Huh! That won't be much. *(Starts to leave)* And if you want me, you can reach me at the bowling alley.
Husband: You know damn well I can't reach halfway to the bowling alley. *(After wife exits)* That's the trouble with her—out every night with the girls to the bowling alley—fooling around with those big old rusty balls. She ain't satisfied to stay home and play croquet with my little set. *(Picks up the phone and dials)* Hello, Operator, I want to speak to Schultzmeir's Drug Store.
Offstage phone voice: Hello.
Husband: Hello, is this Schultzmeir's Drug Store?
Schultz: Schultzmeir's Drug Store!
Husband: Schultzmeir, do you do urinalysis there?
Schultz: Sure, I do urinalysis here.
Husband: I mean, do you personally do the urinalysis yourself?
Schultz: I do the urinalysis myself.
Husband: I'll tell you what to do—wash your hands—I'm coming in for a chicken salad sandwich!
Schultz: Ha, ha, ha!
Husband: All right! I'll tell you what to do, Schultzmeir. Put Montport on the phone.
Schultz: I'll see if he's here.
Husband: Yeah, I'll hold.
Schultz: *(Yells)* Stanislaus, is you here? *(To husband)* Here he is!
Husband: Okay.
Montport: Hello.
Husband: Hello, is that you, Stan? Come right over, I want to tell you what's happened.
Montport: Okay.

Husband: Remember I was telling you about my wife.

Montport: Yeah.

Husband: Well, something's developed.

Montport: What?

Husband: Well, I can't tell you right now.

Montport: *(On phone)* What was it? *(Then Stanislaus Montport comes in the door)*

Husband: *(Does double take)* Just a minute. . . *(Says into phone)* Don't bother coming over, Stan. You're here! Aunt Martha is sending over a new maid and I gotta be here.

Montport: A new maid. . . what happened to the old maid?

Husband: My wife caught me.

Montport: She what?

Husband: I said I caught my finger in the wringer.

Montport: You what?

Husband: I caught my dinger in a swinger.

Montport: What are you talking about?

Husband: It's in a cast now. Oh, for heaven's sake, man! My wife caught me down in the basement.

Montport: Down in the basement.

Husband: That damn pool table gets me into more trouble lately. . . I think we'll start shooting pool on it from now on. You know what happened?

Montport: What?

Husband: I forgot to chalk up and I miscued. . .

Montport: Well, I have the tickets!

Husband: Well, you got the tickets just when I can't go.

Montport: What do you mean you can't go?

Husband: I gotta stick around the house.

Montport: Why?

Husband: Something came up.

Montport: Congratulations!

Husband: No, not that old thing.

Montport: You were supposed to meet me here at 12:30 last night.

Husband: Oh, last night at 12:30. . . Oh, I was over at your house taking a bath.

Montport: Taking a bath! Oh, no you weren't. My wife takes a bath at 12:30.

Husband: Yeah, ain't she skinny?

Montport: Yeah. *(Pause)* Now, wait a minute. I love my wife.

Husband: Well, so do I!
Montport: What did you say?
Husband: I meant I love my wife.
Montport: I want to ask you a question.
Husband: What's that?
Montport: Are you getting any on the side?
Husband: I didn't know they moved it! You son-of-a-gun, you always drag me out to burlesque shows. Okay, I'll go!
Montport: All right, sure.
Husband: Is it a good show?
Montport: Good show—they have that cute little strip dancer, Paddy Wagon.
Husband: Paddy Wagon. Isn't that the girl I read about in the newspaper?
Montport: What about it?
Husband: Had a horrible accident. As I remember it, she was on stage doing a shake number. Shook so hard she fell through a hole in her pants and strangled herself to death. . . It was on the front page of the *Daily Worker*. . . I understand all the chorus girls are now wearing their G-strings at half mast.
Montport: *(Laughs)* Ho, ho, ho.
Husband: You know, it sounds like a very well-balanced show.
Montport: It is, oh, it is.
Husband: It should please the men and the women.
Montport: It should please both sexes.
Husband: The others will just have to dance up and down in the aisles. . . There goes the doorbell!

(Doorbell then rings)

Montport: Now, how did you know that bell was going to ring?
Husband: I write these things as I go along.
Montport: Oh, I see.
Husband: Would you mind answering the door?
Montport: Not at all.
Husband: I gotta go to the bathroom.
Montport: What for?
Husband: To change my tie! *(Muttering)* What for!
Montport: *(Groans, goes to door, opens it and attractive maid enters)* Ohhhh. Come in. What can I do for you?
Maid: Is this Mr. Hyman's residence?

Montport: Yes, but you don't wanna pay any attention to him—
he's a, ha, ha, ha.

Husband: *(Re-enters)* That bathroom runs all over the joint. *(Sees
maid)* How do you do?

Maid: How do I do what?

Husband: I'm Irving Hyman. What can I do for you?

Maid: Is this the place where I'm to be maid?

Husband: Yes. . . Yes, you couldn't be maid in a nicer place. *(They
walk to centre of the room)* Tell me something. Did you come by rail-
road or did you come by train?

Montport: *(To maid)* Is this your first trip to the city?

Husband: No, I've been here before. But I'd like to say a few words
about Texas.

Montport: What words?

Husband: Directions on how to get to Texas.

Montport: Okay, how do you get to Texas?

Husband: Go west until you smell shit, that's Oklahoma. Then go
south until you step in it. That's Texas.

Montport: Be quiet! No one's talking to you. *(To maid again)* Is this
your first trip to the city?

Maid: Yes, I was with Aunt Martha but I thought I'd take a whack
at this. . .

Husband: Boy, I'd like to take a whack at that. . . Or take a whack
at Aunt Martha, I don't care. *(To Montport)* You're beginning to
look all right to me, too, lately.

Montport: Now, looka here. . .

Husband: I'm going home to dad.

Montport: I have a proposition for you—a great suggestion. Why
don't you take the two tickets, get a friend and go and see the burlesque show?

Husband: Well, I'll see if I can. . .

Montport: And I'll stay here with the maid.

Husband: Just a minute, not so fast, Montport.

Montport: What?

Husband: You take the tickets and go to the theatre.

Montport: Damn. Okay, sure.

Husband: Sit in the front row and get a bag of popcorn.

Montport: Popcorn be damned!

Husband: And when you come back, don't forget to ring the bell.

Montport: Don't worry, I'll ring the bell. But I have my doubts about you.

Husband: I'll do all right.

(Exit Montport)

Husband: I imagine you're a little tired after your trip. Would you like to take a bath?

Maid: Well, I am a little dirty!

Husband: And I'm a little filthy myself. Would you mind stepping in here? *(Tries to take her into bathroom, which is merely a stage door)*

Maid: Where do you think you're going?

Husband: I was merely trying to help you, sis. I was going to show you where the soap was.

Maid: I can find the soap myself. *(Goes into bathroom)*

Husband: Well, don't lose it. *(Pause)* Do you mind if I help you with your grip?

Maid: *(Offstage)* No, not at all.

Husband: I imagine when you take a trip, you. . . *(Pause)* My, this is lovely luggage you've got here. *(Looks at beat-up old luggage)* Is that airplane luggage?

Maid: Yes, it is.

Husband: *(Pause)* When did you crash last? *(Opens up suitcase and looks in)* I imagine you must have just. . . *(pause, pulls out bra)* What the hell is this? Oh, a slingshot—a double-barrelled slingshot, eh? I'll tell you what—you just relax and I'll look after these things. *(Pause, goes to bathroom door and shoves the bra through)* You may need this. *(Pause)* Oh, is that where that goes?

Maid: Take your hand off my *(pause)* shoulder.

Husband: *(Fiddling with her clothes, improvising some remarks)* I must get a road map. You never know what the weather's going to be. . . *(Trying on the maid's clothes—panties, bra, hat, etc.)* You know, if you reinforce these things in the right places, you—*(wife enters)*

Wife: Honey, I missed the bus and it wouldn't wait, but. . . *(Pauses as she sees him in women's clothing. He goes into a dance when he sees her)* What are you doing?

Husband: I was just doing my dance.

Wife: Dance! I didn't know you could dance.

Husband: I didn't know it either until you came in. . .

Wife: What have you got back there?

Husband: I got a dame.

Wife: What?

Husband: I got a pain. . . I'll be honest.

Maid: *(Singing loudly, then comes through bathroom door wrapped in a bath towel)*

Husband: Sex o'clock, eh?

Wife: Well, I like that!

Husband: I thought it was all right, too.

Wife: And just who is this woman?

Husband: Honey, this is the new maid your Aunt Martha sent over.

Wife: Huh! That's a likely story.

Husband: It's the truth, so help me. If I'm lying, I hope to get paralyzed. . . that's *(pauses as he becomes temporarily paralyzed)* I could have sworn it was her.

Wife: Young lady, you must think you're in pretty fast company. Well, let me tell you something—you're FIRED!

Maid: I'll say I'm in fast company! In the past five minutes I've been hired, tired, fooled and fired!

Husband: You might have been hired, tired and fired, but this is one time you're not going to be fooled! *(Chases maid off stage)*

(Curtain)

THE TORSO SLINGERS

A hot-blooded chorine named Fawn
Could make love from dusk till dawn,
She let no one slip past, but took on the whole cast,
Cause she'd heard that the show must go on!

In the war between the sexes, men have always been excited by the struggle to get women to take off their clothes. As early as Salomé and her dance of the seven veils, there have been women who have understood and exploited this desire.

Stripping, introduced into burlesque theatre in the 1930s, may have been the art form's last desperate attempt to retain its patrons. It worked for a while, until stripping became the dominant feature of the shows, relegating the comedy to the background.

For one version of how stripping started, take a gander at Robert Friedkin's 1968 movie The Night They Raided Minsky's, with Britt Eklund playing the lead in the tale of a religious girl's involvement, much to her father's dismay, with a burlesque comic (Jason Robards). It's a nice look at what early burlesque was like, with good performances by all, including Norman Wisdom and Elliot Gould.

Once numbering in the dozens, strippers soon began to be counted in the tens of thousands, even in countries where people once sneered at the practice or registered shock, contempt or distaste. The French have always had a calm acceptance of the female body. In Paris clubs, the strippers wear more clothes than they wear at the beach, yet arouse far greater interest, which is proof that stripteasing, if not an art form, is a technique that has little relationship to nudity.

A really good strip act is far from a hook-and-eye affair where slithering, sensuous, seductive damsels shed their costumes. Done properly, the strip is a highly skilled performance requiring as much know-how as a successful rendition of a Beethoven sonata. There were and are two schools of stripping: the romantic and the energetic. Maybe you could add the ballet type, likely invented by Valerie Parks. Or the comedic strip, illustrated by the reverse strip, in which the dancer starts out naked and puts on all her clothes. June Taylor once hurried down the theatre aisle in her street clothes as though late for the performance, and took those off instead of the usual exotic garments.

Burlesque almost totally disappeared from the entertainment scene. But it didn't die, it just went into limbo for a great many years, and has now gradually managed a small comeback, as witness the rising number of burlesque nights at nightclubs across North America. And if the Cactus Pricks rock 'n' roll band can draw a crowd in the Rat's Cellar, there's hope for any kind of entertainment.

Live burlesque will kill you with laughter, from baggy-pants jokes and provocative sketches, the raised eyebrow, the punchlines, the nuance, the double and single entendre to the off-colour joke. And just maybe, some of the best humour from the heyday of burlesque can be revived in a well-performed show.

But don't let your kids read this book; these are adult jokes. Your kids may know more than you ever did about sex at their age, but let them invent their own appreciation of sexual humour. After all, some things must be kept sacred.

Listen to Blossom Deary on Ben Bagley's vintage record, DeSylva, Brown and Henderson's Burlesque Revisited:

"Okay Harry, hit me with the surprise pink! That's no surprise, Harry! There aren't many surprises left. . . Whaddaya mean, 'Take it off'? It *is* off! I could be bakin' cakes for the Elks! It's comin' out of those cakes that kills ya. Oh, oh, I nearly bumped myself off!"

I recently came across a sheriff's report of a police raid on a burlesque show back in the days when strippers had first infiltrated the medium.

"The show consists of an orchestra, playing such songs as Your

Lips Tell Me No No, But There's Oui Oui in Your Eyes', and 'Tain't
No sin to Take Off Your Skin and Dance Around in Your Bones, a
chorus line and so-called comedy routines, starring comic
Rhomboid Muckfuster, such as the following:

Judge: Oh, boy, you're a beautiful blonde. I'll bet you're Swedish.
Girl: Well, I'm part Swedish, part French and part Irish.
Judge: *(To audience)* Whew! I'd like a standing ovation for the man
who assembled these parts…

"But I understand the department is only interested in the
strippers. These girls were found by deputies to be ingeniously
covered at strategic points, barely adhering to only the letter of the
law. However, on closer investigation, deputies were shocked to
find a recording company brazenly documenting the performance,
with their microphones placed in an indecent position for pickup.
Inspecting this disgraceful situation, Deputy Smith burned his
chin on the footlights and has a red mark on his chin to prove it. In
the second row, Acting Deputy Jones lost his balance. His opera
glasses flew over and struck the violinist, breaking the female
musician's G-string, and she had to play the rest of the evening
without it. This covers the strippers.

"Concerning the inflammatory effects of such sights of count-
less lovely muscles on the audience, this officer was surprised to
find practically no caterwauling, lewd or otherwise, until, going
backstage, I found that the batteries in my hearing aid were dead.
Twenty-three deputies failed to report back after the midnight show
and one of them fell out of one of the boxes during a comedy routine and strained his knee. From now on these silly investigations
will be conducted only by myself. I have enough trouble keeping
deputies without this, Horace. If you want to help, meet me there.

"Expense accounts for these activities are enclosed.

The Sheriff

"P.S. Since my investigation, I now view the subject in a new
light. Supported by a large core of enthusiasts, the medium is
healthy escapism for the populace, and should continue to supply
name talent for Broadway and TV."

There was always an element of comedy in the North
American version of stripping. Here's one way it was presented in
our show.

The Stagehand and the Tramp
with Girdles Lovejoy

MC: Welcome to the *Sorry 'Bout That* burlesque revue of 1982. We wonder if you have ever wondered two things. First, what goes on in the mind of a stripteaser as she does her act, and, secondly, what happens in the wings or backstage when the stripper is doing her act? Someone has to be there to take her clothes when she throws or hands them offstage. So let's pretend that here we are backstage *(points to sign which has suddenly been thrust out on stage from wings)* and here is the star stripper of our revue, Miss Girdles Lovejoy, dressed in a thousand-dollar creation designed especially to enhance her lovely figure. She has three numbers you're going to be wild about—39-25-36. . . And those figures you couldn't miss if you're out front there to see the revealing, enticing, voluptuous Miss Girdles Lovejoy. She does a very unusual dance—the only thing on her is a spotlight. However, you can hear her thoughts over our public address system while she puts on her stripper costume and warms up to go into her strip routine with the help of our unsung hero, the stagehand. *(MC exits)*

(Girdles Lovejoy enters from the wings, seductively crosses the floor and sits at a dressing table, which is lighted at one side of the stage. She proceeds to put on a costume—in effect undressing, then dressing, in front of the audience as if she were in her backstage dressing room. The Thirties burlesque tune I Want to Be Bad is playing, expressing what might be going through the stripper's mind. The lyrics can be lip-synched. The music changes to whatever number Girdles is theoretically dancing to when she makes her entrance, which she now does, going through the main curtain and disappearing from before the real audience and appearing before the imaginary one behind the curtain. Sound effects of wild applause here. Recorded burlesque band music starts over the PA , but it's not loud enough to cover the following thoughts coming from Girdles Lovejoy)

Girdles: Well, here I go again. I wonder if it's a good group. They look like a bunch of stiffs. Well, we'll soon find out. Hmm, now, there's a good looking group of guys. Hi there, you little crotch watchers... Bet that table cost them a bundle. Back later, baby, gotta spread it around. Look at that bunch of stags—cab driver

give you a bum steer, you horny little mothers. . . Now you're cute
—is that your wife or is this a pleasure trip? You're a doll—love
him, hate her. . . Why, there's Dirty Harry. . . Don't pretend you
don't know me, honey. I wonder if he ever got his car started. Ha!
Ha! Ha! That blonde he's with doesn't know what she's in for. I
can't wait till this is over and I can have my hot pastrami on rye—
and with a big pickle—unless something better comes up. . . Well,
gotta get to work now. . .

*(Burlesque music louder at this point. A comic stagehand comes onto the
real stage with a broom in his hands, pushing it to the sound of the music
coming from behind the curtain as Miss Lovejoy proceeds with her act and
her broadcast remarks before the imaginary audience. The stagehand's
comic routine is performed as pantomime. Sundry items are handed back
to the stagehand through the centre slit of the curtain by the stripper
doing her act on the other side.*

*The mime sweeps the floor, dusts the curtains. The cloak comes through,
and the stagehand unceremoniously throws it on the floor and sweeps it
over to the wings.*

*One silk stocking is handed through, then a second silk stocking, then a
third. The stagehand ponders this. He balls the stocking up, throws it on
the pile with the other two and sweeps them off to the side of the stage.*

*The G-string comes through. The stagehand handles it gingerly with his
thumb and forefinger, throws it on the floor and starts beating it with the
broom before sweeping it aside.*

*An object the shape of a woman's derrière is thrust against the curtain
from the other side and begins to do a grind. The stagehand watches for a
while, then hits it with the broom.*
*Now he lets go of the broom in order to pick up the pile of clothing to take
into the wings in a bit of audience misdirection, but the broom is now
rotating in the air on its own. This is achieved by having another stagehand on the other side of the curtain grab the handle of the broom and
wrap the curtain around it with both hands from the other side of the curtain. This makes it appear as though it's stuck up the stripteaser's butt.*

A great oversized brassiere is the final touch)

There's a smooth segue out of the Girdles Lovejoy pantomime routine into this next front-of-curtain skit. The manager is in the wings, the stagehand is already onstage working and the tramp wanders in, demanding a seat in the theatre.

The Tramp, the Manager and the Stagehand

Stagehand: Now look, you scruffy-looking reprobate, we can't have people like you coming on stage here and spoiling the show. You'll have to leave right away.

Tramp: Well, I got a seat *(points to his ass)* and I've got to find a place to park it!

Stagehand: Man, *(pause)* you've got a hole in it—hang it up.

Tramp: Can I have a seat in the back?

Stagehand: Certainly not. The seats are five dollars each, and I don't suppose for a moment you have five dollars, or even five cents.

Tramp: Is that so? Don't let appearances fool you, mister. For all you know, I might be a millionaire travelling incognito.

Stagehand: Oh, so you're a millionaire, are you? Okay, go to the box office and get yourself a five dollar ticket and you can sit yourself down in the audience and watch the show.

Tramp: You're only saying that because you know I haven't got five dollars. You know very well that millionaires never carry any money on them. Their credit is always good.

Stagehand: Your credit isn't any good in this theatre. If you don't go away, I'll have to call the manager.

Tramp: I bet his credit isn't any good, either.

Stagehand: I've had enough of this. *(Shouts into wings)* Mr. Ramsbottom, Mr. Ramsbottom, are you there?

Tramp: Most people would be satisfied with enough—if other people didn't have more. Who's Mr. Ramsbottom?

Stagehand: Mr. Ramsbottom is our manager. He'll soon deal with you, my friend.

Tramp: Don't call me your friend. I'm particular about the people I'm friendly with.

Manager: *(Enters from the wings, looking authoritative)* Now then, what's your problem? Who is this, this disreputable person?

Tramp: You ought to know. He says you're his manager.

Stagehand: He's just a lazy no-good layabout, trying to see the show for nothing. I can't get rid of him, Mr. Ramsbottom.

Manager: Oh, is that so? Have you told him to buy a ticket?

Stagehand: Yes, but what's the use? He won't have any money. He's a tramp, he's unemployed.

Tramp: (*Mimicking the stage hand*) What's the use, he won't have any money. Flippin' know-it-all, that's what he is. According to the latest statistics, there are three million Canadians who aren't working. Even more, if you count civil servants…

Manager: Well, if you have some money, why don't you get a ticket to watch the show in comfort from the audience. The price to you is a measly five dollars.

Tramp: You call that comfort? Well, I'll tell you what I'll do. If you'll just lend me ten dollars for ten seconds or so, I'll pay for a ticket for the show and give you your ten dollars back, and it won't hurt either of us.

Manager: That sounds rather complicated.

Stagehand: Oh, for god's sake, do as he says and let's get him off the stage. Lend him ten dollars.

Manager: For ten seconds?

Tramp: Yes.

Manager: And I'll get it back? And you'll pay for your ticket like a decent citizen? Honestly?

Tramp: Who said anything about honestly? Just give me the ten dollars.

(*The manager does, and the tramp proceeds slickly into the sequence with the notes, without fumbling*)

Tramp: Thanks, mate. You're a gent. (*Turning to stagehand*) Not like this over-stuffed nitwit. Can you split this ten dollars into two five-dollar bills, mate?

Stagehand: (*Cautiously looks into his wallet, finds he only has one five-dollar bill. He drags it out*) I'm afraid I only have one five-dollar bill.

Tramp: Well, give me that, and you can owe me five dollars. Here's the ten-dollar bill. (*He hands the ten-dollar bill to the stagehand and takes the fiver*) Right. Now you owe me five dollars, right? And the seat costs five dollars. So I've paid for the seat, correct?

Stagehand: *(Uncertainly)* Well, yes.

Tramp: Right. The manager's responsible for the money, so give it to him. Give him the ten dollars and get change. *(Stagehand hands the manager the ten-dollar bill and receives five dollars in change)*

Tramp: Now the seat's paid for, which settles that.

Manager: But what about the ten dollars I loaned you?

Tramp: Don't worry. Everything's under control. I've paid for the seat. *(Turning to stagehand)* I just gave you the ten dollars and you gave me five dollars and you still owe me five dollars, right?

Stagehand: Yes, that's right.

Tramp: You've got five dollars in change now, so hand it over and we'll be quits.

Stagehand: *(Hesitantly hands over the five-dollar bill)*

Tramp: *(Puts the second five-dollar bill with the first one already in his hand and turns to the manager)* Here's the ten dollars you loaned me. I'm sorry it's in two five-dollar bills.

Manager: *(Reluctantly takes the two five-dollar bills)*

Tramp: Now everybody's satisfied and I can go and pick my seat *(Scratches his ass as he says this)* Here, give me that broom *(takes broom from the stagehand)*, I'll even do some work before I find that spot to hang my seat. This show had better be good, or I'll want my money back.

(Tramp goes through stage centre curtain as it opens onto full stage and the band strikes up with King of the Road. The chorus, dressed in skimpy tramp outfits, comes onstage and joins the tramp, singing the lyrics: Trailer for sale or rent, Rooms to let, fifty cents. . . I'm a man of means, by no means, KING OF THE ROAD)

(Curtain)

Let's go back to the present-day stripper situation. Strip club marquees pander to male sexuality with titles like Hot, Hard and Horny and Naked, Naughty and Nasty, featuring Attila the Honey. Inside, a dancer gyrates on a stage ornamented with a pole and a disco ball and often, dry-ice vapour, while other strippers work the room looking for lap-dance customers.

Some strippers are becoming militant, forming local chapters of the Service Employees' International Union, in an attempt to promote more respectful behaviour among the customers, i.e. refusing to put up with certain types of shit. They've even picketed certain clubs in San Francisco, chanting, "Two, four, six, eight, don't go here to masturbate!" and "No contract, no pussy!"

Bill Seaman (left) as Robert Service and Hal Sisson as Twelve Foot Davis, performing in **Twelve Foot Davis Nites.**

(From left) Doreen Sisson, Bill Seaman, Linda Pelchat and Hal Sisson in the burlesque skit A Place to Park the Car. In the skit, both men covet girl A (right), while girl B proves to be the greater challenge.

Bill Pobuda (left) and Hal Sisson performing a blackout, a fast-paced bit of front-of-curtain frenzy to keep the audience warm while the crew changes the set.

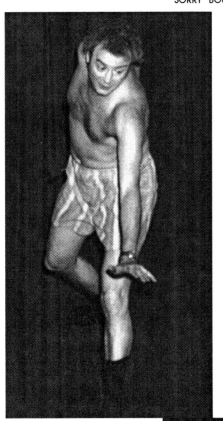

Hal Sisson doing a strip in the ever-popular skit Moe and the Cop. The skit was made famous by veteran burlesque comic and musician Tommy "Moe" Raft.

Candy Butchers Bill Seaman (left) and Hal Sisson hawking their wares, lobbing various objects into the rows of spectators.

(From left) Peace Players Lindy Sisson, Doreen Sisson and Pearl Baldwin vamping in the dressing room.

(From left) Doreen Sisson, Bill Seaman and Hal Sisson in Old Judge Montfort Rides Again.

BLACKOUTS

She was only a clergyman's daughter,
but you couldn't put anything pastor.

She wore a wreath of roses;
Her clothes were in the wash.

The blackout forms an integral part of a burlesque revue. These quick and funny vignettes provide an opportunity to change the set, as they're always performed front curtain in the spotlight. Blackouts are enacted jokes that end with a punchline. For some blackouts, you might need a minimum of props like chairs or a small bar to set the scene and make it work, although you can always leave the setting to the imagination of the audience. Six blackouts makes a standard set, but you can throw one in whenever it's needed. As the laughter from one dies, another blackout can hit the stage.

A Fine Figure

CHARACTERS: Husband and wife.
PROPS: Chair, newspaper
SCENE: Husband is sitting in a chair reading the paper. Wife enters, moves around like a model admiring her own figure.

Wife: I've just come from the doctor's.

Husband: *(Doesn't look up or stop reading)* Uh-huh.
Wife: He gave me a complete physical examination.
Husband: Uh-huh.
Wife: *(Continues to parade around, trying to catch husband's eye)* He says I have a very fine figure for a woman my age.
Husband: *(Finally looks up and says, sarcastically)* Did he say anything about that big, fat ass of yours?
Wife: *(Pause)* No, your name never came up.

(Blackout)

The Bedtime Story

CHARACTERS: One woman dressed as a granny in a rocking chair; two others as little girls, Fanny and Dolly. Granny is knitting as she babysits the little girls, who are working on a colouring book. Tiring of this, they go over to granny's rocking chair. Fanny curls up on the floor and Dolly climbs up onto granny's lap

Dolly: *(Begging)* Tell us a story, Grandma.
Granny: Not tonight, it's too late.
Fanny: Aw, come on, Granny.
Granny: Well, okay *(puts knitting aside)*, what story shall I tell you tonight?
Both girls: Grandma, tell us our favourite story—about the time you were a whore in Montreal.

(Blackout)

When and Where

CHARACTERS: Two men. A comes on with an obvious black eye.

B: What happened to you?
A: You oughta know. That was some advice you gave me about kissing my girl.
B: What was wrong with it? I told you to kiss her when she least expected it.
A: Oh! I thought you said WHERE. . .

(Blackout)

The Lucky Seat

CHARACTERS: Bartender; guy.

Bartender: Well, well, if it isn't the guy who used to be my best customer.
Guy: Yes, it's good to be back in the old bar again.
Bartender: I haven't seen you in a month of Sundays. What happened? Did you go on the wagon?
Guy: No, I didn't go on the wagon. I was just going to a family bar down the street.
Bartender: Wait a minute! You goin' to some other bar now? Didn't I always give you good service here?
A: Yes, good service, yes.
Bartender: Good drinks?
Guy: Good drinks, yes.
Bartender: Cash your cheques?
Guy: Yes.
Bartender: Then what's the attraction down the street?
Guy: You're not going to believe this. They got a seat down there they call the lucky seat.
Bartender: Yeah?
Guy: They move it around every night—you never know where it's going to be.
Bartender: Yeah.
Guy: And whoever sits in that lucky seat that night gets laid.
Bartender: Wait a minute! Let me get this straight. If you—ha, ha—if you happen to sit in that particular seat, they guarantee you're gonna get laid?
Guy: Yep.
Bartender: You believe that?
Guy: I know it's true!
Bartender: Let me ask you this—did *you* ever get lucky?
Guy: No, not yet—but my wife has three times.

(Blackout)

The Cornflake Breakfast

CHARACTERS: Dad; two kids, Bobby and Dougy
SCENE: Kitchen, minimum props—table and two chairs

(Kids engaged in sight gag when scene opens and spot hits them)

Dougy: Hey, Bobby. . . Hey Bobby, you know what one of my favourite things is?
Bobby: No. What's one of your favourite things, Dougy?
Dougy: I really like to have breakfast with Dad.
Bobby: I like to have breakfast with Dad, too. Why don't you call him down, eh?
Dougy: Do you think I should? I will. *(Goes to make-believe door and shouts as if to upstairs)* Hey Dad! *(Returns to seat)*
Bobby: *(Yells, very loudly)* Come on down for breakfast, Daddy.
Dad: *(Enters, really hung over, just out of bed, feels his way along the wall, grimacing as if he has bad taste in his mouth)*
Dougy: Morning, Daddy.
Bobby: Morning, Daddy.
Dad: *(Yells)* Shut up! Just shut up! *(He makes strange noises as he searches for something in imaginary cupboards, fridge or liquor cabinet. He mumbles about needing some juice or a drink)*
Dougy: Do you ever have funny eyes, Daddy.
Bobby: I love you, Dad!
Dougy: I love you too, Dad.
Dad: *(Snarling at them)* What do you want for breakfast?
Dougy: I'll have some of them Fucking Cornflakes!

(Dad attacks Dougy right on the spot, karate chops him to the floor, to teach him not to say that word. Meanwhile, Bobby jumps out of his seat and cowers against the wall)

Dad: *(Loudly)* And what do you want for breakfast?
Bobby. I sure don't want any of them Fucking Cornflakes!

(Blackout)

TWA Tea

CHARACTERS: Female flight attendant; man
SCENE: Inside an aircraft, sign saying TRANS WORLD AIRLINES hangs in prominent place.

FFA: Excuse me, sir, would you care for something to drink?
Man: Yeah, okay. It's TWA we're flying here, eh? Got any TWA coffee?
FFA: Yes, would you like some?
Man: Oh, no! You got any TWA milk?
FFA: Yes, we do, would you like some?
Man: No. What else have you got?
FFA: Well, we have alcoholic beverages—beer, scotch, rye, gin, rum, and also 7-UP, coke and ginger ale. Would you like any of them, sir?
Man: What I'd really like is a little T.W.A.T. . . .
FFA: *(Slaps his face and exits)*

(Blackout)

Carnation Milk

CHARACTERS: Husband and wife

Husband: *(Sitting in chair, reading paper)*
Wife: *(Enters, holding letter in her hand)* Honey, this is very strange. I've just received a letter from the Carnation Milk Company saying I've won Honourable Mention in their slogan contest.
Husband: Well, congratulations.
Woman: And they say I would have won first prize if they'd been able to use it.
Man: That is strange.
Wife: That's not the strangest part. I don't recall even entering the contest. You see, the contest was to complete the last two lines of a verse about Carnation Milk. The first two lines were: *Here I stand in my kitchen grand, A can of Carnation in my hand,* and you had to finish the verse.
Husband: So?
Wife: Well, I never finished it. My recollection is that I left the

paper on my desk with an envelope, meaning to finish the verse and send it in. But I never did.

Husband: Honey, I remember now. I did it for you. I completed the verse and sent it in. Sorry I didn't tell you.

Wife: What did you say, for heaven's sake?

Man: Hmm. . .

Here I stand in my kitchen grand,
A can of Carnation in my hand,
No tits to pull, no hay to pitch,
Just punch a hole in the sonofabitch!

(Blackout)

The 300 Club

CHARACTERS: Lady; yokel named Giles; husband.

Lady: My, but that's a fine bull you have there, Giles.

Yokel: Yes, my lady, he be champion and father of champions.

Lady: Go on, tell me all about him.

Yokel: Well ma'am, this here bull went to stud 300 times last year.

Lady: Indeed? Well, go over to my husband, my good fellow, and tell him that there's a bull here that went to stud 300 times in one year, will you?

Yokel: *(Crosses stage and spot picks up husband)* Sir, your wife says to tell you that there's a bull over there that went to stud 300 times in one year.

Husband: Very interesting indeed! Always with the same cow, I presume?

Yokel: Oh, no indeed sir, 300 different cows!

Husband: Aha! Go tell that to my wife, will you?

(Blackout)

The Researcher

Woman: I want fifty yards of material for a nightgown.
Clerk: Fifty yards—for a nightgown? Why on earth would you want such a lot of material? Fifty yards—for a nightgown?
Woman: Well, my husband is a researcher—and he'd rather look for it than find it.

(Blackout)

Paul Revere

SCENE: One man dressed as American soldier Paul Revere. Fake upstairs window of house with stepladder behind curtain. Woman climbs up the ladder and sticks her head through the curtain break to say her lines. Front curtain door below. Paul Revere is riding a stage variety cardboard and foam fake horse. Horse riding music.

Paul: *(Rides across front of curtain, stops in the middle and yells)* Is your husband at home?
Woman: *(Sticks her head out as if from window)* Yes.
Paul: Then tell him the British are coming. He's got to get dressed so he can fight the British. *(Paul rides offstage and comes around for another pass, repeats routine, then comes around for a third pass)* Is your husband home?
Woman: No, he'll be gone for a week.
Paul: *(Starts to ride off, but when he hears this, he yells)* Whoa-a-a-a! Whoa-a-a-a!

(Blackout)

Three Dates

SCENE: Father, onstage. Three voluptuous daughters walk on.

Daughters: Father! Father! Father!
Father: Yes, what is it?
Daughters: Dear Father, don't wait up. It's Friday night and we all have a date.

1st Daughter: I'm going out with a boy named Joe and he's going to take me to the picture show.
Father: Have a good time, dear.
2nd Daughter: I'm going out with a boy named Pete. We're going to a restaurant for something to eat.
Father: Have a good time, dear.
3rd Daughter: I'm going out with a boy named CHUCK–
Father: YOU GET BACK UPSTAIRS!

(Blackout)

The Stolen Car

CHARACTERS: Drunk; cop

Drunk: *(Has a shirttail sticking out of his fly)* I say, Oshifer, I want to report a stolen car.
Officer: Where did you park it?
Drunk: Dam 'f I can 'member!
Officer: Well, when was the last time you saw it?
Drunk: *(Holds up key)* Lass time I saw that car. . . was on the end of this key.
Officer: *(Smiles)* Look, I'll notify you if we get any news on your car. We'll carry out an investigation. Meanwhile, why don't you go home and get some sleep? And by the way, before you leave, you'd better zip up your fly. . .
Drunk: *(Looks down at his trousers and the shirttail sticking out of his fly)* My God, they stole my girlfriend, too!

(Blackout)

Time to Get up for School

CHARACTERS: Man; woman
SCENE: Man lying on stage in fetal position, fully clothed, covered by a blanket. Enter woman, motherly type.

Woman: Come on, Harold, time for you to get up and go to school.
Man: *(Voice muffled by blanket)* I don't want to go to school today.

Woman: No nonsense now, you've to get up and go to school.
Man: Do I have to? Why?
Woman: Well, there's two good reasons you have to go to school.
Man: What are they?
Woman: Well, for one thing, you're 42 years old *(pause)* and for another—you're the PRINCIPAL!

(Blackout)

Give Him Some Whiskey

SCENE: Man crosses front curtain and collapses centre stage. Several other pedestrians gather around offering suggestions.

Old Lady: Give him some whiskey.
Second man: What he needs is air. Stand back and give him some air.
3rd Man: We should call an ambulance.
Old Lady: Give him some whiskey.
4th Person: He needs a doctor.
Second Man: Anybody here know first aid? He needs some first aid treatment.
Old Lady: Give him some whiskey.

(Sundry remarks—do this, do that)

Collapsed Man: *(Raises his head)* Will you all shut up and listen to the little old lady!

(Blackout)

Speeding

SCENE: Man in mock-up car; cop beside his window.

Cop: I'm giving you a ticket.
Man: Look, officer, the road was clear and I was only doing 67 miles per hour.
Cop: Never mind the arguing and whining. That's seven miles over the speed limit.

Man: *(Friendly tone)* You know, I tried to join the police force once, but I was refused.
Cop: *(Snarly)* Failed your medical, did you?
Man: No.
Cop: Intelligence test then, I suppose?
Man: No. Actually, I passed everything. They rejected me when I told them my parents weren't married

(Blackout)

The Brooch

SCENE: Couple dancing across stage. They suddenly stop.

Girl: Oh! My brooch has come unfastened and I think it slid down the back of my dress.
Guy: Oh, that's too bad.
Girl: Could you help me get it, please?
Guy: Well, ah, well, yes. *(Somewhat embarrassed but determined to please, he reaches down the back of her dress. After a moment he says)* I'm awfully sorry, but I can't seem to locate it.
Girl: Try further down!
Guy: *(Does so, acutely embarrassed, blushing)* I still can't find it.
Girl: Down still further.
Guy: *(Looks up and gazes around as if suddenly discovering he's being watched by all these people, says in consternation)* I feel a perfect ass.
Girl: *(Snappish)* Never mind that! Just get the brooch!

(Blackout)

Stick 'em Up!

SCENE: Stacked gal is standing on a street corner. Enter comic who sees, at the same time as the girl notices, that her shoelace is undone.

Man: *(Gestures)* Can I do that up for you?
Girl: Yes.
Man: *(On his knees, doing up her shoelace)*

Hold-up Man: *(Enters in mask and gun, puts gun to comic's head)* Stick 'em up!
Comic: *(Runs both his hands up inside the girl's skirt. Both comic and girl smile)*

(Blackout)

The Professional Worrier

CHARACTERS: Two men: comic and straight man. The comic plays the professional worrier, who will worry for you if you tell him your problem, thus saving you the trouble of worrying. He wears a sign saying PROFESSIONAL WORRIER.

Straight: Could you show me, like, what would I get for fifty bucks?
Comic: *(Adopts worried expression, paces up and down, mops brow)* Now, that's for a little worry. But I have $100 worries and $300 worries.
Straight: What would I get for $100?
Comic: *(Demonstrates—bangs his head against the proscenium, acts out series of more physical signs of worrying)*
Straight: Well, what if I had a really big worry? What would I get?
Comic: Oh, the $300 worry. It's really something. *(Rolls on the floor, breaks things, takes off shoe and hits himself over the head)*
Straight: I've got a worry and I need your help, but I can't really afford anything more than maybe about a $25 worry.
Comic: Well, okay, business has been slow, so maybe I can do that for you. What's your worry?
Straight: It's my girlfriend. She's not as good in bed as she might be—and it worries me—I mean, she's not bad, but she really could put out more—if you know what I mean. I worry, is it her or maybe me? Could you worry about that for me?
Comic: I guess so. But it would help if I saw her picture.
Straight: Okay. *(Pulls picture out of wallet and shows it to comic)* That's my girlfriend there.
Comic: *(Looks at picture. Keeps looking at picture. Then goes into an even more horrendous performance than the $300 worry routine)*
Straight: Hold it! Hold it! I told you I could only afford a $25 worry. Why are you giving me a $500 performance?

Comic: *(From convoluted position on floor)* I'm not worrying for you, man, I'm worrying for me! That's a PICTURE OF MY WIFE!

(Blackout)

Timbuktu

SCENE: Two guys trying to pick up a girl, front curtain, spot. Poetry contest to decide which guy she'll date

Girl: Stop bickering! I'll go out with the smartest one of you— whoever can make up the best poem using whatever word I choose. Agreed?

Guys: *(Both mutter, reluctantly agreeing to this condition)* Okay, what's the word?

Girl: The word you must use in the poem is *(thinks)*. . .Timbuktu.

Guys: *(Facial expressions and body language show they're thinking hard. Pacing the stage)*

1st Guy: Got it. *(Stands next to gal and recites)*
> As I was walking down the strand,
> I spied a ship not far from land,
> Its sails were taut, its lines were true,
> Its destination—TIMBUKTU!

Girl: Oh, that's so very good. That's sure to be the winner. *(Grabs the guy by the arm and is about to walk off)*

2nd Guy: Just a minute now. Hold it. Don't I get a chance in this competition?

Girl: Sorry. Certainly. Go ahead, let's hear your poem.

2nd Guy: *(Recites)*
> Tim and I went down to Kent,
> We spied three girlies in a tent,
> Having naught else to do,
> I bucked ONE and TIMBUKTU!

Girl: *(Releases arm of 1st guy and marches off with second guy, smiling)*

(Blackout)

OPENINGS

I've met my love,
I'll never ask for more,
She's deaf and dumb, over-sexed
And owns a liquor store.

Openings were rehearsed routines designed to warm up the audience, performing much the same role as an introduction and warmup by an emcee.

The Candy Butchers

SCENE: Two fake old-time candy butchers working the hall up separate aisles. One flogs candies, ice cream or packets of raisins, alternating actually selling the items or throwing empty cartons at the audience. The other offers "dirty postcards"—plain white cards smeared with brown dirt or paint—and underarm deodorant in an old-fashioned fly spray gizmo that he pumps with a plunger. The butchers work their way to the front of the hall, then come up and stand to one side of the stage. The house lights dim and the spot hits them.

Butcher A: If you want something to munch on, I have here in this box some delicious chewy chocolates, which you may purchase for the small sum of twenty-five cents, one quarter of a dollar. Not only do you receive this box of chocolates, but you will also receive our big combination offer. Another part of this big combination offer is this book which has been banned at all the newsstands throughout the United States and Canada. We are not permitted to sell this book—but there is nothing in the law that says we cannot give them away free *(pause)* with each box of delicious chewy chocolates.

Butcher B: At the last performance the book that was in the box of delicious chewy chocolates was entitled Bend Down, Honey, and Touch Your Toes and I'll Show You Where the Wild Goose Goes.

A: But tonight we are offering an even more stirring sexual drama. It's all about love below the border. Our hero, who is a world traveller, decides to go into a dance hall, where he meets the heroine, a lovely dance hall queen named Mexicali Rose.

B: They start to dance and it's love at first sight. He looks at her and he says, "Rose, you're beautiful. In fact, I've seen girls in Montreal, Toronto, Winnipeg, Calgary and Vancouver, and I've never seen a girl quite so beautiful as you are."

A: She invites him to come home to her apartment. He walks in and he says, "Rose, I've seen beautiful apartments in Montreal, Toronto, Winnipeg, Calgary and Vancouver, but I've never seen an apartment quite so beautiful as this one."

B: Rose excuses herself and leaves the room and comes back five minutes later in a negligee. Our hero says, "Rose, I've seen beautiful negligees in Montreal, Toronto, Winnipeg, Calgary and Vancouver, but I've never seen a negligee quite as exquisite as this one."

A: They have a few drinks to get better acquainted, then she invites him into her boudoir. He says, "Rose, I've seen beautiful boudoirs in Montreal, Toronto, Winnipeg, Calgary and Vancouver, but I've never seen a boudoir quite so beautiful as this one."

B: They turn the lights down low and they lay *(pause)* lie down on the bed, and then they start to make love. And when they start to make love, FROM THEN ON, IT'S THE SAME DAMN THING.

Both: *(Louder)* MONTREAL, TORONTO, WINNIPEG, CALGARY AND VANCOUVER. . .

A: In the combination offer is this telescope. . . *(to someone in audience)* what are you giggling about? This telescope comes direct from Paris, France. You don't believe me! If it doesn't come from Paris, France, may I drop dead on this spot! *(Jumps back a couple of steps from where he was standing, which gets a laugh)* Now this telescope, when you hold it up to the light, you can see a beautiful model in a two-piece outfit *(pause)* Gloves! Now she wiggles and shakes and she shakes and wiggles and we call her Candy because she makes your peanut brittle. . . And now the final item in this combination offer. Here it is, here is the biggie. This is the biggie. Virility pills.

B: Yeah, virility pills come to us from the Upjohn Company. . . go ahead, take your time. . . I'll wait. . . and these virility pills are really potent. I warn you, when you take one, swallow it fast, or you'll get a stiff neck. If you take two, you'll pole vault down the bedroom. . .

A: Now the waiters and waitresses are going to come out into the crowd and sell, and when they do that, please give them a break because they're working their way through reform school. And remember, every night, we are selling one box which has a special gift inside. So try to be the first one to buy a box. Only twenty-five cents, one quarter of a dollar. Who'll get the gift? *(At this point, a couple of performers begin working the aisles, selling the combo offer)*

A: You can't tell what it will be. It may be a valuable watch, it may be a gift certificate for a Cadillac car—you can't tell. One lucky guy got a dime and ring. So ladies, get your boyfriend to buy a box— you may get a dime and ring. Dime and ring. . .

B: Anybody got a gift yet? *(Excited)* Someone over there? There's one now. What did you get, sir? Did you get a watch? What kind of a watch did you get, sir? Did you get a Gruen—that's the best Gruen you ever got, sir. . . Sir. . . What, sir? What's that? I'm a fake? I'm a fake!? How dare you, sir! I'm on the level. The stage may be crooked, but I'm on the level.

A: *(Comes to the rescue)* Certainly he's on the level, and to prove it I have for you a proposed gift for a hundred dollars. How's that? Here's our bonus for any man—or woman—that has one of the little packages with a yellow ticket in it. The yellow ticket in any one of the boxes of candy is worth $100. Did anybody get it?

Voice from audience—a plant: I've got a yellow ticket.

B: Where the hell did he come from? Who in blue blazes let him in here? Did you pay to get in, sir?

A: Well, he's got a yellow ticket, so *(pause)* you will get the $100. . . if. . . you can answer one question correctly. Here's the question, sir: What is the last thing your wife says to you at night before you get into bed?

Voice: That ain't hard!

B: *(To A)* That's not a proper question, so he doesn't win. And that must be an old joke of your father's.

A: Well, what are you—an old joke of your mother's?

B: Now listen here! Aw, forget it. *(Produces letter and says to A)* Here, read this letter for me, will you please? I don't have my glasses and without them I'm a bit blind.

A: *(Takes letter and reads aloud)* Dear sir, I want you to leave my wife alone or I shall shoot you on sight!

B: What?

A: *(Repeats letter's contents, then says to B)* Why don't you leave his wife alone?

B: How can I? He hasn't signed his name. . . I don't know who he is. I'm a devil with the women. Did you see the bird I was with last night? She thinks I'm a solicitor.

A: Why does she think you're a solicitor?

B: I made her alter her will. . .

A: Okay, how do we end this act?

B: I think what we need is a new manager. At least you do.

A: Why's that?

B: So you can stop handling yourself!

A: That does it. I've had it with you. I'm getting a new straight man.

B: What makes you think you're the comic? Good-bye! *(Each go to exit, but then turn toward each other and meet at centre stage, spots following them)*

A: *(Hangs head)* Wouldn't work, Bill.

A: You're right, Hal.

B: What will we do?

A: How about that famous old music hall tune by Bud Flanagan of Flanagan and Allen, Underneath the Arches.

B: Great song. Okay.

(Piano music, then they sing in unison)

> *Underneath the arches*
> *We dream our dreams away*
> *Underneath the arches*
> *On cobblestones we lay*
> *Every night you'll find us*

Tired out and worn
Happy when the daylight
Comes creepin'
Heralding the dawn
Sleepin' when it's rainin'
And sleepin' when it's fine
Trains rattling by above
Pavement is our pillow
No matter where we stray
Underneath the arches
We dream our dreams away.

(Curtain)

The next opening makes a good segue into the skit that follows.

Ladies' Night

MC: *(Front curtain)* We don't have a packed house here tonight because I asked a lot of people not to come. Did you ever notice that the bigger the crowd, the more people are in it? And that small crowds are poorly attended? Now, before the start of tonight's show, I would like to inform you of the policy of this theatre. Performances every night of the week, except Monday. Now, on TUESDAY *(fanfare)* Tuesday night is Garter Night. To every lady accompanied by a husband—whether hers or not—we shall give, absolutely free, an intimate article of feminine apparel. Now, on WEDNESDAY *(fanfare)* Wednesday night is Chorus Girl Opportunity Night, and on that night—

(Enter comic, who comes onstage)

Comic: Pardon the interruption, but I think the folks here at the burlesque theatre would like to know that Miss Fifi La Touche was released from the police station on Sunday. . . It seems she went a little too far on Chorus Girl Opportunity Night and the police raided the joint. She was supposed to be released Friday night, but she couldn't make it.

MC: Why not?

Comic: She went over so well down at the police station, they held her over for two more nights. . .

MC: As I was saying, Wednesday night is Chorus Girl Opportunity Night, and all chorus girls will compete for your applause with a dance of their own choice.

Comic: Hey! The management has asked me to make a special announcement.

MC: Well, what is it?

Comic: Starting this Thursday—every Thursday will be known as Mothers' Night. All you ladies who want to be mothers can meet the manager in his office after the show. . .

MC: Now on Friday Night *(bad fanfare)*, Friday night will be Ladies' Mud Wrestling and Boxing Night. So all you ladies who plan to attend on Fridays, please bring your box. . . But now, the moment we've all been waiting for! We have some thespians who are just dying to get on stage and present to you some serious drama. Mesdames and Monsewers, we have here with us tonight the Moose Jaw City Art Players in a literary creation called:

Come Fly With Me

CHARACTERS: French maid (Louise); Gaston the lover; husband; author; wife. Costumes: outlandish
SCENE: Bedroom/living room. French maid is onstage, dusting. Husband enters.

Husband: Hello, Louise, have you seen my wife?

Maid: No sir, she hasn't come down yet.

Husband: Well, when you see her, you tell her I'm going on a vacation for three weeks. I'm going to the El Rancho Grande Hotel. It's in Ploughsville. Got that, Louise? *(Maid nods)* See you later. *(Exits behind a screen; he doesn't really leave. Wife enters, in sexy dress)*

Wife: Oh, Louise, have you seen my husband?

Maid: Yes, madame. He told me to tell you that he was taking a three-week vacation at the Ploughsville hotel, El Rancho Grande.

Wife: Has my lover Gaston called?

Maid: He called, but I did not wish to disturb you so I asked him to call back. *(Phone rings)*

Wife: Never mind, Louise, I'll take it. That must be Gaston now. And by the way, Louise, you can take the winter off.

Maid: Thank you, Madame.

Wife: *(On phone)* Is that you, Gaston? Oh, darling, it's so good to hear your voice. Where are you?

Gaston's voice, from backstage: Just in the next town.

Wife: Well, hurry right over. *(Hangs up)*

Gaston's voice from backstage: Is that same audience out there?

Wife: Yeah, they're still here. Is it any wonder I fell in love with Gaston? He has everything a woman could want. The face of Rock Hudson, the charm of Cary Grant, the physique of Burt Reynolds.

(Enter Gaston, who is none of these handsome actors. He has on an old tux and top hat and carries a cane)

Wife: Oh, darling, I'm so happy I could fly.

Gaston: Well, my dear, let's fly, and we'll fly from here to here to here to here *(Whacks the bed with his cane with each "here")* We will fly like we never flew before, my sweet.

Wife: Oh, Gaston, you must control yourself.

Gaston: How can I control myself when you keep shifting gears?

Wife: Oh, Gaston, I love you.

Gaston: Let's lay down and talk this over, just the two of us, because when I get through with you. . .

Author: *(Comes to edge of stage from out of the audience)* All right, all right *(Shouts)* Both of you! What in hell's going on up there? Of all the atrocious acting I've seen, this is the worst. What the hell's the matter with you two?

Wife: Don't blame me, it's him.

Author: Oh! Hey, Stupid! *(Pause, then louder)* Hey, Stupid! *(Gaston motions toward wife as if it's her that's supposed to answer)* Not her! I'm talking to you, Stupid!

Gaston: Me? You callin' me stupid?

Author: I am.

Gaston: Who the hell are you?

Author: I happen to be the author. I wrote this thing.

Gaston: Wrote this thing?

Author: Yes.

Gaston: I seen better writing on the wall in the men's room!

Author: Well I've seen better acting there, too. . .

Gaston: How would you like me to raise a lump on your head with this? *(Threatens author with cane)*

Author: Not only did I write this thing, but I've played every part in it.

Gaston: You're kiddin'.

Author: Yessir!

Gaston: You play my part?

Author: Yes.

Gaston: Play the maid?

Author: Yes.

Gaston: Play her part? *(Pointing to wife)*

Author: Naturally!

Gaston: Let's you and me fly, boy!

Author: Look, I'm talking business to you.

Gaston: I'm makin' you a damn good offer. Come on there. . . You really wrote this thing, eh?

Author: I did.

Gaston: Maybe it's none of my business, but has this turkey got a name to it?

Author: It doesn't need a name.

Gaston: It needs something. How about some Saniflush, Airwick, something.

Author: This happens to be a beautiful story about love in outer space.

Gaston: Love in outer space?

Author: Yes.

Gaston: What do you call it? Moontang? *(To audience)* Am I a little too fast for you? *(To author)* You really wrote this thing, eh?

Author: That's right.

Gaston: You, sir, have a hernia in the head. Besides that, you're an imbecile.

Author: I'm an imbecile! You're an imbecile.

Gaston: You're an imbecile!

Author: You're an imbecile.

Wife: Gentlemen. . .

Gaston: Shut up, this is between us imbeciles.

Author: You have the audacity to call me an imbecile?

Gaston: Yep.

Author: Well, that ties it. Let's take this turkey out of the show. Strike the props. Bring on the elephants.

Wife: Oh, Mr. Muckfuster, give us another chance.

Author: No!

Wife: Please, please, give us another chance!

Author: Absolutely not.

Gaston: Aw, give us another chance, you knucklehead. What the hell are you squawking about? These idiots *(indicates audience)* paid to get in here tonight, didn't they? Maybe they'd like to see it. Would you like to see it again, folks? *(Scattered applause)* You see, it's unanimous! *(Laughs)* Everybody wants to see it. I may throw up, myself.

Author: All right, I'll give you one more chance. Miss De Lovely, you're playing this part a bit too falsely.

Gaston: You're damned right she is.

Author: You shut up!

Gaston: You can kiss my bingo card.

Wife: Look, how do you expect me to make love to a guy who's been eating garlic?

Author: Have you been eating garlic?

Gaston: Well, yeah.

Author: Why?

Gaston: I happen to like it. *(Has been leaning on his cane but at this point, the end of the cane slips off the stage and he nearly falls into the pit)*

Author: That's right, why don't you just fall off the stage. You might get your first laugh.

Gaston: How do you think you're going to look with this thing sticking out of you, bud? You know where, too!

Author: Okay, I'll direct this thing. We'll take it again from the top. You behind the screen, come out here. You behind the screen, will you come out here?

Husband: *(Pokes head out)* Who, me?

Author: Yeah, you. Are you going away on a trip?

Husband: *(Dumbly)* Huh?

Author: A trip!

Husband: *(Dawns on him)* Oh, yeah!

Author: Well then, where the hell's your paraphernalia?

Husband: *(Looks all around, then down at his fly)*

Author: Your grip!

Husband: Oh, I never get the grippe. I had pnoo-monia once. Also a hysterectomy.

Author: I mean your bag!

Husband: *(Looks at wife)*

Author: Not that kind of bag! I mean a suitcase. Now, get behind the screen to await your discovery of the lovers. And when you see that man making love to your wife, you come out and shoot him. *(To Gaston and wife)* Now, get back here, you two. Take your positions.

Gaston: Now you're talkin'. Come here, honey. I'm gonna be great cause I've got my truss on tonight. I got it on upside down—I figured for the weekend I'd go sporty, you know what I mean?

Author: What are you doing there?

Gaston: My position is here with her.

Author: Your position is not there, your position is offstage.

Gaston: Oh, yeah?

Author: Yes.

Gaston: Hey, when do the babe and me get to *(mouth noise)* on the bed. . . you know.

Author: You'll get there in due time!

Gaston: Well, if I get there, I'll do time, all right, but I'd like to take one shot at it before I go.

Author: Hold it!

Gaston: I'll send her right back. I'm pretty fast, you know.

Author: No.

Gaston: I hop on, I'm right off. I'm a guy who gives pep talks to rabbits.

Author: No!

Gaston: Pronto Tonto they call me.

Author: How would you like a shot in the head?

Gaston: I don't drink in the men's room.

Author: Get out of here.

Gaston: See you later, Kemosabe. I'll be back after awhile, honey, and give you my silver bullet. And this goddam audience better not be here then, either!

Author: All right, we're all set to run through it again—please.

Wife: Oh, Gaston, I'm so happy I could fly.

Author: Oh, my gawd, honey, be an actress. You're about to make love. Whoever told you you knew how to make love?

Wife: That's not what you said at the hotel last night.

Gaston: *(Steps out from behind curtain)* Oh, so that was you runnin' round those halls last night without any clothes on. Whooee! I saw you, you son of a gun. Naked as a jaybird and twice as cocky.

Author: I was talking to the chambermaid.

Gaston: And what did she say?

Author: No soap!

Gaston: Hey, Milford!

Author: Yes?

Gaston: I'll tell the jokes up here, if you don't mind.

Author: When?

Gaston: As soon as we get an English speakin' audience, that's when. *(Gaston motions and whistles to wife to get on the bed)*

Wife: No.

Gaston: *(To author)* How about you?

Author: No.

Gaston: *(To guy in audience)* Sir?

Author: Will you do me one favour?

Gaston: Yes.

Author: Just go off stage and come bouncing in on your cue.

Gaston: *(Pause)* What do you think I've got, a pogo stick?

Author: May we try it once again, please, and this time, please put a little more feeling into it.

Wife: Oh, Milford, I could put so much more feeling into it, if you would come up and play the part. *(Audience applauds)*

Gaston: Why, you dirty doublecrossers! You can all go to hell for all I care. I don't need you, I don't need you and I certainly don't need her.

Author: No?

Gaston: No, I got all kinds of women falling at my feet.

Author: You have?

Gaston: Yeah, I go out with the clumsiest broads.

Author: Get out of here. *(Gaston exits)*

Wife: Oh, Gaston, I feel so happy—*(Sound of shot offstage)*

Gaston: *(Enters)* Excuse me, are there any animals around here? About this big *(indicates six feet)* all black with a band of white fur around the neck?

Author: No.

Gaston: Are you sure? My god! I've just shot Bishop Pierce!

Author: Get offstage! Now, once again, my dear.

Wife: Oh, Gaston, I'm so happy I could fly. And I'm hungry and I need something to eat *(starts to laugh)*. This is so ridiculous!

Author: Stop clowning around and let's get on with the rehearsal. Take it from the top and get into the love scene.

Wife: Oh, Gaston, I'm so happy I could fly.

Gaston: *(Enters again)* We'll fly from here to here to here *(whacks the bed with each "here")*. Come here, my sweet. We will fly like we never flew before. *(They sink down onto the bed)*

Wife: Gaston, you must control yourself.

Gaston: My darling, what is it about you that arouses within me this mad passion?

Wife: Oh, my goodness!

Gaston: No, it ain't that.

Wife: I like your style.

Gaston: I like your smile.

Wife: I like your clothes.

Gaston: I like your nose.

Wife: I like your class.

Gaston: *(Long pause)* What's new?

Author: All right, you behind the screen, that's your cue. You behind the screen, will you come out here? *(To Gaston)* Will you do me a favour? Will you go see what he's doing back there?

Gaston: Glad to. *(Looks behind screen, pauses)* He'll be through in a minute.

Author: Get him out of there!

Gaston: I'll get him out the hard way.

Husband: *(Runs out)* I quit, I quit.

Gaston: *(Pokes him in the ass with the cane, then checks cane)* He's down about a quart.

Author: Well, you two, step down in front. This is your big scene.

Gaston: It is?

Author: I want you to make mad, passionate love to her, I want you tell her that the skin on her neck is as soft as the down on a duck's stomach. Let's see you do it.

Gaston: My dear! *(Pauses, says to author)* What was that again?

Author: I said tell her that the skin on her neck is as soft as the down on a duck's stomach.

Gaston: My darling, the skin on your neck *(pauses)*. What the hell were you doing under a duck's stomach?

Author: Will you make love to her?

Gaston: Darling, the first time I laid eyes on you I said *(pause)* you're getting a little hippy there, kid.

Wife: Don't get smart with me.

Gaston: Do you want to lose ten ugly pounds?

Wife: Yeah.

Gaston: Cut your head off!

Wife: Look, wise guy, just to show you how smart you are, while you were making love to me, I stole your watch. *(Pulls out watch and shows it to him)*

Gaston: How do you like that? Stole my watch! I didn't even know it, either. *(Pause, then he pulls out garment from behind him and dangles it in front of her face)* Here are your panties.

(Curtain)

SONG AND DANCE

Thanks for the memory,
Of the night when I came home
and found you not alone;
You said it was a nudist,
come in to use the phone,
Oh, thank you, so much.

People think if you're an entertainer you must be an alcoholic, a skirtchaser, a pervert or a dope smoker. That's what attracted me to the business in the first place.

For me, performing comedy is like sex—I'm done before you are. Actually, comedy is better than sex. Some nights you get to perform for forty-five minutes to an hour. After a comedy show I always feel good, satisfied, like I've accomplished something. After sex, I feel, I don't know, like it just wasn't worth the money.

I can't sing worth a damn but I could rhyme a simple song or two. I was thinking of a little song entitled, Last Night I Was In the Mood, But Tonight I Must Get Some Sleep.

Vaudeville and music hall went in for more songs than burlesque. One of the most famous music hall masters was Max Miller. He'd say: "Here's a song called The Girls Who Do," then ask the piano player, "Shall I start it off?" The pianist would say, "Yes, you start it off." Max would reply, "And you'll creep in, won't you?" The piano player would say, "I'll creep in," then Max would say, "He'll creep in. . . I'll give you the key. Well now, he might be home before me, see?"

Then Max would launch into the song:

Oh I like the girls who do,
I like the girls who don't
I hate the girl who says she will
And then she says she won't.
But the girl I like best of all
And I think you'll say I'm right--
Is the one who says she never has
But looks as if she. . . Listen 'ere now!

You don't hear those kinds of songs much anymore, but at one time they were very popular in music hall and burlesque theatres. They're reminders of yesterday, when they were on a lot of trouper's tongues.

Here's a song that can be worked very well into a short burlesque skit.

Two Jerks from Jericho

CHARACTERS: Two male singers
A: *There were two jerks from Jericho,*
   There were two jerks from Jericho
(*Pause, then A says to his partner Z*) Come on, you're not singing with me.
Z: I don't know this piece.
A: It's an old piece.
Z: I know a lot of old pieces. . .
A: It's a hundred years old. Try it, will you?
Z: I don't know any pieces that old.
A: Try it. Every time I point at you, you sing.
Z: Okay, I'll try it.
A: *There were two jerks from Jericho*
Z: *Jericho.*
A: *There were two jerks from Jericho*
Z: *Jericho.*
A: *Jeri, Jeri,*
Z: *Cho cho cho*
A: *Jeri, Jeri*
Z: *Cho Cho Cho*

A: *There were two jerks from Jericho.* That's the idea! Now we'll go a little faster. They both had girls, see?

    Their girlfriends came from Amsterdam.

Z: *Amsterdam.*

A: *Their girlfriends came from Amsterdam.*

Z: *Amsterdam.*

A: *Amster, Amster,*

Z: Dam *(Stops)*

A: Come on, you gotta sing your part. Here we go—*Amster, Amster,*

Z: *Darn, Darn, Darn.*

A: *Their girlfriends came from Amsterdam.* Come on, now, you gotta do your part. *The two guys came from No-or-folk*

Z: *No-orfolk*

A: *The two guys came from No-orfolk*

Z: *No-orfolk*

A: *The two guys came from Norfolk*

Z: *Norfolk*

A: *Nor, Nor,*

Z: *(Stutters and splutters)*

A: Come on, you're killing the whole song. Now, we'll do it right. Here comes the big part. They climbed up on top of the wall and fell off the precipice.

    They both fell off the precipice.

Z: *Precipice*

A: *Preci, Preci,*

Z Oh, no! *(Stops)*

A: Oh, come on, you can do your part fine. *Preci, Preci,*

Z: *Wee, wee, wee*

A: Here's your last chance—*Preci, Preci,*

Z: *Number 1*

A: *They both fell off the precipice.* He's a good sport. So okay, let's end it. We're gonna end it.

    And now we're gonna finish it

Z: *Finish it*

A: *And now we're gonna finish it*

Z: *Finish it*

A: *Fini, fini,*

Z: *Shhhhh (Stops)*

A: Oh, come on! *Fini, Fini,*

Z: *Poo, Poo, Poo*

A: *Fini, Fini,*
Z: *Number 2*
Both sing: *And now we've got to finish it!*

JaDa

Ja Da Ja Da
Ja Da Ja Da Jig Jig Jig
Ja Da Ja Da
Ja Da Ja Da Jig Jig Jig
Now that's a sexy melody
It's so soothing and appealing to me
It goes Ja Da Ja Da
Ja Da Jig Jig Jig

Matches, Matches
M A T C H E S,
Matches, Matches
M A T C H E S
You strike 'em on the window
You strike 'em on the glass
I even met a girl who could strike them on her—
Ankle...
Matches, Matches
M A T C H E S

She had a, she had a,
She had a pair of BVDs
She wore 'em, she wore 'em
She wore 'em down below her knees
Now she wore 'em in the winter
She wore 'em in the fall
When she ran around, didn't wear 'em at all
She had a, she had a,
She had a pair of BVDs...

Have a Good Time in Your Prime

(Duet)

Have a good time
While you're in your prime
Cause it don't mean a thing when you're old
Hey fellows, take a chance
Find romance with Susie and Jane
Don't wait too long, boy,
You'll have to carry a cane
Get out and make hay
While you're feeling okay

Don't be like this old friend of ours
He went up to the lake
And he hired a canoe
His girlfriend was 18
But he's 82
They paddled and they paddled
What else could they do
So have a good time in your prime.

Have a good time
While you're in your prime
Cause it don't mean a thing when you're old
Hey fellows don't be shy, you can try
Hey what can you lose
Don't wait too long, boys
You might blow a fuse
Go out and get looped
Before you are pooped
Don't be like this old gal of ours
She went into a nightclub
And to her chagrin
The nightclub was crowded
But she walked right in
She went in with two Swedes
But came out with a Finn

So have a good time in your prime.
Have a good time
While you're in your prime
Cause it don't mean a thing when you're old
Ah, be a man, while you can
And this you will learn
Modern girls like to deal
With an old established firm
Wherever or when
You are feeling a yen
Don't be like this old friend of ours
By cracky, he was so old
That his knees were bent and creakin'
But he went out one night
And found what he was seekin'
When they found poor Mr. Wetzell
He was bent up like a pretzel
So have a good time,
Have a good time,
Have a good time
In your prime!

I used to have a dressing room right next door to the chorus line. There was a hole in the wall between our dressing rooms and I was going to plug it up, but I figured, why bother? Let them enjoy themselves.

You know, I've been in show business so long that I could tell just by looking at an audience whether it was a good audience or a bad audience. If it was a good audience, I'd sing a song. If it were a bad audience, I'd sing five. This next one is a sad song, so when I performed it, I'd ask the audience to cry in tempo.

A sweet young girl was jilted by her husband
He left her and he went his merry way
With tearful eye she wrote a final letter
And here is what her broken heart had to say:

(three-bar intro with change of pace in music here)

I'm returning every present that you gave me
I'm sending back each letter that you wrote,
The locket that I wore around my throat.
Enclosed you'll find the mortgage on the house, dear,

That I'm fair you must admit is true
I'm returning everything except the baby,
That's the one thing that I didn't get from you.

The Thingbee Song

Sometimes we'd advertise a two-hundred-voice choir in the program for *Sorry 'bout That.* We didn't have two hundred voices up on stage, but we did in the audience. So I'd lead them in song.

MC: I'll sing, *Gold is the colour of my true love's hair*
And then you'll sing, *Thingbee! Thingbee! Thingbee!* You want to try it? Okay! *Gold is the colour of my true love's hair*
Audience: *(voices weak) Thingbee! Thingbee! Thingbee!*
MC: That's not loud enough, let's just try your line, eh?

(Leads them until they're shouting)

MC: Ah, that's better. Okay, we'll give it a fling now. *Gold is the colour of my true love's hair.*
Audience: *Thingbee! Thingbee! Thingbee!*
MC: *If gold is the colour of my true love's hair*
Audience: *Thingbee! Thingbee! Thingbee!*
MC: Then what can the colour of her. . . *(Stops)*
Audience: *Thingbee. (Several start to laugh)*
MC: I have my doubts about you bunch. Well, we've got a real bunch of singers here this evening. You are something else.

Burlesque songs were suggestive, allusive, sexually oriented and blue, but they were not bawdy or obscene. They don't come under the heading of dirty songs. For those, you really have to go to the military. In that great movie Bridge On the River Kwai with Alec Guinness, when he led his hardy band over the bridge, they only whistled the tune of the so-called Colonel Bogey March. British soldiers had some choice lyrics to fit that stirring march. Should I quote them? What the hey! You all know the words, so sing along:

Bullshit, was all the band could play,
Bullshit, they played it night and day,
Bullshit, the same old bullshit
Ta da, da da da, da da da, ta da!
Hitler—has only got one ball,
Goering's—are rather awf'lly small,
Himmler's—are somewhat sim'lar,
And Goebbels has no balls at all!

Colonel Bogey was tame compared to most dirty songs, where the language isn't smoothed over and couched only in the vaguest of terms. Folk is a four-letter word, and a lot of folk songs were bowdlerized, expurgated and edited, in short, cleaned up. To what purpose? When cleverly contrived, the dirty song is as valid a work of art as any other folk song, work song, historical ballad, protest song or love song. Dirty ditties aren't just a string of obscenities set to music, they often constitute social commentary. They often have an irreverent take on great figures of history, roar defiance and tell impossible tall tales. The good ones last—the bad ones are soon forgotten.

These songs persist underground over the years, passed on from generation to generation. The hypocritical Judeo-Christian-Puritan ethic damns them in the pulpit and sings them in the pub.

Please don't burn our backhouse down,
Mother says she will pay
Brother's away on the ocean blue
And the cat's in the family way
Father's gone and lost his job
Things are mighty hard
So please don't burn our shit house down
Or we'll have to go in the yard!

Lili Marlene

This is a song combined with a funny bit. It mixes a nostalgic song, sex and comedy with a punch ending. One of the chorus girls would sing it. If she was a singer, all the better, but the whole thing could be lip-synched to Marlene Dietrich's own voice singing Lili Marlene. The singer is dressed to kill—red velvet gown with a slit skirt and matching hat. She'd stand in a blue spot under a lamppost pool of light. She doesn't move in this number, and as she sings, after a few bars or a verse, fake snow begins to slowly fall from above the streetlight. The snow starts to fall more heavily, until by the end of the song, it's falling very thickly and completely covers her. At the climax of the song, we'd hit her with a bucket of snow.

Dance, Ballerina, Dance

Dance number for comic ballerina, with a singer and a pianist, or to recorded tune of Dance, Ballerina, Dance.

> *The ballet was starting at Carnegie Hall*
> *As the last ticket stub had been torn*
> *And the maestro was frantically giving his all*
> *A star was about to be born.*
> *As the new ballerina appeared*
> *She did a high kick (rim shot) near the lights.*
> *The women all fainted, but the men stood and cheered,*
> *She'd forgotten to put on her tights.*
> *Her poor little heart was filled with fright*
> *But the maestro said, "This is your opening night!"*
> *So dance, ballerina, dance*
> *You mustn't miss your chance*
> *Though you forgot to wear your pants.*
> *Show what you're made of, lass*
> *Your time soon will pass,*
> *So whirl around and show your class.*
> *If it is fame you seek*
> *Don't let them think you're meek*
> *Show them you have lots of cheek,*
> *Then just pirouette with grace*
> *The critics in the place will shout,*
> *"Good Lord, a brand new face!"*
> *You must pretend you're in the Ballets Russes*
> *What if your dying swan*
> *Looks like a dying goose (whoo whoo)*
> *Then just do a nice arabesque*

Though you may look grotesque
Who knows, it might bring back burlesque
So dance on without your pants.
The critics are aghast
You've even shocked the cast
You may be embarrassed
But ballerina, dance, dance, dance!

Here's another tune, one the reader will no doubt recall from school days, with the MC once again leading from the stage.

MC: *Row, row, row your boat, gently down the stream,*
You all remember this one. Here we go—EVERYONE—please join in.
MC and audience: *Row, row, row your boat*, etc.
MC: Well, that's not so good. We can do better than that. I'll tell you what we'll do. Let's divide things up. I want just the ladies over 40 to sing. *(Audience laughs)* We do have some, don't we? Now only the ladies over 40. *(Sings)* Hey, I'm talking about your age, not your bust measurement! Okay, now all the virgins! And I thought I was the only one. Come on, surely there's more here than in Moose Jaw. All right, just the oversexed women *(sings)*. No prostitutes, now *(sings)* I think we lost about four there. We'll try it again. This time just the oversexed MEN will sing *(MC and men sing Row, row, etc.)* Let's hear it, bassos. . .Okay, now all the men who never cheated on their wives. Hey, there's one in trouble—the wife is digging him in the ribs, saying, "Sing, damn you, sing!" Now all the fairies. *(Pianist stands up and waves a hanky with a languid wrist)* He's not really like that. He used to wear the Golden Gloves *(pause)* came right up to here *(illustrates gloves up to the elbow)*. They were beautiful. . . Okay, let's wrap this up—All the GOOD LOOKIN' PEOPLE will sing. Oh, BULLSHIT! OH, MAN! A bunch of you shouldn't have been singing. I won't point you out, you know who you are. . . I'm only kidding, folks. Half of this crowd is more beautiful than the average, and the rest are sitting out there tryin' to look better now.

(Curtain)

HERE COME DA JUDGE

I met a girl the other night,
What a time, what fun, no sorrow;
I'll not forget the other night,
My case comes up tomorrow!

Courtroom scenes played a big part in burlesque programs. In fact, that's likely where the comic phrase "Here come da judge" originated.

A prime illustration of a judge and courtroom skit is this one, a short one-act comedy, really, that I got from Irving Benson, who performed it as part of a bigger show in one of the main rooms in Las Vegas—maybe the Frontier—back in about 1969.

Wise Child Court

SCENE: Interior of a courtroom, breakaway drop.
CHARACTERS: Judge, who takes occasional surreptitious swig from a bottle; straight man DA; two putative fathers; one mother; one female baby.
PROPS: Four chairs, judge's bench, gavel, phone book, judge's robe. At opening of scene, straight man is on stage.
DA: Hear ye, hear ye, the court is now open. All hail the judge. All hail the judge.
Judge: *(Comes onstage)* That's not a very nice thing to say.
DA: What's that?

Judge: Ah, the hell with the judge.

DA: No, I said 'All hail the judge.'

Judge: The hell with you, too. *(Gets behind bench)* Hear ye, hear ye. This Court is now open. What's the first case on the docket?

DA: The first case today is a very strange and serious one. It concerns two men who claim to be the father of the same child.

Judge: Two men claim to be the father of the same child?

DA: Yes, your Honour. Rather unique, don't you think?

Judge: No, it happens every day over in Mousefart, North Dakota. Say, Mr. DA, wasn't there a case like that in history?

DA: Yes, your Honour, in Biblical history. In the time of King Solomon, the wise king, only the case was reversed. It concerned two women who claimed to be the mother of the same child. So what did King Solomon do?

Judge: How should I know? I was out of town that week.

DA: King Solomon summoned the two women before him and told them he couldn't give each of them the child, so he told them that he was going to cut the baby in half and give each an equal share. He commanded one of his soldiers to do the deed. The soldier placed the baby on a marble slab, raised his sword over his head and was about to cut the baby in half when one of the women screamed, "Stop, I lied, I'm not the mother of that baby," and pointing to the other woman, she said, "There's the real mother." And King Solomon, being a wise king, knew by the supreme sacrifice that the woman was making that she was the real mother, and he awarded the baby to her.

Judge: That's all very well, but please remember that this is a courtroom and not a slaughterhouse, and I'm a judge and not a butcher. Now, let's get on with the first case. The two men who claim to be the father of this child, are they here?

DA: Yes, your Honour. They are in the anteroom.

Judge: Well, get them off auntie and bring them in here. *(Echo of voices offstage)*

DA: Yes, your Honour, two men to the bar. *(Two men enter stage right and sit in chairs to the right of the bench)*

Judge: *(Looking at the men)* Oh, this is going to be a tough case. The mother and the baby, are they here?

DA: Yes, your Honour. Mother and baby to the bar. *(Two women enter from stage left, one dressed as the mother, the other dressed as a little girl)*

Judge: We have to get the case over as fast as we can, because I don't want to keep the child up too late. She's got to get her proper rest. *(Judge is now looking at "baby")* She has to go back to school tomorrow and if she doesn't get her proper rest she'll be cranky. *(Takes a longer look)* So before we go any further, I just want to say—get a load of the size of that kid! *(To DA)* Are you sure this is the right case?

DA: Yes.

Judge: *(To mother and child)* You may be seated, please. *(Both sit. Mother pulls skirt above knees. Judge does double take, lying on top of his bench to get a good look)* This is going to be an interesting case.

DA: Your Honour.

Judge: Take a peak at the old lady here. The legs are a little skinny, she's got a few Syracuse veins, but not bad. *(Sings) You made me love you, You woke me up to do it.*

DA: Judge. The men are over here.

Judge: Yes. Who is the first witness?

DA: The first witness is Mr. Figgwiggin.

Judge: Mr. Figgwiggin, stand up and tell the court why you claim to be the father of this child.

Man A: Well, your Honour, I met this woman through a harmless flirtation.

Judge: Yes, they all start that way. Go on.

Man A: After a short acquaintance, we wanted to get away for a weekend, so we decided to take a boat ride.

Judge: Oh, a boat ride. Did you ever try the local excursion boat?

Man A: That's the one.

Judge: That's a damn nice trip. I made it four times one Sunday. They carried me off the boat.

DA: Please, your Honour. Remember who you are.

Judge: Oh, yes. Go on with your testimony.

Man A: As soon as we got aboard we went up on the poop deck.

Judge: Hear, hear. We'll have no profanity in this court. That's a kid sitting there. You know how kids pick things up, like dirty words. These things fall on her little ears and before you know it *(looks at baby)*. Are you sure this is the right case?

DA: Yes, yes.

Judge: *(Turns to man A)* One more crack like that and I'll poop your deck. I'll deck your poop.

DA: He's right, your Honour. Poop deck. That's the upper deck.

Judge: Well, say that.

Man A: Soon as we got up on the poop deck, we started to perambulate.

Judge: You admit that?

Man A: Yes.

Judge: You admit you were perambulating on the poop deck? Three days in the electric chair. *(Judge leaves bench, goes over to mother)* Come on, Ma. This case is over, we're closing up the courthouse. You come with me. You want to make thirty-five cents? Bring the kid along, I'll make it half a buck.

DA: Your Honour, what do you mean?

Judge: *(Returning to bench)* He used a dirty word. He admitted he was perambulating on the poop deck.

DA: But your Honour, that's not a dirty word. Perambulating means he was walking on the upper deck. Up and down. Up and down.

Judge: That's what did it, that up and down. That's how come the kid's here.

Man A: Well, your Honour, after a while we got tired, so we found two deck chairs and we sat down.

Judge: Certainly you have to sit down. You can't perambulate standing up. Ask me, I tried it a couple of times but the back of my legs started to hurt, then I got a pain in my head.

DA: Your Honour!

Man A: And that, your Honour, is why I claim to be the father of that child.

Judge: Your story don't make a damn bit of sense, but I'm dumb enough to believe you. *(To man B)* Will you please tell the court why you claim to be the father of this child?

Man B: Well, your Honour, I'll explain it so thoroughly that even you, as stupid as you are, will understand.

Judge: *(To DA)* That last remark, did it do me any good?

DA: It was very derogatory.

Judge: It was? Thank you very much. Go ahead.

Man B: I was driving down the street and stopped for a red light. This woman was standing on the corner and she started to flirt with me. Well, your Honour, I wasn't going to let her get away with that, so I flirted right back.

Judge: You're damn right. Two flirts are better than one. Go on, please.

Man B: She asked me to give her a ride, and judge, what a ride I gave her.

Judge: I'll bet you did at that. You're a manly little bugger.

DA: Judge, your Honour! Remember where you are.

Judge: Oh, yes, I'm sorry. Please go on with your testimony.

Man B: We were riding along and all of a sudden I found myself on a lonely country road and the car stopped.

Judge: All of a sudden you found yourself on a lonely country road and the car stopped? *(To DA)* This guy knows his business, that's an old trick of mine. I used to have a switch on the floorboard, and I could kick off the motor and the girls never knew what happened.

DA: Your Honour, what are you saying?

Judge: *(Catches himself)* I'm giving away my secrets. Go on, please.

Man B: After the car stopped, I found that I had a flat tire.

Judge: Oh, the lady said no. *(To woman)* Madame, you must co-operate.

Man: No, your Honour. The tire on the car was flat.

Judge: Oh, the car had a flat tire. Go on.

Man: Well, I got out of the car to look and found it wasn't as serious as I thought. It was only flat on the bottom. *(Judge mugs)* Then I found I had no tools to fix it, so I decided to walk to the nearest gas station. But before we started, for no good reason, I picked up the backseat and put it under my arm and started to walk.

Judge: Just a minute, you say for no good reason you just picked up the backseat and put it under your arm? You had a damn good reason. I know, I lost four backseats one summer.

DA: Your Honour, please. Watch what you're saying.

Judge: *(Catches himself)* I'm sorry. I got carried away. Go on.

Man B: After a while we got tired of walking, so I put the seat down on the ground and we decided to lie down and rest a while. We had no sooner sat down when that woman started to fiddle around. Well, your Honour, I wasn't going to let her get away with that, so I fiddled right back. Well, she fiddled and I fiddled then she fiddled and I fiddled.

Judge: *(Banging gavel)* Just a minute. There's too damn much fiddling going on here. *(To DA)* He thought he was Nero. He fiddled while she burned. *(Catches himself again)* Go on, please.

Man B: And that, your Honour, is why I can claim to be the father of that child.

Judge: That's a better story than the other guy had. *(To woman)* Madame, what is your name?

Woman: *(Very coy)* Oh, Judge, you know my name.

Judge: I don't know your name, and if I knew I wouldn't ask. Now what is your name and where do you live?

Woman: Oh, Judge, you know where I live. You've been there many times.

Judge: *(Very coy)* Yeah, third floor in the back. . . *(Catches himself, then to DA)* that woman is contaminating my court. She won't answer my questions. She won't talk.

DA: That's the trouble, your Honour. Silence, silence, that's all we get. There that woman sits with her lips sealed, when one word from her will clear up this entire mystery. But will she talk? *(DA pounds bench with hand. Judge pounds bench immediately after DA)* Your Honour, I ask you, is it right that she not tell the court who the father is? No, it is not. Your Honour, that woman has a secret buried deep down in her heart and she alone knows who buried it there. But will she tell? No. *(Pounding business again by DA and judge)* Your Honour, I want you to look at that innocent little baby. Shall she be permitted to go through life with a veil hanging over her head? I say no. Your Honour, shall she be permitted to walk the streets and have people point the finger of scorn at her and say, there goes a fatherless child? I say no, no, a thousand times no. *(Judge loves the gavel and gets to pounding again, resulting in the break-away drop falling onto the judge and the bench)*

Judge: *(Getting up)* Why don't you come back tomorrow and see the regular show. *(Goes back to bench)*

DA: Your Honour, I rest my case. I leave it in your hands.

Judge: I don't know what I'm going to do with it. After all, I'm not too smart you know. *(Mugs)* I shouldn't even be here. This is a political job with me. I was supposed to be a guard at the playground, but they were all filled up, so I took this. It's all they had. You being a learned attorney, maybe you can come forth with a suggestion that will help us clear up this mystery.

DA: Since you mention it, your Honour, I believe I can. It's like the old adage, two heads are better than one, even though one is on a jackass.

Judge: What the hell are you looking at me for? Watch your talk.

DA: Your Honour, why not have the baby tell the court who her father is?

Judge: Have the baby tell the court who her father is? Can she do this?

DA: She can do this very easily, your Honour.

Judge: Why?

DA: Because she is a baby and a baby has a natural instinct. Your

Honour, I suggest you let the baby walk over to these two men, look into their eyes, pierce them right down into their very souls, then turn around and tell this court who her rightful father is. Your Honour, it is in your hands.

Judge: Thank you, Mr. DA, for a brilliant summation. Little baby, stand up. Look at the size of that kid! *(To DA)* Are you sure this is the right case? *(To baby)* Little baby, this might seem as confusing to you as it has been to me. I just want to say that I am the judge and this is a court of law. Now, before we go any further, I just want to say *(To DA)* Are you sure this is the right case?

DA: Yes, yes.

Judge: Little baby, we are here to see that justice is meted out in the legal juicy prudence of this court.

DA: Jurisprudence!

Judge: The Jewish prunes of this court. Little baby, I have here a book of law. Many great men have contributed to this book. As a matter of fact, in the words of that great statesman *(looks confused for a moment)* who said on his last visit to Peace River: "Remember as you go through life that he who pulls hardest gets most of the blanket." Little baby, you represent the future youth of this nation. We in this court want you to feel free to go home at night and put your little head on your pillow so you can get up in the morning and romp and play with the other children. And this kid's got one helluva romper! Little baby, you might not think so, but I know what's going on in that dirty little mind of yours. But before we go any further, I would like to say a few words about poontang. *(Catches himself)* Little baby, I am the judge, this is my court and I believe in capital punishment and I think that women should be hung like men.

DA: Hanged!

Judge: So little baby, don't you worry and fret because it is always darkest before the dawn. *(To DA)* What's the darkest thing in the world?

DA: *(Exasperated, holding his head in agony)* I don't know. What is the darkest thing in the world?

Judge: Looking up a Mau-Mau's muu-muu! *(To baby)* If I may digress and be serious for a moment, I would like to say that our God-given right in this world is freedom of speech, freedom of worship, freedom of religion, freedom of the press. This is the land of the free and the home of the brave. This is life, liberty, and the pursuit of happiness. This is your land, my land. This is the land that I love. *(Sings a few bards of O Canada)* Little baby, we are not going to let you go through life with a pail over your head.

DA: No, your Honour, a veil hanging over her head.

Judge: We are not going to let you walk the streets of life and have people fingering your scorn.

DA: Pointing the finger of scorn.

Judge: Little baby, we are going to let you tell the court who your father is. You can do this. Why? Because you are a baby and a baby has a natural stink.

DA: Instinct!

Judge: Well, everything stinks around here. So, little baby, in view of this court, I want you to walk over to these two men, gaze down deep into the souls of these two heels, turn around and tell the court who your rightful father is.

Baby: *(Walks over to the two men, looks at each one, shakes her head as each man says, "Baby!" She turns to the bench, puts her arms out to the judge and says)* "FATHER!!!!"

(Curtain)

Old Judge Montfort Rides Again

SCENE: Front curtain, dialogue between a man and a woman about to get married before a justice of the peace.

Woman: They'll walk all over you—they'll put you right under their feet.

Man: Shut up, shut your Adam's apple, before I clip you. You want me to slug you? I don't know what's the matter with you, baby. I don't understand you. Here we are on our way down to the justice of the peace's office to get married. Today should be a happy day in our lives, but ever since we got off the bus, you've been screechin', "After we're married you gotta be the boss, your mother says you gotta be the boss!" Well, I've made up my mind, once and for all that after we get married today *(pause, looks her over)* you can be the boss. Satisfied?

Woman: All right.

Man: So everything's all right. We'll go down to the—wait a

minute, I just remembered that there's something I've got to tell you before we get married. It's sort of a confession I have to make about my past.

Girl: A confession.

Man: It's not easy to say, but I've got to tell you. Ah, well, you know I run a grocery store and every day a lot of good-looking girls used to come into my store. The girls would be young and pretty and bein' a young fellow, naturally I had a lot of oats to sow. They were in my store, and I had the oats on hand—so I figured I might as well sow them while the girls were there—and save the girls an extra trip. *(Pause)* No, no, that didn't come out right at all. What I'm trying to say is that after we're married today, I want you to go to my grocery store, see, and in the back room you'll find a barrel and in that barrel you'll find a potato—a potato for every time that I've been untrue to you. Now you know; I've confessed all.

Girl: Well, how many potatoes are there?

Man: I don't know, there's probably a barrel and a half back there. Or there may be a few potatoes laying around on the floor that I forgot to throw in the damn barrel. You know how it is, trying to sow wild oats, wait on customers and throw potatoes in the barrel, it's not easy, but now you know. If you want to jilt me, all right.

Girl: Well, I'm glad you told me, because I sort of have a little confession for you, too.

Comic: Yeah. *(Pause)* Yeah?

Girl: After we're married I want you to go to my place, and upstairs in the attic you'll find a bucket. And in the bucket you'll find a bean, a bean for every time I've been untrue to you.

Man: There's beans in the bucket—well, ah, how many?

Girl: Half a bucket.

Man: Well, I mean——if that's all—what's a half a bucket? A half a bucket. A half a bucket of those big beans?

Girl: No! Little bitty ones!

Man: Oh! Well, they don't take up any room. That's more than a barrel and a half of potatoes! That is, I knew I'd get the worst of this. Let's go to the justice of the peace office and get this over with. *(Both exit as music comes up . Curtain opens on next scene, the JP's office)*

Judge Montfort: *(At his desk)* This justice of the peace thing ain't what it's been cracked up to be. I've married over two dozen couples today and believe me, I'm tired. *(Sees couple enter)* Oh, no!

Man: The door was open so we came right in. Are you the justice of the peace, sir?

Judge M: I do.

Man: Yessir, well, we want it, boy!

Judge M: I suppose you want to be joined in the holy bonds of matrimony?

Man: We don't know anything about the fancy words, we just want to get the little piece of paper that says *(pause)* Hoo boy!

Judge: I see. Sit down, please. *(Goes over to woman)* My, my, you're very charming!

Man: Isn't she, though!

Judge: That's a cute little hat you have on.

Woman: *(Coyly)* Thank you.

Judge: And those gorgeous cheekie weekies, oh, yes! *(Tweaks her cheek)* Those snappy little eyes—oh, oh, yeah!

Man: Hell, fella—buddy boy—I wish you wouldn't handle the merchandise there. See, I'm going to marry the girl and I don't want your cotton pickin' prints all over her.

Judge: Why don't you be quiet and sit down.

Man: Well, I'll sit down, but just keep your hands to yourself. I'm going to marry the girl. You just marry us and get it over with, that's all.

Judge: Aw, be quiet.

Man: I could learn to hate you real easy, ya know that?

Judge: *(To woman)* Now I'll have to ask you a few questions, which you won't mind, now, will you?

Girl: *(Coyly)* No.

Judge: No-o-o-o-.

Man: Well, goo, goo, ga ga!

Judge: Tell me, have you been married before?

Girl: Yes, three times.

Judge: *(To man)* Ha Ha! Do you hear that?

Man: What?

Judge: She's been married three times before.

Man: That's all right. I like to do business with an old established firm.

Judge: *(To woman)* Are your husbands living or dead?

Woman: Well, two are dead and one is living in New Brunswick.

Judge: Hmm.

Man: Mark 'em all three dead—nobody lives in New Brunswick. Well, there are people known to be existing over there, but you couldn't call it living. I spent a month in New Brunswick one Wednesday, I'll never forget it. That's where they shot the mailman last week—they thought he was a Confederate soldier. Did you read about it? It was in the paper.

Judge: Did your husbands die natural deaths?

Woman: Well, I poisoned one and one I cut his throat from ear to ear. . .

Judge: *(Laughs loudly)*

Man: Yeah, she cut his throat from *(tapers his sentence off slowly)*

Judge: *(To man)* Now I'll ask you a few questions.

Man: Yes?

Judge: Have you been married before?

Man: Yeah, but my wife's been dead for five years.

Judge: I'm sorry to hear that!

Man: That's all right, she's dead, to hell with her. Forget about it.

Judge: I said I was sorry.

Man: So you're sorry! What do you want from me? She's dead. You want to worry about her? Have a good time. Don't bother me with it. She's dead, that's it. She's no good to herself now, or anybody else. She wasn't much good when she was alive *(pause)* she's dead now. I can just picture my wife now, lying on her deathbed, gasping for air, and I came and shut all the windows. I walked over and looked down at her and she looked up at me and she says, "Joseph" *(pause)* it's a funny thing, she always called me Joseph.

Judge: Why?

Man: It's my name. . . she says, "After I'm dead and gone" *(pause)* she knew she was going to die.

Judge: Oh, she did?

Man: Oh, she saw me fixin' her medicine. . . she says, "After I'm dead and gone, if you ever go out with another woman or look at another woman," she says, "I'll know about it and I will dig my way out of my grave and haunt you for the rest of your life." Well, naturally, her threatening me like that, when she did die, I had to use some precautionary measures.

Judge: Oh, yes?

Man: *(Laughs)*

Judge: What did you do?

Man: I buried her face down. She must be damn near to Hong Kong by now. It's just as well, she always did like to travel.

Judge: Do you have any children?

Man: Children? Yes, I have a little girl, three years old.

Judge: A little girl three years old.

Man: Oh, she's a cutie pie.

Judge: Wait a minute—if I'm not mistaken, you just told me your wife has been dead for five years.

Man: That's right.

Judge: And now you tell me you've got a little girl three years old. How do you explain that?

Man: I said my wife's been dead for five years, not me. I get around, Bub.

Judge: What do you do for a living?

Man: I'm a garbage man.

Judge: A garbage man?

Man: Okay, a sanitary engineer, I'm still a garbage man, what do you want?

Judge: How much do you make?

Man: I don't make it, I just collect it. Yeah, I have a big truck I put it in, see?

Judge: I mean, what is your salary?

Man: Oh, how much do I get?

Judge: Yes.

Man: Forty dollars a week and all I can eat. . .

Judge: You mean to say you eat that stuff?

Man: Well, I certainly can't live on forty dollars a week.

Judge: Ohhhh!

Man: *(Cries)* God knows I've tried, but with car payments and taxes, there ain't nothin' left.

Judge: Who cares? *(To woman)* Now, what is your name?

Woman: Peggy O'Mara.

Judge: Peggy O'Mara. Where are you from?

Woman: Medicine Hat.

Judge: Medicine Hat. Not little Peggy O'Mara from Medicine Hat!?

Woman: Yes.

Judge: Don't you remember me?

Woman: No, I don't think I do.

Judge: Stanley Montfort!

Woman: Oh, Stanley! *(Rushes toward him)*

Judge: Well, I'll be hornswoggled! *(Rushes toward her)*

Man: Now I know I hate you!

Judge: Quiet!

Man: You look so familiar to me.

Judge: Yes?

Man: Yeah, I was just lookin' at you. Yeah, you look just like a second lieutenant I had in the army.

Judge: Could be.

Man: Looked just like you.

Judge: Yeah?

Man: Yeah, I can't remember his last name now, but his first name was Chicken.

Judge: *(To woman)* No, you wouldn't know the old place now.

Man: *(Aside)* I hate that guy, I hate him. *(To judge)* We had a major by the same name.

Judge: Yeah, well forget about it. *(To woman)* No, you wouldn't know the old place now.

Man: Chicken Smith!

Judge: Oh, shut up!

Man: I'm workin' on it. It's a short name, I know that.

Judge: Yes, yes.

Man: Chicken Shit!

Judge: Never mind.

Man: I'll think of it.

Judge: You don't have to.

Man: You bring your own beans when you come and visit us, Bud.

Judge: *(To girl)* Tell me, have you been home lately?

Man: This guy's got a bean in the bottom of that damn bucket. Oh boy, I'm emptying that bucket and we're startin' from scratch.

Woman: Oh, Stanley, I haven't been home in years.

Judge: You haven't? You certainly wouldn't know the old place now. Remember the little candy store on the corner, where they used to sell the jawbreakers and the jelly beans?

Woman: Oh, I certainly do, Stanley.

Judge: They put up a 57-storey hotel there.

Woman: A 57-storey hotel.

Judge: That's right.

Woman: Is that right?

Man: In Medicine Hat?

Judge: Yes.

Man: Oh yeah, oh sure—only, they built the damn thing long ways *(demonstrates)* like that. in fact, it's the world's longest hotel. That hotel is 18 storeys longer than Medicine Hat. I know, cause I had a room on the top floor one time and I was out past the city limits. I used to have to wait for the bus to come by in the morning to bring me into the lobby.

Judge: Keep quiet, will you, I'm conversing with Peggy.

Man: It was a nice trip, though.

Judge: I said SHUT UP!

Man: I enjoyed it. Hey, do you remember the main street that used to run north and south?

Judge: *(Very interested)* Yes.

Man: Still does. What did you expect, STUPID?

Judge: *(To woman)* Remember the little red school house?

Woman: Oh yes, Stanley.

Judge: They tore that down.

Woman: Did they?

Man: That's right. Now instead of going to school, the kids all go to the shoe factory. Turned out to be a bunch of little heels. . .

Judge: Remember the day I was carrying your books home from school? I dropped one of your books in the mud and you slapped my face?

Man: Oh, things sure have changed in Medicine Hat.

Woman: Oh, yes.

Judge: Remember what I did to you, though?

Woman: No, I don't.

Judge: Oh, I put you across my knee, I lifted your little dress, and I gave you *(claps his hands)* a darn good spanking.

Woman: Yeah, I remember.

Man: YOU WOULDN'T KNOW THE OLD PLACE NOW!

(Fast music as they run offstage)

BITS OF BUSINESS

You may know some girls named Annie
That are quite divine,
But you never saw a fanny
Half as pretty as mine!

Sometimes we'd use the ladder trick to create a memorable entrance for *Sorry 'bout That*. We'd place a ladder directly behind the curtain break, and the player would climb the ladder and stand on the top rung facing the curtain. When he heard his cue in the MC's introduction, he'd stick his head through the break and walk down the ladder. All the audience saw was a head travelling down the front of the curtain, apparently without support.

The Old Lady and the Sausage

CHARACTERS: Two men.

A: *(To audience)* Live it up! They've got your money, you can't leave, so you might as well stay and suffer along with everybody else. I know what you're thinking, here comes a burlesque comic. First thing he's going to do is come onstage and say, where are the broads? I'm not going to do that. Tonight I'm going to tell you how stupid I am! I was backstage and a joker came up to me and said,

"Hey, funnyman, do you like to gamble?" And I said, "I'll bet on anything." He says, "I'll bet you twenty dollars you can't say sausage to three questions I ask you." I said, "Fire away, soldier." He said, "An old lady's walking down the street with a basket of sausage on her arm and an automobile hits her, right between the post office and the drug store, knocks her down. Who would you pick up, the old lady or the sausage?" I said, "Sausage." He says, "A fire breaks out in a twenty-storey building, there's a little boy up there on the 18th floor with a sausage in his hand. You dash up the fire ladder. Who would you bring down, the little boy or the sausage?" I said, "Sausage!" "Now," he says, "in case you should win this bet, which would you rather have, the money or the sausage?" Well, hot damn, sometimes I wonder why I get up. Well, the first live wire that comes along, I'll get my money back. Here comes one now.

(Enter B)

A: Hello, bud.

B: Hello.

A: Hi!

B: You speaking to me?

A: Yes I am, fella.

B: Fella. Hey, what's the matter with you? First it's Bud, now it's Fella. You lookin' for a fight?

A: Look, brother–

B: Brother! Who the hell're you calling brother? I'm not your brother.

A: What the hell are you so mad at?

B: I am not your brother. My brother's in jail. You bad-mouthin' my brother?

A: Look, drop your brother, will you?

B: Drop my brother. Did you hear that? Drop my brother!

A: What the hell's going on? Look, I just want to make you a little bet and you get all mad about nothing.

B: Make a bet, you mean gamble?

A: Sure!

B: I don't bet on things, unless they're sure things.

A: Well, all right, I'll bet you twenty dollars.

B: You've got money? You look like a bum to me.

A: I've got plenty of money.

B: You have?

A: Yeah! I've got a room over a bank! My assets over a million.

B: Well, what are we betting on?

A: I'll bet you twenty dollars you can't say "sausage" to three questions I ask you.

B: Sausage.

A: Yeah.

B: Oho! You're on.

A: Now, here's question number one. Look, there's this old lady. . .

B: How old?

A: How the hell do I know how old she is?

B: Well, I want to know.

A: What difference does it make?

B: Look, has she got a name?

A: Sure.

B: Was she born?

A: Yes.

B: Is she living?

A: Yeah.

B: Then how old is she?

A: Goddamn it, she's 98, all right?

B: Okay.

A: Now, the old lady's walking down the street–

B: What street?

A: Now, you son of a bitch, I–

B: Well, what street was she on?

A: How should I know? What difference–

B: Well, there's a lot of streets in this country, she's got to be on some street. What street?

A: *(Yells)* Diffenlicken Avenue, all right!?

B: Never heard of it!

A: Sounds good, anyway. Now, can I continue?

B: Sure.

A: Now, the old lady's walking down the street–

B: Which side?

A: She's walking on the left-hand side.

B: What's the matter with the right-hand side?

A: The old lady doesn't like the right-hand side, do you mind?

B. Yes, I mind. I always walk on the right-hand side. Every day of the week, while your old lady doesn't like the right-hand side.

A: To hell with it, run her up an alley.

B: Oh, you ran her up an alley! What did you do, mug her?

A: No, the old lady said. Look, damn it, I was up the alley all by myself.

B: What were you doin' up an alley?

A: Takin' a short-cut! Now, the old lady has a basket on her arm.

B: Which arm?

A: She had it on her left arm.

B: How do you know?

A: It's the only damn arm she had left. Now, she had the sausage in the bag.

B: What sausage?

A: I don't know.

B: What kind of sausage? And what kind of a story is this? You don't even know what kind of sausage this is.

A: Liverwurst! All right?

B: All right!

A: Now, she has the sausage in a bag in the basket and here comes an automobile.

B: What kind of an automobile?

A: A Chevrolet with a Studebaker rear end. Let's see you argue about that. It was going forty miles per hour.

B: How fast?

A: Sixty miles per hour.

B: How fast?

A: The damn car was running sideways.

B: Now, let me get this straight. The little old lady was walking down Dickenlicken Avenue.

A: Yeah. No, Piffenliffen.

B: Well, whatever it is. Yeah.

A: Lickindippin.

B: And this car hits her. Well, say where it hit her—in the front or in the rear?

A: Dammit! It hit her right in the ass. Right in the rear.

B: Hurt her much?

A: Yeah, they found the motorcycle but the kid's missin'. Anyway, there's the old lady laying down there with her sausage on the ground. Who are you going to pick up, the old lady or the sausage?

B: The sausage!

A: Good! Now, question **number** two. A fire breaks out (*pause*) I

don't know who started the damn fire, on the 28th floor of this building and there's a little boy up their shaking his sausage in the breeze. Now you dash up the ladder, who are you going to save, the little boy or the sausage?
B: The sausage!
A: Good! Now, in case you win this bet, which would you rather have, the money or the sausage?
B: The sausage!
A: Goddam you, you little s.o.b. You got it. There you are, pal. *(Pulls out a sausage and chases B offstage, hitting B with the sausage)*

When You Gotta Go, you Gotta Go

PROPS: Some folding money, real or fake.
SCENE: Front curtain opens on two guys standing against wall with backs to the audience, in a position that looks as if they're taking a leak. Hold this for a few seconds, long enough for a laugh. Then one guy motions with his hidden hands and body language, indicating he's through with his business, jiggling and zipping up.

A: *(Turns and comes toward the audience. He's now seen to be counting some folding money. He goes back to the wall and taps the second guy on the shoulder)* Do you have change for a hundred dollar bill?
B: *(Still in peeing position against the wall, gives himself a shake, turns his head)* I ain't got no money!

Cops and Robbers

SCENE: Strobe light effect. Man comes running across the stage. Cop suddenly appears and fires his pistol four or five times. The man goes down to his death. The cop runs over to him, still pointing his gun and yells, "FREEZE!"

The Minister Takes a Walk

A man of the cloth, dressed in a long black clerical robe and hat, walks slowly out of the wings across the stage, all the while solemnly engrossed in reading the Bible. He looks up and down stage to see if anyone is watching, then faces audience and does a couple of bumps and grinds à la stripper, accompanied by the drummer's *bump-bump-ba-dump*. The minister then resumes his solemn poise, carries on reading the Bible as he then continues to walk slowly to other side of stage and off.

A "Put-On"

A raucous burlesque music number suddenly blares out of the PA system and a naked performer runs across the stage with his hands cupped over his genitals, his bare cheeks flapping as he exits. Two or three seconds later, he runs back onto the stage, this time wearing a skimpy pair of black briefs. He stays onstage, moving from side to side as stagehands hand him various articles of clothing to put on. He does so in the same seductive manner that strippers usually use to take off their clothes, but at speed. He dons shirt, tie, breeches, boots, then a mounted police tunic and finally a Mountie hat. The cop then points at the audience and yells, "You're all under arrest for watching an obscene performance!"

The Topless Accordion Player

MC: And now, *Sorry 'bout That* is proud to present the latest in West Coast entertainment. Miss Ole Galore performing topless on the accordion.

(Gal proceeds to play the accordion. You can't actually see if she's topless, except that as the squeeze-box moves in and out, the humour is in the expressions on her face as she mimics the pain of her breasts getting squashed into the folds of the accordion, and her relief as the motion is reversed. She's paired with the barefoot tap dancer, who has taps taped to the bottoms of her feet)

The Baritone Single-Octave Toilet Plunger

PROPS: One baritone single-octave toilet plunger and one violin case to contain the b.s.o.t.p. A toilet (cistern optional) on a wooden

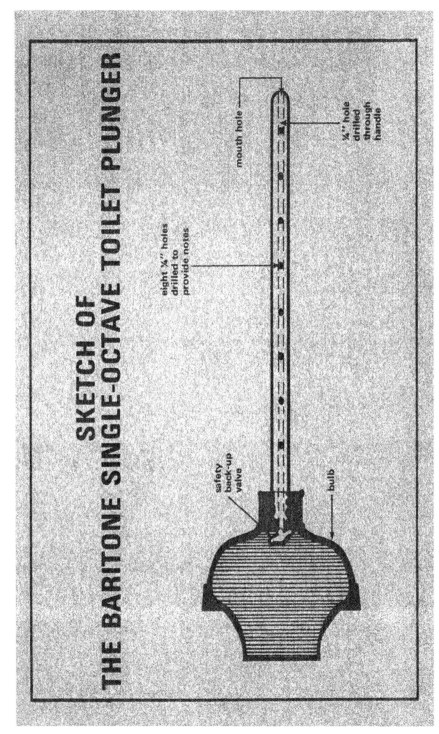

board fitted with casters. A cassette recorder with a recording of the b.s.o.t.p being played, placed inside the toilet bowl. A pre-recorded tape of water sounds—someone gargling a tune with accompanying sounds of bubbling and splashing water.
SCENE: Curtain open. The performer enters carrying the violin case with the toilet plunger inside, which he places on stage beside him.

Performer: Ladies and gentlemen, we are living in an age of revisiting the past in the style of clothing. There has also been revived an interest in old musical instruments—the zither, the lyre, the recorder. One can often hear instruments such as these in today's modern music recordings. This evening, then, I would like to speak to you about another little-known instrument—one that I have here in this case. (*He bends down and opens case and takes out the b.s.o.t.p.*) This, ladies and gentlemen, is a baritone single-octave toilet plunger. Any domestic plunger is suitable for adaptation. The one I have here is of a size sufficient to produce rich baritone notes. The smaller varieties would be suitable if one wished to play in the upper register.

The adaptation is simple and merely involves drilling a quarter-inch hole the length of the handle with eight evenly spaced quarter-inch holes in a straight line bored into it from the outside. You see these here. (*Fake dark spots on handle*) These form the finger stops with which the notes will be produced. A very important and essential feature is the safety backup valve at the lower end of the handle. (*Points with a finger inside the bulb*) This prevents water from travelling upward toward the mouth-hole. . . which every player would prefer to avoid.

Now that you are acquainted with this intriguing instrument, I would like to talk to you about the playing of it. (*To offstage helpers*) Would you bring on the toilet, please? (*A stagehand wheels in the toilet on a board base. The performer adjusts its position and continues*) For effective playing, the instrument should be placed with the bulb under water, the player facing the toilet and in the kneeling position. Like so. (*He kneels and places the b.s.o.t.p. as described inside the bowl*) I want to emphasize that this position is most effective for the production of a full-bodied sound and the posture of supplication establishes the sense of reverence with which the instrument should be played. If desired, the music can be placed against the upright seat. The bubbling notes produced are unique, being a cross between the sound of the Scottish fife and the North

American gargle. Let me show you what I mean. *(After taking time to adjust and compose himself, he reaches into the bowl on the pretense of getting the height right and switches on the cassette. He "plays", getting lost in the playing, his body swaying in time to the music. He finishes his playing when the tape ends, and promptly lowers the toilet seat and sits down on it. He wipes his brow with a long piece of toilet paper)*

Performer: Playing this instrument always leaves me a little flushed. *(He sits with legs crossed, begins chatting amiably to the audience)* Any type of toilet is suitable, but those with a small water capacity should be avoided, as they limit the variety of bubble-sounds which can be obtained by varying the depth to which the bulb is submerged. This engaging instrument lends itself to the performance of almost any kind of music. Handel's Water Music is an obvious choice. . . In a lighter vein, one could hardly do better than I'm Forever Blowing Bubbles.

I have just made a recording with this unique instrument. One side is by Johann Strauss and the other by Sebastian Bach. Personally I prefer the Bach side. . .

The number of people who have attended a performance on the single-octave toilet plunger is regrettably very small. This is because of the restricted size of the average washroom. There was once, however, a performance of single-octave toilet plungers en masse in a public convenience in Munich. Every cubicle contained a player and a capacity audience was in attendance. Unfortunately, the public convenience was situated next to a beer garden and the rendition was continuously interrupted by visits from the revellers with consequent ruination of the quiet mood and the gentle quality of the performance.

I hope some of you, at least, have been sufficiently impressed to make your own single-octave toilet plungers. If you do, your efforts will be rewarded with many hours of joy. *(He swivels around and paddles his way offstage)* Happy bubbling!

The Big Bet

SCENE: Front curtain skit for three men.

A: For those of you folks who've never seen burlesque, they

always had to have a rube comic. And here he is, Hal Sisson. Nice to see you, Hal, and it's certainly, certainly great to have you here!

B: What makes you think I'm here?

A: Well, that's. . . that's ridiculous. Of course you're here.

B: I'll bet you ten dollars I'm not here.

A: Look, you're a guest and I can't just take money from a guest.

B: Put your money where your guest is. Ten dollars says I'm not here. There's my ten. Right there.

A: Here's mine right here.

B: Okay.

A: Go ahead, if you want to throw away good money!

B: I'm not in Ottawa?

A: Of course not.

B: I'm not in Vancouver?

A: Of course not!

B: All right, if I'm not in Ottawa and I'm not in Vancouver, I must be someplace else.

A: That's right.

B: Right! Now if I'm someplace else, I can't be here! (Takes money, exits)

A: (Shows chagrin, then continues) On with the show. Burlesque always had to have a top banana, and we have a real slippery banana here tonight . He's now a star of TV, motion pictures and–

C: (From offstage) Broadway stage!

A: And Broadway stage! Here he is, Bill Seaman (C).

C: (Enters) Thank you for that lovely introduction, and man, what a thrill this is for me. Burlesque. The atmosphere—I sincerely mean it—it's just great to be here. I know you're going to pay me and everything, but just to be here. . . it's. . .

A: It's great to be WHERE?

C: Here!

A: What makes you think you're here?

C: Snow again, I didn't get your drift!

A: Bill, I'll make you a bet.

C: Bet, you want to bet?

A: Yes. How about ten dollars?

C: Ten dollars?

A: Yep, ten dollars (slaps down a bill, C does the same) And ten more. (They keep slapping down the bills)

C: Ten dollars more.

A: And ten more.

C: Ten more.

A: Ten more.

C: Ten more

A: Okay, ten dollars more.

C: Ten dollars more.

A: Ten more.

C: Hold it! What are we betting on?

A: I'm betting you that you're not here.

C: *(Pauses in disbelief)* Ten dollars more.

A: Right, ten more

C: All right already, we have a wager.

A: Now, I'll prove it to you. You're not here.

C: All right.

A: You're not in Ottawa, are you?

C: What would I be doing in Ottawa? I'd like to see Paul Martin, but I'm an NDP supporter and I'd rather see him in hell!

A: Just answer the question. You're not in Ottawa, are you?

C: No, not in Ottawa.

A: And you're not in Vancouver.

C: In Vancouver at this time of year, it's too wet.

A: Just answer yes or no, that's all.

C: Okay, I'm not in Ottawa, and I'm not in Vancouver.

A: Right! Now if you're not in Ottawa and you're not in Vancouver, you must be someplace else.

C: That is only too true!

A: So! If you're someplace else, you can't be here!

C: Ha ha ha! Certainly. *(Grabs all the money)* Thank you and goodbye. *(Starts to leave)*

A: Hey, hold it, wait a minute, no, no, don't hold it, I won the bet! Give me the money.

C: Ho, ho. No.

A: That's my money you got.

C: Just a moment! Not so fast.

A: But you just took my–

C: What, what, what, what?

A: What?

C: You, in your own words, didn't you say I'm not in Ottawa?

A: Of course.

C: And I'm not in Vancouver?

A: That's right.

C: If I'm not in Ottawa and I'm not in Vancouver, I must be someplace else.

A: That's right.

C: Now if I'm someplace else, how the hell can I have your money?

Running Gags

These gags are usually told in pantomime, often in conjunction with some other action on stage, such as someone singing a song. The pantomime action or story is continuous or occurs intermittently throughout various sections of the revue. The action can be front curtain, at backdrop of stage, or through a double door set-up at centre rear of stage.

When combined with a song, the singer stands in front and off to one side to give the audience a clear view of the centre doorway. During the song, a busy waiter goes through the doorway, carrying a towel on his arm and an order book in his hand. He comes back out again, heading in the opposite direction. In a moment he returns and passes through the doorway with a stein of beer. He comes back again and returns with a tray of bottles and glasses. Again he passes through the doorway and comes back with a pole, on which he's dangling several buckets of beer. He returns again, and this time comes through with a keg of beer.

The keg serves as the climax and finish, but sometimes the waiter comes back again with a hose with a show card hanging on it, saying, BREWERY PIPELINE.

The most famous running gag was in the variety show *Hellzapoppin'*, in which a messenger comes marching through various parts of the theatre, calling, "Flowergram for Miss So-and-So," and each time, the plant he's carrying gets bigger and bigger until at the end of the show, when the audience is filing out through the lobby, he's standing next to a full-grown tree.

We once used a running gag where a shot was heard offstage, and then a hunter crossed the stage carrying a very small wooden bear. Each time the shot was heard the bear he was carrying got bigger until, on the fourth or fifth time, he was dragging a bear of humungous size.

Song Tearing

A method of rendering or tearing apart a song that involves repeatedly interrupting a song for the purpose of comedy effect and laughs. The leading proponents of the song-tear were Frank Fay and Jimmy Durante. The two had different approaches, as described in Maurice Zolotow's No People Like Show People.

In his day, Frank Fay was considered the finest vaudeville and café monologue artist and the master of repartee. His most creative role was that of Elwood P. Dowd in the fantasy film Harvey.

For the song tear, Fay would announce he was going to sing Tea for Two. The band would give him the intro and he'd chant,

> *Just picture you upon my knee,*
> *Tea for two and two for tea*

He'd extend his hands and quiet the orchestra, then screw up his mouth in a puzzled way and say bitterly, "Ain't that rich? Here's a guy who's got it all figured out. He's got enough tea for two, so he has two for tea. I suppose if a third person walks in, they have to stab him."

The band would pick up the melody again and Fay would continue:

> *Just me for you*
> *And you for me*
> *Alo-o-o-ne*

"What does he mean 'alone'?" Fay would ask, growing more amazed. "I've heard of guys inviting dames up to see their etchings or their nylons, but this is the first time I heard of a guy inviting a dame to come up to take a peek at his tea leaves."

Jimmy Durante's take on the interrupted song, which he may have invented, was to enter and begin singing one of his favourites, like Inka-Dinka-Doo, then after the introduction and a few bars of the chorus, stop singing and launch into a joke, while the orchestra kept playing in the background.

"I goes intew da Automat and I puts in a lead nickel. Whaddaya t'ink comes out? The manager!"

Then he'd resume singing, but suddenly stop again to remark, "I asks dis guy for a loan of twenty-five thousand dollars. But he didn't have that much on him. So I took a buck and a half. I was in no mood ta dicker."

Another chorus of the song, and then, "So I goes on a cruise and a girl comes up ta me and says, 'Where can I find the captain?' and I says, 'Da Captain is forward, miss.' And she says ta me, 'I don't care—this is a pleasure cruise.' "

In Durante's case, unlike Fay, the jokes have no connection to the song. Jimmy's theory was, "I like to tell a joke in with a song, because I avoid the monogamy of just tellin' straight jokes. When I finish up da joke and then pick up on the song again, it's like givin' da joke a boost over da fence." Apparently, it took him years to get his jokes perfectly synchronized with the music.

I tried the song-tear on occasion with my version of Margie, which went something like this:

Sisson: Now it's not commonly known, but I am a singer of sorts myself and every once in a while I get the urge. . . of course this could make a nonentity of me in one easy lesson. I sing not only in A flat, but in anybody's flat. *(To band)* Give me an A, please *(try to hum the note but I'm off-key)* That's close enough. I want to dedicate this song to everybody's first girlfriend, and especially my own. You men know that everybody remembers his first girlfriend the best—no matter what happens later, ladies. Therefore, this is a nostalgic song. Ah, yes, my first girlfriend, what was her name? *(Pause while band plays a few notes of Margie)* I remember now—Margie! *(To band)* Can you play some sad music? (Nostalgic mood music ensues) I said sad, not pathetic! Okay, dim the house lights and give me a sexy spotlight! *(This is the cue for band to break into the opening of Margie)*

> *Margie, I'm always thinking of you, Margie,*
> *I'll tell the world I love you,*
> *Don't forget my promise to you. . . music fades)*

Sisson: What a girl! Speaking of promises, she made me promise that I'd always fight for her honour. I don't know why, that's more than she ever did. I don't remember where Margie and I met. In fact, we didn't really meet. As I recall, I had my wallet open and was counting my money and suddenly there she was. I later found out that's why everybody called her young and carefree. She didn't care as long as it was free. Nevertheless, you would always fascinate me, Margie. That's why I always tried to unfascinate you. When I first met Margie, I asked her if she would be free that evening. She said no, but that she would be reasonable. So I asked her where she would meet me that evening, and she said, "Halfway." She was one girl who would only neck within limits—the city limits. She was one of those goody-goody girls—every time someone turned out the lights she said, "Goody-goody!"

(Intersperse with a little verse)

Sisson: Margie told me she was just a little country girl who only went out with city fellows because farm hands were too rough. Her family had a nickname for her. They called her Daisy, because she grew so wild in the woods. Yes, we were star-crossed lovers, for when I looked at her, time stood still. In other words, she had a face that would stop a clock. The odour of faint perfume clung tenderly to her. I say faint perfume, because that's exactly what it made you want to do. And her clothes! Why, those low-cut evening gowns she wore were enough to make a baby cry. I used to wonder why she wore such wrinkled stockings. Then I found out she wasn't wearing any stockings. Speaking of clothes, she always complained about the high price of clothing, and I agreed with her—nylon stockings should be within reach of every man. But then we had a lover's quarrel and Margie became moody, morose and down in the dumps, always down in the dumps. Later I found out why—she was in love with the garbage man.

OLD FAVOURITES

Here's to Eve, mother of all races,
She wore a fig leaf in the most personal of places.
And here's to Adam, daddy of us all,
Johnny on the spot when the leaves began to fall.

Back in the Seventies, Bill Seaman and I took a trip to Vegas and saw a number of shows, including many of the burlesque variety. The Silver Slipper, a small casino on the Strip, now long gone, featured this type of entertainment. It was there that I saw the following skit, played by an old-time burlesque comic and musician named Tommy "Moe" Raft. As chance would have it, we saw his last performance, for later that night or early the next morning, he died of a heart attack. He was a great loss to burlesque.

Moe and the Cop

CHARACTERS: Moe; straight man; cop; girl A; girl B.
SCENE: Front curtain or full, minimal props

Moe: I just got back from the Established Cleaners—the local racetrack. I go there all the time, but I lost all my money. I don't mind losing a race, but when a horse starts from a kneeling position. . . I should've gotten suspicious when I saw that jockey packing a lunch. A tout comes up to me and says, "I got a hot tip for you,

Moe. A horse called Shot in the Dark in the third race at Northlands. It's a sure thing, it can't lose. Don't worry about a thing—bet it!" I said, "Are you sure?" and he said, "Moe, listen to me, this is it! Bet the bundle!" Ladies and gentlemen, I want you to know that I bet the horse. . . the horse won. It paid $2.85. . . I took the $2.85 and bought a hamburger. That was two days ago. I haven't eaten since. I know what I should've done. I should've eaten the horse. Don't laugh, horse meat isn't bad, tastes all right, as a matter of fact. Only trouble is, after you eat it you want to pee in the street. I hope somebody comes along here soon that I can put the touch on. Oh-oh, here comes a guy now.

(Enter straight man, crosses the stage)

Moe: Say, buddy, can you spare twenty bucks for a cuppa coffee?
Man: Twenty bucks for a cup of coffee? Coffee's only a buck.
Moe: I don't tell you how to run your business, don't tell me how to run mine! Anyway, I get horny after I drink coffee!
Man: Are you a panhandler?
Moe: *(Astonished)* Panhandler? Panhandler?
Man: You don't have to explode!
Moe: Don't call me a panhandler.
Man: You sound like you don't even know what a panhandler is.
Moe: Oh, yes I do! A panhandler is an intern down in the *(Says this slo-o-wly)* General Hospital.
Man: Aren't you ashamed of yourself, standing on the streets like this—begging? You don't see me begging anymore.
Moe: No?
Man: No, I got it made.
Moe: How come?
Man: Yeah, a buddy of mine showed me how to do it. I got myself a room, soft bed, three meals a day, nobody bothers me, I live like a king. Ah, gee, it's great!
Moe: Yeah? where do you live?
Man: In JAIL . . . *(Goes to walk off)*
Moe: You're kiddin' . . . where you goin'?
Man: Back to jail.
Moe: Wait for me, I'm goin' witcha.
Man: You can't. You can't just walk in and say, "Put me in jail." You gotta do something to earn that honour.

Moe: Earn it?

Man: Sure. Kill a jug, commit a misdemeanour, slug somebody, start something, cause a riot, anything—they'll throw you in.

Moe: Where you goin' now?

Man: How'd you know I was goin'?

Moe: I dunno, I just thought you looked like you had to go.

Man: Well anyway, like I said, I'm goin' back to jail. *(Starts to leave)*

Moe: *(Yells)* Jail! Listen, what time do you have supper?

Man: Five o'clock.

Moe: I'll be there at 4.30!

Man: Better make it 4 o'clock.

Moe: What for?

Man: We'll have a little drink before dinner.

Moe: You tellin' me you can get anything you wanna drink in jail?

Man: Are you kiddin'? They got bars in every cell. . . *(Leaves)*

Moe: He should get twenty years for that joke alone. . . I gotta find some way to get locked up there. I know what I'll do, I'll make believe I'm drunk. They don't allow drunks in this town. *(Peers out into audience)* Although maybe I'm wrong about that. A cop'll come along, throw me in for disturbing the peace. *(Starts to act drunk, yells, staggers)* That's to alert the nodders. *(Sings and shrieks)* If you're not paying attention, how do you expect to get bored?

(Cop comes onstage)

Moe: Hey! Cop, there!

Cop: *(Looks around as if he's looking for a cop)* Hey, wait a minute, I'm a cop. *(Goes over to Moe)* See that? *(Shows his badge)* That's headquarters!

Moe: See that? *(Turns and lifts his coattails, showing his rear end)*

Cop: What's that?

Moe: That's Hindquarters! Shay, I'm drunk. I'm stoned, I want you to lock me up.

Cop: So you're a little drunk. Havin' a ball, eh?

Moe: Yeah!

Cop: Disturbing the peace, eh?

Moe: Sure thing.

Cop: Makin' a lot of noise.

Moe: Correctamente, el capitan.

Cop: No more whiskey?

Moe: No!

Cop: *(Takes out a mickey and hands it to Moe)* Here, kid, swing!

Moe: *(Steps slowly forward toward audience)* What kind of a cop is that? *(To cop)* Hey, you!

Cop: Yes?

Moe: What the hell's the matter with you?

Cop: Nothing.

Moe: Look, I don't want to drink this stuff, you know. I just want you to lock me up.

Cop: And why should I lock you up?

Moe: Because I'm drunk.

Cop: I don't care. All the more reason I can't lock you up. *(During this bit, cop has come up to Moe on his right).*

Moe: Right-toh!

Cop: You see, my father–

Moe: Right-toh!

Cop: What's with this "Right-toh?"

Moe: You're standing on my right toe!

Cop: As I was about to tell you a moment ago, before you rudely interrupted me with your toe, my daddy was a drunk.

Moe: Is that so?

Cop: *(Emotionally)* And I. . . every time I see a drunken man, I think of my dear old daddy lying on his bed of pain, stoned out of his bird. Daddy looked up at me and he said, "Son" *(pause)*, he always used to call me Son.

Moe: Did he ever finish it?

Cop: And he said, "Son, I want you to promise me you'll never arrest a drunken man." So every time I see a guy like you, I think of that silver-haired daddy of mine *(cries)*. When I think of it I gotta cry. *(Moe cries along with him, then cop leaves)*

Moe: WHAT KINDA COP IS THAT? I don't want to drink this stuff. Well, maybe I'll try a little sip. *(Takes a swig, splutters, coughs, holds it in his mouth, puffs out his cheeks then suddenly lets go)* My God, it's Liquor Control Board gin! I gotta figure some way of getting locked up. *(Pause)* I know what I'll do *(pause)*. I'll steal something from somebody. They don't allow theft or larceny in this town. They'll scream.

(Girl A enters, crossing stage with umbrella tucked under her arm. Moe grabs the umbrella as she passes him)

Moe: Here, gimme that umbrella!

Girl: *(Starts into hysterics)* I didn't mean to steal your umbrella, really I didn't. Please don't turn me over to the police, I didn't mean it. Oh, please, really I didn't. An impulse just came over me. I shouldn't have done it, please have mercy on me, oh, please, please, please. *(Girl leaves)*

Moe: *(Thunderstruck)* Who the hell was that? Gertrude Lawrence? You give 'em one line and they try to star.

(Cop enters at opposite side of stage)

Moe: Hey! Keystone!

Cop: *(Indignantly)* Keystone? *(Goes over to Moe)* Whaddaya want?

Moe: I just stole this *(holds up umbrella)* I just stole this umbrella from a lady. Lock me up! I don't want it.

Cop: You're telling me that you just stole this umbrella from a lady and you don't want it?

Moe: That's right!

Cop: Well, give it to me, my wife can use it. Oh, by the way, if you come across any hot jewels, hot pearls, hot girls, hot anything, you get in touch with me. *(As he leaves)* See ya, kid!

Moe: *(Flabbergasted)* WHAT KINDA COP IS THAT? I know what I'll do, I'll get fresh with somebody, I'll insult somebody. They don't allow indecent assault in this town.

(Girl B, scantily clad, swings her way across the stage). Moe gooses her as she passes)

Moe: Hiya, Petunia!

Girl: *(Turns, cuddles up to him)* Why, hello, baby!

Moe: What the hell is this? Listen, I'm getting fresh with you!

Girl: I like 'em fresh, honey.

Moe: But you don't understand. I want you to scream, I want you to holler. *(Girl has been making circles on Moe's chest with her hand)* I want you to make bigger circles.

Girl: Okay, let me holler. *(Chucks him under the chin)* Eany, Meaney, Miney, Moe.

Moe: *(Looks down at his zipper)* Better stay away from Smokey Joe. *(Enter cop)*

Cop: Don't move!!! Okay, that's it, what are you trying to do, make a fool out of me? *(Pause, while Moe makes faces)* That's the last straw. I've had it up to here! *(Cop indicates his neck)*

Moe: Wait till the boat comes by *(pause)* and don't make waves.

Cop: I've told you once and for all. Day in and day out it's the same damn thing. Well, you're goin' in now and you're goin' in for a long time.

(Pause. Moe has been looking as if the cop is talking to him. They pass each other as cop goes to girl while Moe stands there, flabbergasted again)

Cop: Aw, what the hell. Hey, Mahitabelle, get out of here, will ya?

Girl: Okay, okay. All right!

Cop: Go on, get out of here or I'll call the wagon. *(Girl leaves and cop says to Moe)* Now, if anyone else gives you any trouble, you just call on me and I'll take care of it. *(Cop leaves)*

Moe: *(Pause)* WHAT KINDA COP IS THAT? What can you get arrested for in this town? Jaywalking, sure, but I'd never stoop to that. I know what I'll do, I'll take off all my clothes. I'm bound to get arrested for that. They don't allow indecent exposure in this town. *(To band)* Heathcliffe, give me a note!

(Band starts to play A Pretty Girl is Like a Melody and Moe begins to strip in a funny manner as if it's a choreographed dance. Gets down to his shorts, which are long and loud, with cherries hanging in front. Cop enters at this point)

Cop: What the hell are you doing?

Moe: I'm doing a strip *(laughs)*, I'm taking all my clothes off!

Cop: What?

Moe: I'm taking my clothes off!

Cop: Well, when you get them all off. . .

Moe: Yes?

Cop: You can take me behind the fence!

Moe: *(To audience)* NOW we know what kinda cop that is!

(Curtain)

Fangs for the Mammaries

CHARACTERS: Comic narrator; Dracula; girl; Igor
SCENE: Front curtain

Narrator: There was a time when people were very, very superstitious. Particularly in the 18th century in a European province known as Transylvania—where the Transvestites come from. Cobblestone streets, horses and buggies, the clock on the corner cathedral is striking midnight *(Musician in orchestra pit hits drum three times)* Daylight Savings Time. A group of young groupies are standing on the corner singing the top-ten song Transylvania 6500. *(Band plays a few bars of Pennsylvania 6500 à la Glenn Miller)* Is that a little too hip for this show? At the edge of town is a damp and swampy area. A huge cottonwood tree dips its huge roots into the water, a bat flies nimbly through the branches. Off in the distance we see an eerie greystone mansion around which the fog creeps on little cat's feet.

(Curtain starts to slowly open here, and a buildup of fog, thanks to a fog machine in the wings, begins to seep out and around the stage)

Narrator: Yes, in the middle of the damp dark forest, a castle. Way up in the castle, only one little light coming out of a window. It is flickering back and forth. It is the drawing room of the castle of the infamous Count Dracula. And what do we find waiting for him but his many brides.

(Dance number by chorus line. Narrator heads off to wings at this point as curtain fully opens onto a crypt-like scene with coffin, which is placed between first and second curtains. Dracula's brides dance to the Bumblebee Boogie. The name is misleading, but the record has a good beat and is on the scary side. Costumes are sexy, gossamer stuff suitable to the low-lying fog shrouding the scene. As the dance ends, the crypt scenery moves back quickly and in darkness, opening onto the scene behind the second curtain. The sound of wind howls over PA. A spotlight hits a standing coffin. Spooky music as the lights dim and the coffin lid creaks open. A hand comes into sight first and Dracula emerges.)

Dracula: *Cocks one ear as he notices the music)* Sounds like Bat-hoven to me. *(Dracula has a white face, red lips, fangs, slick, black greasy hair, cummerbund, cape, the works)*

Narrator: *(Steps out of wings)* A bat has landed on the second-storey window of the grey mansion. He drops inside. The butler comes and picks up the drops. He doesn't like those damn bat droppings inside. The bat, as you see, has turned into the most horrifying, most horrendous wampire his victim shall ever see in her life, with long fangs and a mad red gleam in his eyes. And where is this wampire's victim?

(Curtain now opens fully on scene behind second curtain. Over in the corner is a candle, which casts an eerie shadow. Across the room is a bed with a beautiful girl lying on it.)

Narrator: Dracula looks across the room. There is a four-poster bed with a canopy on top *(pause)* and a can-or-pee underneath. No plumbing in those days. He looks closely and on the bed there is a gorgeous girl. He knows he must have her as his bride. He goes closer to the girl. *(Dracula looks at the girl)* She is asleep. *(Dracula goes out to front stage and looks at the audience)* The audience is asleep....No.... they are getting ready to attack the WAMPIRE *(Dracula turns back and approaches the girl)* The girl in her sleep feels the Wampire's presence. HA! HA! Well, he is not really close enough for her to feel his presence, but you know what I mean. Suddenly, Igor, an ugly hunchbacked figure, jumps out of the bed and Dracula is shocked to find Igor has been in bed with his bride.

Dracula: *(Shocked)* What is the meaning of this?
Igor: It means, master, that it's the first time I've smoked in bed without a cigarette.
Dracula: How could you, Igor? After all I've done for you—you ingrate, you love thief!
Igor: Well, she kissed me and I kissed her back *(pause).* Too late I discovered how tall she was.
Dracula: *(To bride)* Did he get anything, my dear?
Bride: *(Crying)* Yes. It was dark when he crawled into bed, and I thought it was my lover. Oh, what is going to happen to me now?
Dracula: Did Igor promise you anything?
Igor: I promised her a watch, but actually, I only gave her the works!
Dracula: You may have to marry this girl, Igor.
Igor: But sire, marriage is like a box of candy—you have to buy the whole box to get one little piece.

Dracula: It's called a piece because nobody gets all of it. I've had it with you, Igor, right up to here (*makes throat-cutting gesture*).

Igor: (*Cringing*) Couldn't we have a drink and talk this over, Dracula?

Dracula: What do you suggest?

Igor: (*Pulls out a bottle of red wine*) Blood and bitter lemon, sire. I have a bottle here.

Dracula: No thanks. You have a glass of that and I'll have a glass of her (*Bares his fangs as he looks at bride*).

Igor: (*Looks at bottle*) Well, I'd rather have a bottle in front of me than a frontal lobotomy. (*Takes a pull at the bottle and puts it back in his pocket*)

Dracula: (*Looking at Igor in disgust*) You're not pretty, Igor, and you're not ugly. You're just pretty ugly. Also, you are ignorant, and I cannot tolerate ignorance, Igor.

Igor: But master, I went to a famous English public school.

Dracula: Which one?

Igor: I was brought up at ETON!

Dracula: You look as if you'd been Eton and then brought up. And those clothes that you wear, is that a camelhair coat?

Igor: Yes, sire.

Dracula: I could tell by the hump! Igor, with a little study, you could go a long way—so why don't you start right now?

Igor: Please, master, don't send me away! Have I not served you well in the past? (*Grovels in front of Dracula*)

Dracula: I'm not so sure, Igor. Remember the last time you got me up out of the coffin? I thought night had fallen. It was only an eclipse of the sun. Turned out to be high noon. You nearly killed me.

Igor: But master, I do my best!

Dracula: Your best? You dolt! Remember my last honeymoon? It was a disaster. There was no bed in the room, Igor.

Igor: Ah, yes, master, I remember—no bed in the room. You had to stand up for your conjugal rights. Look at it this way, master, a honeymoon is just the tail end of a wedding.

Dracula: Very funny, Igor. And how about that bride you lined up for me who liked to do jigsaw puzzles? All the time doing jig-saw puzzles—and losing the pieces.

Igor: Could I help it, master, if she kept giving me a piece on the side?

Dracula: Have they moved it? (*Pause*) And at meals, quit asking

me how I like my steak. You know how I hate stakes—they give me heartburn. No, I've had about enough of you, Igor. You have fouled me up for the last time. You know I like virgin blood, and yet I find you here in bed with my bride! *(Igor is on his knees begging for mercy)*
Igor: No, master, no, no!

(Dracula strangles him to death then and there. Dracula then comes forward and addresses audience)

Dracula: Ladies and gentlemen, I have very sad news for you. Igor has just suffered a heart attack and cannot continue in this skit.
Plant in audience: Give him an enema!
Dracula: I know it's very shocking news, and I'm sorry to have to be the one to announce it, but Igor is dead. Your suggestion to give him an enema could not possibly help him.
Voice: Can't hurt him!

(Dracula goes back toward girl in the bed)

Girl: Oh, sir, what is it that you want?
Dracula: *(Comes closer)* Don't be afraid. I bet I can touch your breasts without ever touching your nightgown.
Girl: But that's impossible.
Dracula: No it's not.
Girl: You bet you can touch my breasts without touching my negligee? Impossible!
Dracula: Wanna bet?
Girl: What do you bet?
Dracula: Five hundred dollars.
Girl: Okay, it's a bet.
Dracula: *(Grabs her by the breasts)* Well, you can't win them all.
Girl: *(Screams and backs away from Dracula)*
Narrator: She screams and opens one eye—it is a wooden eye. The vampire looks at her and says, "Wood eye!" *(Pause)* You didn't think I'd throw in that crappy joke, did you? Once again, Dracula starts to advance. *(Excitement builds in narrator's voice)* The girl knows that there is only one thing left that can save her life at this moment. . . a different audience. No, the only thing that will have any effect is the CROSS. She leaps from the bed—she's a leaper.

(Girl leaps out of bed) She runs across the room to get the cross. She runs back across the room with the cross *(Girl carries out actions as narrator speaks)*. She shoves the cross into the wampire's face, and the wampire looks at her and says

Dracula: *(With Jewish accent)*, "That won't help you lady, I happen to be a Jewish Wampire."

Girl: Is there nothing, then, that will save me from a fate worse than death?

Dracula: *(Continues to use Jewish accent from this point on)* No, you got the wrong vampire this time, snookey!

Girl: What if I crossed my heart? *(Does so)*

Dracula: Wouldn't help!

Girl: *(Pauses, then asks in desperation)* What if I crossed my legs?

Dracula: *(Pause)* Dammit! That'll do it every time!

(Curtain)

COMEDY MAGIC

Hope for the best
Expect the worst,
Life is a play,
We're all un-rehearsed!

In a burlesque revue, even the magic is funny. In a prestidigitation routine, the conjuror is the comic, as in the following sketch.

Professor Mundane

CHARACTERS: MC/Professor Mundane; Anita, the beautiful female assistant.
SCENE: Characters enter simultaneously from opposite sides of the stage under separate spotlights. The magician is wearing a tux, the girl has a magician's assistant costume under a shirt and slacks.

MC and girl (*In approximate unison*): Ladies and gentlemen, tonight it gives us great pleasure—(*they notice each other and realize there's some kind of foul-up in the introduction proceedings. They move to the centre of the stage and the spotlights merge*)

MC: I thought I was supposed to announce this next act!
Asst.: No, Don told me to do it. Obviously there's a mix-up! You go ahead and do it.

MC: Well, okay. *(Girl starts to leave stage)* Anita, just a minute. You're not wearing a brassiere under that shirt, are you?
Asst: No.
MC: What kind of a show do you think this is, anyway? You come out here jiggling! Don't you read the bulletin board? Everyone has to wear a brassiere. Now, put this on! *(Pulls a bra out of his pocket and hands it to her)*
Asst: Now?
MC: Now. We can't have this sort of thing. Do you want our audience to think this is a burlesque show?

(Anita takes the brassiere, turns her back to the audience, her face close to the curtain, takes off her shirt and puts on the bra, with the professor helping her do up the back)

MC: Do I have to help dress you, too? I have to do everything myself. So let's get this on.
Asst: No problem!
MC: No problem now *(peeking at her décolletage)* but a BIG problem before, eh? *(She turns to go)* Wait a minute, Anita. You're not wearing any panties under those slacks, are you?
Asst: Well, no!
MC: What did they tell you about that? The director definitely said everyone must wear panties in this show. Now put these on! *(Pulls a pair of panties out of his pocket and hands them to her)*

(Anita shrugs and starts to take off her slacks. Blackout briefly, but long enough for Anita to exit stage, then bring spot back up on the professor)

MC: What would a show be without a magician? And the answer immediately comes back—much better. But we happen to have one here tonight, so now it gives me small pleasure to introduce the magician on tonight's show, that sterling performer, that stalwart personality, that star of stars, one of the most outstanding magicians in western Canada. In fact, he's out standing in the wings right now. So let's put our hands together and give a big, warm welcome to. . . *(he gets right over to the curtain break at stage left as he says)* PROFESSOR MUNDANE!

(Fanfare, big long drum roll. MC disappears through left curtain break, as spot moves slowly over to stage right curtain break and holds there. The MC has dressers immediately behind the curtain who whip him into long magician's cape of many colours, a top hat with a tall peacock feather in the band that sticks high up in the air. He crosses as quickly as possible and makes stage entrance right, having thus introduced himself)

Prof: Good evening, folks, how do you feel? Now that you've found out that I am Professor Mundane. . . That bad, eh? Well, you don't feel half as bad as I did when I found out you were the audience. . . But what's more important, you smell good—like human beings. You're packed in here like human beings. . . When people go out for an evening on the town, man, they want those armpits to be charmpits. The guys smack on the aftershave, the left and the right guard. And the women, they have on all that cologne and perfume, and Lord knows what else! Do you remember that perfume they called SHHHH!—which, when spelled backwards, was *(He places a finger to one nostril and sniffs deeply and loudly).* And when you get all that stuff in one room, WOW! Everyone take a deep breath. Doesn't that smell nice! *(Pauses, does a skull and sniffs the air a couple of times)* Except for one or two of you, of course. . .

(Magician takes notice of orchestra)

Prof: Good evening, orchestra. *(To audience)* They've been practicing all night. *(To orchestra)* Didn't mean to interrupt your practice, God knows you need it. *(Smiles, says to audience)* They think I'm kidding. *(To orchestra)* The white part is the paper, the black parts are the notes. . . *(To audience)* Okay, let's have a big hand for the orchestra. Is there anyone here from Moose Jaw? *(Pause)* None? Cheap bastards, they never leave Moose Jaw.
The management has asked me to announce that a little later in the show, the dancing girls have agreed to perform an extra dance number for this audience only. They are going to come out one more time and do the Dance of the Voluptuous Virgins *(pause)* of course all but one of these girls do it entirely from memory. . . They come to us directly from the meat department at Safeway. Now, the management has also asked me to announce that during my act, please do not dance in the aisles. And for those of you who have hygienic duties to perform, now would be as good a time as

any to go to the can so you don't miss the finale. . . which comes later and is very good! Now I dress up like this, classy, because I do magic. I'm a Magician *(Pronounces it MAG-ICK-CAN)* or if you'd rather, a MA-JICK-EN. Magic, of course, is many centuries old *(Pauses, looks into wings as if expecting someone to make an entrance)* I said, magic is many centuries old. *(To offstage, louder)* That's your cue, Anita! *(To audience)* She's supposed to be out here with my equipment. I think she must have gone to the can, too. Now, I suppose you haven't seen a real live MAG-ICK-CAN for some time. Particularly a Western MAG-JICK-EN, which is rather refreshing, as there's not too many of us around anymore.

(Enter Anita with the magician's stuff, a deck of cards. She's now showing some leg and skin. Her outfit is sufficiently low-cut in front to conspicuously display a playing card in her cleavage. Short skirt, starter's pistol stuck in the garter around one thigh)

Prof: *(Sarcastically)* Thank you, my dear. Where were you?
Anita: I don't care to say, and it's none of your business.
Prof: Urinate!
Anita: *(Indignantly)* What did you say?
Prof: You heard me. I said, you're an eight!
Anita: And just what do you mean by that?
Prof: I mean you're an 8, but if you had bigger boobs you'd be a 10.
Anita: You know, I can tell by your ready wit that you're a bachelor. Not only that, I bet your father was a bachelor, too.
Prof: *(To audience)* Don't laugh at me, folks, I didn't pay to get in. Now, as a Mag-ick-can, I am going to try and fool you at every opportunity. So I'm warning you to watch me very closely. I have nothing up my sleeves but my arms, but I'm working at a disadvantage. As a matter of fact, my hands don't match. *(Demonstrates by holding one palm up and the other palm down and then reversing them several times.*

(Magician takes the deck of cards from Anita)

Prof: These cards are shuffled so thoroughly that you can't tell your ace from a hole in the ground. . . Now, the first trick is a good one. The rest of them are rather crappy, but the first one's a good one. What I need right now is a drink. *(Produces drink from his coat-*

tails. His costume has been prepared in advance. A thread was run through a soft rubber ball and attached to a safety pin, which was pinned into the coattail. The ball fits into the throat of the glass containing the drink. Prof releases the drink by grasping the glass and releasing the ball with his thumb. Prof looks at the drink) Looks more like a specimen to me. . . *(Tastes it)* Okay, who peed in this glass?

Orchestra: We all did!

Prof: *(Pours some of the liquid over edge of stage to prove it's a real drink and not just coloured glass)* Look, I'm not too choked up with you people, either, you know What I need is another drink. *(Produces another)* Now, I want someone in the audience to call out the name of any card in the deck—any card that comes to mind.

Voice from audience: The seven of hearts.

Prof: Are you sure you want the seven of hearts? All right, I'll find it for you. *(He fans through the deck and comes up with the seven of hearts)* Here it is, the seven of hearts. *(Shows it to audience and puts the balance of the deck in his pocket)* Now I'm going to perform a miracle. I am going to change this freely selected card into something entirely different. Watch! *(He tears the card into tiny bits, which he clenches in his fist)* I will now change the seven of hearts into something entirely different! *(Holds fist up in the air and says to Anita)* Can you count to three? *(Anita does not reply)* If that's too tough, can you count to two? *(Pause)* Use your chest! No, that would be 44, that's too long a count.

(Anita gives the professor a dirty look, then pulls the starter's pistol from her garter, counts to three and fires the pistol at prof's fist)

Prof: Look! Confetti! *(He throws the bits of torn card into the air, then sketches an elaborate bow)* Marvellous, is it not? Okay, so it's not! That's really just the warmup. Now I will really do an amazing card trick. I want some man in the audience to remove one card from the deck and one card only. Now don't look at that card, don't tell me what it is, don't flash it. Now come up here on the stage *(man does so)* and place it   *(magician whispers in man's ear telling him where to place the card, man puts card in Anita's décolletage, face in against her skin)*. We have now placed the card, which no one has looked at or knows, in plain view. In fact, placed it in the most conspicuous place in the theatre right now. Without looking at them—I mean IT, the card, that is. . . at no time allow your eyes to wander—You the audience have to CONCENTRATE. This is a test of your combined mental power. Now, will someone in the audience call out the name of a card, any card at all. That's the card we are all going to concentrate on!

Voice from audience: The seven of hearts.

Prof: *(Disgusted expression, says to voice)* Are you some sort of wise ass? Don't tell me that out of 100,000 sperm, you were the fastest? *(To rest of audience)* Name another card, any card.

Second voice: The ace of spades!

Prof: Are you sure you want the ace of spades, sir? You are? Fine! Now, for the most amazing coincidence. The card, which was selected at random and placed with Anita *(goes over and takes gun from Anita's garter, backs off and fires gun at card)* is none other than *(goes back and takes card from her cleavage and looks at it. Registers surprise and embarrassment)* SHIT! *(to audience)* This is all your fault. Some of you weren't concentrating on the ace of spades. It was you men, I'll bet. You loused this up. You were concentrating on the wrong thing. *(Shrugs dejectedly and starts rapidly tearing the card into little bits as before. Tosses pieces in the air)* Happy New Year! *(Takes a bow)* Aw, to hell with it, I can't do card tricks, let's face it. But if other Ma-jick-ens can do card tricks, why can't I?

Loud, sepulchral voice over the sound system: *(With background thunder)*   BECAUSE YOU PISS ME OFF!

Prof: *(Registers shock and awe)* The Great Magician in the Sky! Is that you, Harry? That was Harry Houdini! Well, if I can't do card tricks, Harry, then I'll try some of your old tricks. *(To Anita)* Now, my dear, would you please get me *(pause).* Ladies and gentlemen, isn't she a sight to behold?

> She has beautiful hair,
> She has beautiful eyes,
> She has beautiful teeth,
> Etcetera, etcetera, etcetera.

My dear, will you get me the rest of the equipment, please?

(Exit Anita. As soon as she's gone, magician addresses the audience)

Prof: Etcetera, etcetera, etcetera—those are the best parts. Ladies and gentlemen, the trick you are about to witness, and the *pièce de résistance* of this act is the most dangerous thing you'll ever see for a long, long time. *(Anita returns and hands him four toilet plungers)*

Prof: In my hands are the razor-sharp Renaissance toilet plungers supplied by Jack Jones at the hardware store.

(Curtain opens to disclose, exactly in the curtain break, a slanted eight by four board with four holes in it, which are concealed by the multi-coloured tissue paper that covers the whole board in small squares. Two stagehands are behind the board, one to steady it, the other to ram four gimmicked toilet plungers through those holes from the back side. The holes are strategically placed on opposite sides of where the assistant's head would be and at just above knee level. The extra plungers are glued to the piece of board which was cut out and this is then glued to a larger piece of board to which handles are attached on the back, to give leverage and control when shoved through the first board with the four holes in it. When the stagehand shoves these gimmicked plungers through the holes at the same time as the magician pretends to throw his plungers from the back of the hall, it looks as if he really did throw them and that they stuck to the board but missed the assistant)

Prof: And now, taking her place before the board. . . *(Drum roll)* is my lovely assistant, Anita. And now I am going out into the audience and I am going to throw these four toilet plungers around her beautiful body, missing her by only inches. If I miscalculate by even the slightest bit, she could receive a massive (pause) hickey! *(To orchestra, as he works his way off the stage and out into the audience)* Could you play some dangerous music, please?
Orchestra leader: What tune do you want?
Prof.: How about the Butcher's Song?
Orch: The Butcher's Song, what's that?
Prof: Someday We'll Meat Again!
Orch: Sorry, don't know it.
Prof: *(To Anita as he works his way to back of hall, near door)* Don't worry, my dear. I will throw the plungers at the target without hurting you *(pause)* much!
Anita: *(With tremor in her voice)* Are you sure you can hit the board and not me?
Prof. Is the pope Norwegian? I've wanted to do this act for many years, but this is the first time I've found an assistant who is stupid enough—I mean brave enough to stand against the board. I'm only kidding, folks. I have performed this act many times, and during that time seven people have died in the audience, from various causes—heart attack, acute alcoholism, strangulated hernia—

and during that time no one has died up on the stage *(pause)* although my life has been threatened once or twice. What I'm trying to say is, that with my accuracy, it's safer to be up on stage than in the audience. Are you ready, my dear?

Anita: YES!

Prof: All right! *(On his backswing, a stagehand behind him out of sight behind the door grabs the plunger as he shouts)* I Lunge and Throw! *(Magician's hand flies forward as if completing the throw, and spoken phrase is cue for stagehand behind board to ram a plunger through one of the holes next to Anita's head)*

Anita: Thank the Lord! That was close! *(To magician)* Did you realize that you could be a stand-up comic?

Prof: What did you say?

Anita: Did you realize you could be a stand-up comic?

Prof: *(Pleased)* Do you really think so?

Asst: Yes—if only you were funny and could stand up.

Prof: Very funny. I'll do the jokes around here. And remember, accidents can happen. That's why they have maternity wards. But don't worry, I'm outstanding in my field.

Anita: A lot of people say that's where you should be—out standing in a field!

Prof: If this next toilet plunger hits you, my dear, it will hit you like a sanitary belt!

Asst: And what might that be?

Prof: A shot of whiskey in a clean glass. . . and here comes the chaser! I lunge and throw! *(Pretends to let go the second toilet plunger. Stagehand behind board rams another plunger through the second hole in the board)* A good shot! But sure, I make mistakes. I'm like the civil service—if I don't make mistakes, someone else will. I usually have a little music with this act. *(To orchestra)* My favourite song is She Asked for Some Wine, So I Let her Have Both Barrels.

Orch: Sorry, we don't know it!

Prof: What songs do you know? Head For the Hills like Big-Assed Birds? I lunge and throw! *(Third plunger appears to land on the board)* No applause, please. Just give me a ten-yard running start. I'm so unlucky that if I were doing the sawing-the-woman-in-half act, I'd end up with the half that eats. I bet when I first came out here this evening you thought I was going to be lousy. I will now release the last razor-sharp toilet plunger!

Stagehand behind board: We're out of toilet plungers!

Prof: You Idiot! You turkey-klutz! You're supposed to have four toilet plungers! Don't foul up this act. I lunge and throw!

(There's a pause. No toilet plunger hits the board. Suddenly, the stage-hand runs his hand and arm through the hole in the board and gives the magician the slow finger)

(Curtain)

Jim Robertshaw, looking a bit "flushed", in The Baritone Single-Octave Toilet Plunger.

Hal Sisson perform-ing the Old Fart monologue: " I travel a lot—with this act I have to."

Terry Sheasgreen (left) as Black Pedro, Arlie McGuire as Conchita Lolita Schwartz and Malcolm Sokoloski in Border Town Saloon.

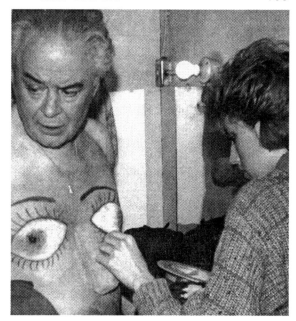

Before

First the eyes, nose and lips are p a i n t e d o n t h e torso, then the top h a t c o v e r s t h e head and finally, the tux is slung over the hips.

After

On stage, the band plays H e a r t a c h e s , b y T e d Weems, while the actor pulses his navel in and out in time to the whistling portions of the song, making it appear as if the "mouth" is doing the whistling.

Phil Prato as one of the three Sonavich Brothers, a parody of famous European acrobatic troupes. Below, Mike Arnold in uniform as the captain in the skit Private Gallagher and Captain Shane.

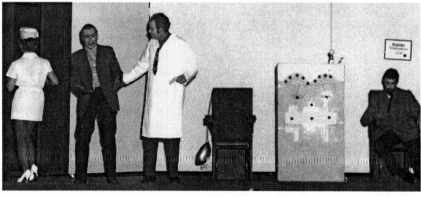

(From left) "Nurse Cuddles", Bill Seaman as a patient, Hal Sisson as the doctor and Jim Robertshaw as the dummy (Danny the boyfriend) in Dr. Cockenlocker's Sickness Transformer.

MIND READING

I've drunk to your health when I'm with you,
I've drunk to your health when alone;
I've drunk to your health so goddamned much
I've just about buggered my own!

Do you need to be the seventh son of a seventh son, or be born with a "veil over your eyes" to be a successful clairvoyant? No sir! Such ability is not inborn, it is achieved! And you can learn the art easily and quickly. You need no preparation, no secret apparatus to utterly amaze them and make sensational revelations that will long linger in their minds.

Madame Gazaza

CHARACTERS: Three comics: Madame Gazaza the mindreader; Cobb, the MC and Gazaza's assistant; the heckler, Alex, who interrupts from the audience

Cobb: *(To audience)* Ladies and gentlemen, tonight we are proud to present a woman who sees all, knows all and tells all, to whom the minds of men are an open book. Tonight, blindfolded, hypnotized and in a stupor, she will tell you your names, tell you your innermost secrets, tell you what you have in your pockets.

Alex: (*Comes down from rear of hall to a stageside table, where a seat has been saved for him for the purpose of the skit*) That must be my wife!

Cobb: Now just a cotton-pickin' minute here! Don't interrupt.

Alex: Hah! Where's the girls?

Cobb: The girls are downstairs changing their clothes—they're naked.

Alex: NAKED!

Cobb: You wouldn't want me to bring them out here like that, would you?

Alex: (*Cheers in unison with the males in the audience*) Hey, what's going on behind that curtain?

Cobb: There's nothing going on behind that curtain.

Alex: Well, there ain't a damn thing going on in front of it, either.

Cobb: Just how did you get in here, anyway?

Alex: I came in on a friend's ticket.

Cobb: Well, where's your friend?

Alex: He's outside looking for his ticket. . . You're pretty nosey, aren't you?

Cobb: So you sneaked in!

Alex: I resent that!

Cobb: Do you deny it?

Axec: No, I just resent it. Bring on the girls! (*Stomps and whistles*)

Cobb: Why don't you just shut up and sit down?

Alex: Well, I got a seat and I got to find the right place to put it!

Cobb: (*Pause*) You got a hole in it. Hang it up.

Alex: You should be arrested for making bad jokes. Come on, what are you going to do?

Cobb: I'm out here to introduce an act, if you'd just shut up!

Alex: You're going to introduce somebody?

Cobb: That's right

Alex: Who are you going to introduce?

Cobb: The Great Madame Gazaza, the world's foremost mindreader.

Alex: Mindreader? Can she read my mind?

Cobb: She most certainly can.

Alex: Can she tell me what I'm thinking about right now?

Cobb: Oh, yes.

Alex: Can she tell the rest of these guys what they're thinking about?

Cobb: Oh, yes.

Alex: Let's get the hell out of here. The police are going to have trouble picking up the whole lot of us. . .

Cobb: She not only is a mindreader, she's a hypnotist as well, and so am I.

Alex: A hypnotist? What's a hypnotist?

Cobb: A hypnotist is someone who can place you under a spell and make you do anything they want you to do, whether you want to or not! Why don't you come up here and let me hypnotize you?

Alex: You ain't gonna get me up there and make no jackass out of me!

Cobb: Hell, no. Nature beat me to it.

Alex: Oh boy, you're gonna get it. Well, go on, introduce somebody.

Cobb: Will you shut up and sit down?

Alex: Okay. *(Sits)*

Cobb: Ladies and gentlemen *(pause)* and patrons, it gives me great pleasure to introduce at this time, one of the foremost mental wizards of the day, the girl with the X-ray eyes. She probes the hidden mysteries of the mind and masters the complexities of telepathy. Ladies and gentlemen *(pause)* and patrons, MADAME GAZAZA!

(Curtain opens as a sexily dressed Gazaza seats herself on a high stool at centre stage)

Alex: *(Mimics loudly)* MADAME GAZAZA! Hey, hot damn, get a load of that Madame Gazaza! Hey, Madame Gazaza, how'd you like to meet Papa Gazaza?

Madame: Young man, I'd like to be your mother for about five minutes.

Alex: Well, I'll speak to the old man and fix it up. . .

Madame: Your type of man makes me sick.

Alex: Well, your type of woman don't make me long for no nightlife, either.

Madame: How'd you like it if we women had all the money and we took you for a car ride and let you walk home?

Alex: Not when it's freezing out, you don't see me walking home.

Cobb: Are you going to shut up?

Alec: Okay, I'm shut.

Cobb: All right, now, first I'll blindfold the Madame. *(Slips silk scarf around Madame's eyes)*

Alex: Blindfold the Madame. Then what're you gonna do?

Cobb: I shall pass amongst you while Madame Gazaza is in this interesting condition. *(Climbs down offstage into the audience)* I'm going to walk out amongst you and I'm going to place my hand on a few small objects.

Alex: What?

Cobb: I said I'm going to place my hand on a few small objects.

Alex: Some of these guys might fool you.

Cobb: Preferably various small, val-u-a-ble objects. The Madame will be able to tell me what they are. *(Calls out)* Madame!

Madame: Yes?

Cobb: This young man here has something on his wrist.

Madame: Yes?

Cobb: Can you tell me what it is? Watch out! *(No answer from Madame)* Take your time. . . Take your TIME.

Madame: A wristwatch!

Cobb: Right!

Alex: *(Boos and groans, in unison with crowd)* What the hell? A man's got something on his wrist, watch out! Take your time! *(Sarcastically)* Well, it could have been a checkerboard.

Cobb: *(To Madame)* Have you the time?

Madame: Yes, but not the inclination.

Cobb: Tell this gentleman the correct time by his watch.

Madame: *(Says anything but the right time)*

Cobb: That's right, Madame. *(To man in audience)* The Madame is never wrong. Your watch must be busted. *(To audience in general)* We want you to know that we use no hidden words, no, nothing to aid the Madame–

Alex: No, you just come right out and tell her.

Cobb: Will you shut up! You've got constipation of the mind and diarrhea of the mouth.

Cobb: *(To Madame)* What's in this gentleman's pocket?

Madame: A hole.

Cobb: I mean in his hip pocket.

Madame: A bottle of whiskey.

Cobb: Where does he buy it?

Madame: He doesn't buy it, he sells it.

Cobb: All right, Madame, now what am I touching? *(Holds hand up in air)*

Madame: Nothing.

Cobb: Incredible! I don't see how she does it! Now what am I touching, Madame? *(Places hand on woman's head)*
Madame: Absolutely nothing!
Cobb: *(Standing next to another man in audience)* What's this man's name? It's not Tom, it's not Dick, it's. . .
Madame: George?
Cobb: If this man didn't shave he'd be. . .
Madame: Harry!
Cobb: Correct! Marvellous, wonderful! You're absolutely incredible. What is in this man's head?
Madame: Dandruff.
Cobb: No, I mean what does this gentleman have on his mind?
Madame: *(Pause)* I'm ashamed to tell you.
Cobb: What did Eve wear in the Garden of Eden?
Madame: She wore a fig leaf.
Cobb: What did Adam wear?
Madame: He wore a hole in the fig leaf.
Cobb: Was it the apple on the tree in the Garden of Eden that caused the trouble?
Madame: No, it was the pair on the ground!
Cobb: *(Standing next to another man in audience)* This is Mr. Dunlop. What is the difference between Mr. Dunlop and Mrs. Dunlop?
Madame: Dunlop tires.
Cobb: *(Next to woman in audience)* What is this lady sitting on?
Madame: Next question, please
Alex: What's the difference between mashed potatoes and pea soup?
Madame: Don't get smart with me, young man.
Alex: Anybody can mash potatoes. . . What's the date?
Madame: *(Pause)* The date is a tropical fruit.
Alex: Here's another question for you. What's the V-neckline on your dress stand for?
Madame: The V stands for Virgin.
Alex: The V is for Virgin?
Madame: It's an old dress.
Alex: What do you call children born in houses of ill repute?
Madame: I don't know, what *do* they call children born in houses of ill repute?
Alex: Brothel sprouts. . . Why are girls like pianos?
Madame: I really don't see any similarity. Why *are* girls like pianos?

Alex: When they're not upright, they're grand.. . What's the similarity between a passionate kiss and a spider?

Madame: Now look here, you're being ridiculous and I'm not going to tolerate this much longer. But rather than have an unpleasant scene, okay, what is the similarity between a passionate kiss and a spider?

Alex: Both lead to the undoing of a fly. . . What sticks out of a man's pyjamas that he can hang his hat on?

Madame: That's a naughty question.

Alex: His head. You've got a mind like an open sewer. Hey, Madame?

Madame: Yes?

Alex: I got hold of something I ain't had in years. Can you tell me what it is? *(Has his hand in his pocket)* It sometimes keeps me up night.

Madame: That's a hard one.

Cobb: You could have fooled me!

Alex: Well, I fooled myself.

Cobb: Are you going to behave yourself and sit down?

Alex: Okay, I'll sit down. *(Sits)*

Cobb: Now, is there anyone in the audience who has something they'd like to put to the Madame?

Alex: Me first. . . me. . . here! *(Waving his hands in the air)*

Cobb: A question?

Alex: I was answering the first question—I have something I'd like to put to the Madame.

Cobb: You knew what I meant.

Alec: No, I didn't! *(Pause)* I'm a man of action!

Cobb: Has anyone got a question?

Alex: I've got a question.

Cobb: What is it?

Alec: *(To Madame)* Where's my father?

Madame: Young man, your father is in Montreal.

Alex: Eh?

Cobb: She said your father is in Montreal.

Alex: And she is full of sh–shellac. My father's been dead for ten years.

Cobb: Madame, there seems to be a mistake. The young man says his father has been dead for ten years.

Alex: Yeah!

Madame: Young man, the man your mother married has been dead for ten years, but your father is still in Montreal.

Alex: Ah, shut up. How the hell was I supposed to know? What the hell are you laughing about?

Madame: You.

Alex: Say, would you like to see a cute little devil?

Madame: Yes.

Alex: Then go to hell.

Madame: I may be a woman, but you'd better look out!

Alex: Oh, yeah?

Madame: If I were a man, I'd come down there and I'd pull out your eyes and eat them for grapes.

Alec: You wouldn't dare.

Madame: I would, too! And I'd pull your nose off and I'd eat it for a plum.

Alex: What?

Madame: And I'd pull out your Adam's apple and eat it for an apple.

Alex: Do you like bananas?

(Curtain)

HENRY & WILLARD REVISITED

Mary had a little skirt, 'twas split just right in half,
And everywhere that Mary went, she showed her little calf.
Mary had another dress; the skirt was split in front,
She never wore that one.

Let's return to a couple of burlesque sketches by those old pros, Hank Henry and Bill Willard, masters of their craft. The first sketch includes a commodious catalogue of jokes and props and tricky bits of business, plus an absurd premise.

Wolfe Larson on Poontang Island

CHARACTERS: Wolfe Larson, the top banana. In the opening sequence, he's in yellow oilskin raincoat with matching sou'wester hat. Beneath that he's wearing a coloured print shirt and striped slacks for the island scene when he doffs the rain gear. He'll also don a yachting cap and tennis sneakers.

First Mate, the second banana, who's a spindly little guy who looks as if he'd run from his own shadow. He's barefoot, wearing a castoff, oversized white sailor suit with navy collar, a white sailor's cap and navy blue jacket.

1st Sailor, also in white sailor outfit, but with hat from a foreign navy. Barefoot, slightly nutty.

2nd Sailor, also in white sailor outfit, hat from another foreign navy.

3rd Sailor, also in white sailor outfit, but wears Dutch seaman's cap. He wears tennis shoes.

Four girls in hula skirts with teeny bras, leis around their necks, flowers over the right ear.

Leading lady, wearing a sarong. So what's sarong about that? Also has flowers in her hair and a lei around her neck (we banished lei jokes long ago).

Lionel, a tall, skinny, mournful character, wearing a white robe tied with a sash. Pale make-up.

PROPS: Seltzer bottle, liquor bottle filled with amber liquid, a horn pipe for Larson, chalk, a prop snake, a tray with mushrooms on it. A carry-on sign with big red letters saying TILT. Fog horn, beep horn, big bell. Two baby dolls, unclothed, a banana.

SCENE: In One.

(Music—Sailing, Sailing Over the Bounding Main—then fades)

Announcer: *(Offstage)* Ladies and gentlemen, we present a mighty drama of the sea, about one of the historic figures of sea lore, a wanderer of the great oceans of the world: Captain Wolfe Larson, who sails through calm and storm with his mutinous crew. For forty days and forty nights, nothing but hell. We now take you on board his frigate.

(During blackout, as announcer speaks, two stagehands carry in the opening set, a portion of a ship's cabin, about six feet wide and six high, with two portholes, one workable with a simulated brass circle that Larson can pull open. A third person is in back of the set, bearing the seltzer bottle. This stagehand stands ready on cue with the liquor and seltzer bottles. When lights go up, the set is rocking like a ship in a stormy sea, up and down, down and up, etc. Captain Wolfe Larson is at centre, rocking in the opposite direction of the background set)

Wolfe: *(Melodramatically)* Here I am, behind the helm of my great frigate, the *SS Caca*, braving the bounding main. There is a terrible storm outside. In all my years at sea, I have never seen such a storm.

(Walks up to the porthole, opens it up and gets a shot of seltzer in the face. Walks back down front centre, dripping)

Wolfe: Oh, those waves, those damned waves! I will call my first mate to warn him of the treacherous waves out there *(gestures)* on the poop deck of the *SS Caca*. He is the bravest of the brave, standing at the helm, fearless and intrepid, washed by spray from the cold cruel sea, helping to guide the good ship *Caca* with muscles of steel. *(Takes horn pipe from pocket, pipes a blast)*

Mate: *(Rushes on from right)* You called me, Wolfe Larson?

Wolfe: Yes. I want you to look out the porthole and see the sea, the terrible storm, the wind, those treacherous waves. . .

Mate: Wolfe Larson, you're a lousy skipper. You don't know the first thing about running a ship.

Wolfe: What do you mean, I don't know anything about running a ship? There's a storm brewing. Look out the porthole. *(Wolfe kicks at mate's ass as he cringes past)*

Mate: *(Goes up to set, opens porthole, looks, comes back)* What a beautiful day! *(The set rocks when Larson walks to the porthole but remains stationary whenever the mate peers out the porthole)*

Wolfe: *(Goes upstage, set rocking furiously)* Beautiful day! I have a feeling there is mutiny afoot. I know there is a storm brewing. I will walk over to the porthole and check it out again. *(Does so and gets seltzer in face again)* Oh those waves, those damned waves! *(Tastes dripping seltzer)* Hmm, tastes just like mixer. If only I had some whiskey. *(Arm comes through porthole, hands Larson a bottle, who does a double take)* What is this? *(Takes a drink from the bottle, then spits it out)* It is of a PISSY colour! *(Holds it up to the light and skulls. He walks back down to centre, set becomes stationary)*.

Mate: If you know so much about running a ship, let me ask you this. Supposing you're out at sea and a gale is blowing 90 miles an hour. What would you do?

Wolfe: I'd throw out an anchor.

Mate: Supposing a monsoon comes up and the wind's blowing 150 miles an hour. What would you do?

Wolfe: I'd throw out another anchor.

Mate: Wait a minute, where are you getting all the anchors?

Wolfe: Where are you getting all the wind?

Mate: Wolfe Larson, you're a phoney. Why, you don't even know our course.

Wolfe: That's a lie. Who doesn't know our course? Turn around and let me show you. *(Mate turns around as Larson draws with chalk on back of his jacket. Larson makes a circle)* Up here's the Cape of

Good Hope. *(Taps top of circle, then points to the middle)* This is the Atlantic seaboard and right here *(gooses the first mate)* is Capricorn.
Mate: Ooooooooh!
Wolfe: Let me show it to you again *(repeats goosing)*
Mate: Ooooooooh!
Wolfe: Hey, wait a minute, are you goosy?
Mate: Only around Capricorn. . . I'd like to ask you a question.
Wolfe: Go ahead.
Mate: If a sheep is a ram and a mule is an ass, how come a ram in the ass is a goose?
Wolfe: Look, Mate, I want my orders obeyed. Bring on my crew.
Mate: Screw the crew. Let's play Capricorn again. *(Hugs Wolfe)*
Wolfe: *(Pushes him away)* Get out of here. Get the men.
Mate: *(Yells)* Yoo hoo, men! You hoo. Hey, men!

(Crew of three bedraggled sailors straggles on)

1st S: Food. Food. This horrible food is driving me stark raving mad. Mad, mad, I tell you! *(Raves on)*
2nd S: *(Hits him over the head with a rolled up newspaper)* Shuddup, you idiot.
Wolfe: Quiet, you miserable fool. What's wrong with the food?
Mate: Wolfe Larson, you dirty dog. For the past forty days and forty nights you've been serving us nothing but penguin meat. Nothing but penguin meat.
Wolfe: Why, you lowdown sons of sea-cooks. Who started the rumour about penguin meat? I've been serving you nothing but steaks, chops and breaded veal cutlets. I don't want to hear anything more about penguin meat. Now, get out of here.

(Sailors and mate exit right, imitating penguin's swaying walk)

(Blackout)

Anncr: *(Offstage)* Land ho! Land ho! Over the starboard port bow, aft of the mizzenmast at the stern, you lubbers. Drop anchor and hit the beach. All ashore that's going ashore. *(Pipes whistle)*

(Curtain opens onto lush tropical setting. Four girls are dancing. They undulate down front to sing a cappella)

We're the virgins of the Virgin Isles
We need no urgin' to use our wiles
Whenever men are cast ashore
We wonder if they're searching for
The virgins of the Virgin Isles.

(Music swells into Hawaiian War Chant for the girls' wild, hip-shaking finish. Leading lady enters from left at finish of dance number, watches girls)

1st Gal: What an island this turned out to be!

2nd Gal: Yeah. Now that we've finished dancing, what'll we do next?

3rd Gal: Just what we always do. Sit around and do nothing.

4th Gal: Five girls on this island and only one man—if you can call him a man.

Lady: He was all right when he came here, but we ought to turn him in for a new model. Wait! Here comes our good old Lionel Strongshaft now.

Lionel: *(Drags himself on, very pale)* Hello, girls.

Lady: Hello, Lionel. What's up?

Lionel: *(Looks down to where his manhood should be)* Oh, nothing much.

Lady: Well, I guess we'll have to put you out to pasture.

Lionel: If you'd only followed my advice, everything would have been okay. All I needed was one day off a week.

Lady: And the bell in the Love Tower has been silent for months.

Lionel: Yeah, it's been a long time since I rang the bell.

(From offstage, Wolfe's bellowing voice: "Hut, two, three, four, hut, two, three, four." Men march in as girls and Lionel give way. Wolfe stops centre)

Wolfe: Halt, one, two. At ease.

Girls: MEN!!!! *(Tumult ensues, with girls scrambling over Wolfe, mate and the sailors. Wolfe tries to restore order. Finally, after chasing gals away, patting each on the rear, he gets his crew back to attention. Lionel remains)*

Wolfe: Okay, crew, screw. Go find some coconuts and make yourselves some Coco Locos. *(Crew and mate exit right)*

Lionel: *(Goes over to Wolfe)* I'm so glad you and your crew came here to help me out.

Wolfe: We came to help you out? How come?

Lionel: Because I'm the only man on Poontang Island. And you got a good look at the women here, didn't you?

Wolfe: *(Starts panting)* A good look, yes, and I also got a definite feeling about 'em, too! *(Hand gestures as if grabbing behinds and boobs)*

Lionel: Poontang is an island of love established by an old tribal legend. There is a mystic bell on a distant mountain that rings every time anyone makes love. But the bell hasn't tolled in many months.

Wolfe: I get you—some dong-dinging to make the bells go ding-dong?

Lionel: That's right. And at this very moment, the women are preparing a feast for you and your crew. You know, I have a good notion you're going to like Poontang.

Mate: *(Rushes in from right, dangling a snake)* Hey, look what we found. A water snake.

Wolfe: Stop dangling that snake at me. Go and dangle somewhere else.

Mate: But Captain, we've made a pet of him. Watch how he plays. *(Works rubber snake to make a lunge at Wolfe's crotch. Wolfe reacts. Mate works snake up to Wolfe's face and squeezes snake as if it were a toy)*

Wolfe: *(Goes up to stage apron and says to audience)* I bet you expected water to come out of the snake, didn't you? *(Goes back to mate, near wings, grabs the snake and tosses it off left)* See? No water. *(At this point, water shoots out from wings hitting Wolfe in the face)* Oh those waves, those damned waves!

(Hula music)

Lady: *(Slithers on from right, wriggling and shaking, bearing a tray of mushrooms)* Here you are. Start eating. Oh boy, the dongs will start dinging tonight. *(Starts bumping and grinding)*

Lionel: Please. Don't be in such a hurry all the time. Take it easy. There's time for everything.

Lady: That's what you've been saying for the past six months. *(Grind hips)* I want what I want when I want it.

Lionel: *(Looking at hips)* You'll get what I got when I got it. And right now, I ain't got it.

Lady: *(Holds out tray)* Come on, call the crew. Everybody start eating this stuff.

Mate: *(Pokes at mushrooms on tray)* What are these—nuts?

Lionel: Not nuts. Those are the rarest treats in all the world. Our special Poontang Mushrooms, guaranteed to get you in the right mood.

Wolfe: What kind of a mood can a mushroom give you?

Mate: Is this the stuff they put in our coffee in the navy?

Lionel: Nothing like saltpetre. Just the opposite.

Mate: Gee, I hope so. That coffee always makes me dream of Kermit the Frog.

Wolfe: What about the mushrooms, Matey? Shall we give it a go?

Mate: I'll tell you what. One of the crew is a noted mushroomologist. He majored in mushrooms at Peace River University. I'll go find him. *(Exits right and returns immediately with three crew members, who are swapping lines)*

1st S.: I was scared stiff and she took advantage of it.

2nd S.: I was always looking for a pair of nice legs, but when I found them I shoved them roughly aside.

3rd S.: The trouble with being a sailor is that you're always getting into things beyond your depth

1st S.: I think of myself as a carefree guy—I don't care who, as long as it's free.

2nd S.: She's no coward—even if she does take it lying down.

Lionel: That sure was fast.

1st S: Food. Food. *(Raves, pulls out a banana)* This horrible food is driving me stark, raving mad. Mad, mad, I tell you.

2nd S.: Shuddup, you idiot, and eat your banana. *(Swats 1st S over the head)*

Wolfe: So, which of you is the mushroom expert?

3rd S: *(Steps forward)* I'm a mushroomologist from the University of Peace River, on sabbatical.

Wolfe: On your what-ical?

Mate: Never mind. So, tell us about poisonous mushrooms, Prof.

3rd S: There are known species of poisonous mushrooms: *Amanitie Maccaria* and *Amanitie Fallowheaties*, for which there is definitely no antidote. They bring immediate death after eating.

Lionel: You have nothing to fear, professor. These mushrooms aren't poisonous.

3rd S: How do you know?

Lionel: We just fed some to the dog.

Mate: How's the dog now?

Lionel: Just fine. Playful and full of life as can be.

Wolfe: That settles it. Okay men, you can eat the mushrooms.

Mate: Just like the navy. If the food's good enough for a dog, it's good enough for us. *(Mate and Wolfe begin to eat the mushrooms)*

Wolfe: Come on, men, these taste pretty good. *(They dive in)*

Lady: *(Goes over to 3rd crewman, starts feeding him)* Come on, professor. Enjoy.

3rd S: Well, all right. *(Nibbles a bit)* Hmm. Not bad.

Gal: *(Runs on from left, breathless)* Lionel! Lionel! Guess what?

Lionel: What?

Gal: The dog just died. Isn't that awful? And what a terrible way to die.

Wolfe: *(Grabs Lionel)* The dog died. You stupid fool! So they weren't poisonous mushrooms, eh?

Mate: Oh my, I don't want to die. I really don't. *(To Wolfe)* You're the captain of the ship. Don't let them die on us. *(Begging on knees. Wolfe knocks him sprawling and goes over to 3rd S)*

Wolfe: Hey Prof, you on your what-ical. How long did you say it will take for me to drop dead?

3rd S: About six or seven minutes.

Wolfe: *(Looks at watch)* Six or seven minutes, eh? *(Grabs lady and starts off left. Stops, does a take, bends her over and talks over her face to the audience)* I'll never make it. If only I had a little more time. We all have to go sometime, but most of us go during the commercials.

2nd S: Men, in a few moments we'll be over the Great Divide into the City of Everlasting Silence.

1st S: Golly gee, we're going to Moose Jaw!

Mate: Wolfe Larson, now that we're all going to die, I have a confession to make. Remember the 100 dollars I owe you?

Wolfe: Forget about it.

Mate: I did.

3rd S: Men, we've been laughing and joking while death is staring us in the face. What courage. *(To gal who brought in the message about the dog dying)* How long did it take the dog to die after eating the poisonous mushrooms?

Gal: Oh, he didn't die from eating poisonous mushrooms.

All: WHAT!!!?

Gal: Not at all. A coconut fell out of a tree and hit him on the head.

Wolfe: You mean we ain't gonna die?

Lady: Die? Brother, from now on you're gonna LIVE. GIRLS! *(Rest of gals rush on from left)*

Lionel: Hey bobba rebop and hubba hubba. The bells will ring in the tower tonight.

Mate: *(Takes a girl and rushes offstage. Bell rings twice. He comes back out of breath)* I don't know what I was doing, but from now on it's my hobby.

(Gals drag 1st, 2nd and 3rd crewmen off, given a push by Wolfe and mate. Bell clacks dully, then a foghorn sounds, then a beep-beep. Girl returns carrying a sign that says TILT and all three men return looking silly. Wolfe grabs lady again and runs off right. Bell starts ringing and clanging like crazy. Wolfe returns with a baby doll cradled in each arm. Stands centre stage looking from one doll to the other)

(Curtain)

This next piece is a burlesque classic. I can't really say whether Hank Henry wrote it. Likely not, because it goes back a long way. The segment can be included with other sketches or it can stand on its own.

Slo-o-o-wly I Turned

SCENE: Waiting room of an insane asylum.
CHARACTERS: Comic; receptionist; inmate; second comic

Comic: How do you do?

Receptionist: How do I do what?

Comic: Do you know Dwart Farquhart?

Recept: Why, sure.

Comic: Well, he told me to come over here because me and my partner were going to put on a show for the inmates of this asylum.

Recept: Oh, I see. Well, what kind of an act do you boys do?

Comic: Oh, I tell jokes and do some funny stuff like that, and also a little dancing. You know, I'm feeling a little faint, can I sit down, please?

Recept: Why sure, sit down right over there.

Comic: *(Sits down on a chair next to a seated inmate)* I wish my buddy would hurry up and get here. *(To inmate)* Hiya, pardner.

Inmate: Oh, were you addressing me? Thank you, thanky, sir. Those are the first kind words I've heard in years. You see, sir, I wasn't always a dirty, scurvy bum like you. . . Mine is rather a sad story. Would you like hear it?

Comic: No sir!

Inmate: Well, then, I'll tell it to you. You see, it began many years ago when I was just a little boy. My father gave me the benefit of a good education—14 years of grade school, preparatory school, college, and the University of Alberta. Did you go to school, sir?

Comic: Oh yes, sir.

Inmate: You passed your examinations?

Comic: No, sir, but I was first on the list of those who failed.

Inmate: Well, then I met her. She was young. She was beautiful. She was desirable.

Comic: A girl?

Inmate: Of course she was a girl! She was wonderful. She was like a flower blooming fragrantly in the garden of youth. And then one day, God in his infinite mercy smiled down on us. A little bundle of pink and white, a baby boy. I worked harder than ever. And then one day—

Comic: A little baby boy, a little baby boy.

Inmate: Yes, a little boy.

Comic: Did he have blue eyes?

Inmate: Yes.

Comic: And brown hair?

Inmate: Yes.

Comic: And was he a fat little fellow?

Inmate: Yes.

Comic: DADDY! Just kidding.

Inmate: My boy, I worked day and night. And then one day, he came into my life. He was an actor, broken in health and spirit. I took him into my home. I said make my home your home (*pause*) and he did. Oh yes, he did. I was a fool. For one day, when I returned from my work as was my wont, I called to her. "Mary" (*Pause, then louder*) "Mary, Mary." There was no answer. "MARY" (*Louder*) "MARY!"

Comic: She's out.

Inmate: (*Yelling and running around the stage*) Mary, Mary, where are you, Mary? (*Goes berserk*) She was gone. My wife, my baby and the stranger. (*Starts to cry*) They were gone. (*Responding to audience laughter*) What are you laughing at? (*Inmate acts wilder and wilder, makes as if tearing up the scenery*) Then began a search that lasted for years. I was only 21 days behind them as they boarded a United Fruit Lines steamship at Buenos Aires. Fifteen days behind them at Rio de Janeiro, five at Madagascar, two and a half at the Cape of Good Hope, seven hours at Port Said, Egypt. And then one day, at the gates of Calcutta, I found him. I was just about to pounce upon him, just about to tear him limb from limb, when in my weakened condition, aggravated by the fierce rays of the tropical sun, well, it just proved too great an obstacle. I sank in a heap on the sand. When I regained consciousness he was gone. Then began a search all through the capitals of Europe: Rome, Milan, Paris, Moscow, Berlin, across the channel to London, then across the Atlantic to America, New York, Pittsburgh, Chicago, Milwaukee.

Comic: Moose Jaw!

Inmate: Moose Jaw? . . . And then Niagara Falls. Finally, at Niagara Falls, I found him again. He was standing there with his back to the Falls, all eternity behind him and retribution finally staring him in the face. When I saw him standing there, the man who had ruined my life, the man who had stolen my wife and my baby, the man who had made me a miserable wanderer across half the face of the Earth, when I saw that miserable cur standing in front of me, years of suffering welled up within me and with murder in my heart, s-l-o-o-o-wly I turned. *(Inmate stands on right leg, raises left leg and places hand on knee, swinging leg and body around to face comic. He moves over to comic, pacing his steps with his words)* Inch by inch, step by step, I crept upon him. And when I felt his hot breath on my cheek, I STRUCK! *(Hits comic)*

Comic: *(Yells and screams as inmate beats him up)* What are you doing? I give up!

Inmate: *(Comes out of his trance)* Oh, you're the gentleman with the kind face.

Comic: What are you trying to do to me?

Inmate: Pardon me, I forgot myself. I'm so weak, I–

Comic: It's my fault. I'd have done the same thing if I'd caught the guy at Niagara Falls.

Inmate: *(Wild light in eye and again goes berserk)* NIAGARA FALLS!

Comic: Me and my big mouth.

Inmate: When I saw him standing there, s-l-o-o-o-wly I turned. *(Same movements as before)* Inch by inch, step by step *(Inmate attacks comic again, comic yells for guy he was supposed to meet at asylum as inmate mops the floor with him, then suddenly stops)* Where am I?

Comic: Cut it out! Never again will I say that word.

Inmate: What word?

Comic: That word that makes you go off your beam.

Inmate: What word do you mean?

Comic: That word, way down east in Ontario.

Inmate: Where in Ontario?

Comic: Where everybody goes when they get married.

Inmate: Where do they go?

Comic: Down—huh! Well I'm not going to say the word you think I'm gonna say.

Inmate: What word are you talking about?

Comic: *(Pause)* Go ahead, try and make me say Niagara Falls.

Inmate: *(Shouts and goes wild again)* With all the pent-up emotion that was in me, s-l-o-o-o-wly I turned. *(Same movements as before)* Inch by inch! Step by step! *(Beats up on comic again)*

(Enter the partner comic was looking for, stops the mayhem)

2nd Comic: What are you doing here?

1st Comic: They told me we were supposed to do a show for the inmates.

Inmate: Well, gentlemen, as long as you're here, you might as well go with the show that you were going to do for the inmates. They're out there waiting for you.

2nd Comic: Okay, let's do it. What'll we do? *(They go straight into intro for the next skit)*

FAIRY TALES

Little Bo Peep mislaid her sheep,
They were eaten by a leopard;
While what she really meant to keep,
She was losing to a shepherd!

The comedy team of Gabe Kellor and Peter Chmiliar entertained Edmonton and area audiences for many years back in the Seventies and later. These easygoing mirth-makers teamed up to do their own original skit, How to Play Baseball, and expanded to make thousands hold their sides with laughter in take-offs on various sports (golf, bowling, pool, fishing, ping-pong and others). Their material and style of humour was irresistible.

A community group in Vegreville, Alberta asked them to write, produce, direct and play in a show in the town's Wellington Park to raise funds for a recreation centre. They accepted the challenge and called the variety revue *The Last Tango in Vegreville*. Working with thirty amateurs, they put together a two-and-a-half-hour show that got a standing ovation from the twelve hundred enthusiastic people who saw it.

After that first eleven-night run, their popularity grew until they were doing the same thing for three other annual shows in three different community centres. These shows ran for a total of twenty-four nights, played to packed auditoriums and were sold out months in advance.

Naughty, subtle and hilariously funny, Gabe and Peter hit you where you least expected it with a rapid-fire assault on your funny-bone and other ticklish places. Their following grew to tens of thousands who lined up to see their productions, and they were in great demand at conventions, staff parties, nightclubs and lounges. They played Edmonton's annual bust-out Klondike Days and national Kinsmen conventions.

Show business was just a fun thing for these two guys, something they did in their spare time, but like all these type of burlesque variety shows, it provided a fun night for the thousands who looked forward every year to seeing the next one.

I've concentrated on the actual material presented in these types of Western Canadian shows, but I know I've failed to include or mention many worthy and hilariously comedic candidates. (You know who you are). And that also applies to the West Coast scene and the shows produced by the great Fran Dowie in historic Barkerville, BC, the centre of the province's 1860s gold rush (See Chapter 20 for more on Fran). Dowie's shows could spin you helplessly out of orbit on a laughter binge.

Dowie's shows sometimes featured Sid Williams, the man of a thousand faces, who for fifty years was the embodiment of the muse of entertainment, wearing both tragic and comic faces, in the city of Courtenay. Both those men could act, design stage sets, costumes and props, and act as stage manager and director as well.

In syndicated episodes of the classic West Coast television series *The Beachcomers*, you might see Williams, along with Jackson Davies, whose comic talents are still a staple of many a BC play, movie or television show. Davies made his name in Edmonton, his breakthrough coming for his outstanding performance as Lennie in *Of Mice and Men* at the old Citadel dinner theatre. He later starred in the annual *Dawson City Revue* at Diamond Lil's Saloon, which for many long years was produced and directed by Jack McCreath of the Alberta department of culture

Let's not forget the annual summer shows at Victoria's Butchart Gardens, presented by Howard "Woody" Woodland. Woody left literally thousands of happy patrons' stomachs aching from laughter, and most of them returned year after year, bringing friends and neighbours to enjoy the hilarious entertainment.

All of the above are in the lead for the title of Canada's funniest comedic performers.

The following Gabe Kellor skit gives a new, burlesque twist to the classic fairy tale:

Little Red Riding Hood

CHARACTERS: Narrator; stooge; Little Red (a comely wench); wolf in sheep's clothing (should be able to sing); woodsman; chorus line

SCENE: Front curtain, narrator and stooge

Narrator: From the wonderful world of fable, tonight ladies and gentlemen we bring you, for the first time ever, the true story of Little Red Riding Hood. (Starts to read from a fairy tale book) Now, once upon a girl there was a time . . . I mean, once upon a time there was a girl–
Stooge: I liked it better the first time.
Narrator: Yeah, well, this girl's nickname was Little Red Riding Hood, but her real name was Virginia. All the boys called her Virgin for short, but not for long . . . Now, the way she got the nickname Little Red was that she would always go fishing with the boys, you see.
Stooge: And she'd always come home with a little red snapper.
Narrator: She had boyfriends by the score.
Stooge: Yeah, and most of them did.
Narrator: She was an outdoors type of girl. She had the bloom of her youth in her cheeks.
Stooge: Yeah, and the cheeks of her youth in her bloomers.
Narrator: Stick to the script. Well, one day she was on her way through the woods to her Grandma's cathouse, where she had a part-time job.

(Enter Little Red in tight red costume)

Stooge: Yeah, she worked sort of a split shift.
Narrator: Well anyway, she was on her way through the woods when she came upon this great big old wolf.

(Enter wolf, his sheepskin thrown over him as a disguise)

Narrator: Now, you all know what a wolf is: it's a man with a strong will, looking for a girl with a weak won't. But the girls called this wolf Jergens because he worked real fast and didn't leave a ring behind. Anyway, the wolf said he would walk Little Red to Grandma's house. So they walked along a little way and then the wolf turned to Little Red and said:

Wolf: I'm tired of walkin' all you pregnant girls to Grandma's house.

Red: What do you mean, pregnant girls? I'm not pregnant!

Wolf: Yeah, and you're not at Grandma's house yet, either.

Narrator: We're going to find out very shortly, ladies and gentlemen, whether the wolf actually does enter Grandma's cathouse before–(Enter sexy chorus girl) Well hello, how are, and who are, you?

Girl One: I'm one of the kittens from Grandma's house and I always say, Candy is dandy, but sex won't rot your teeth.

Narrator: Well, WOW! (Enter another sexy chorus girl) Who are you?

Girl Two: I'm a little kitten from Grandma's cathouse and I always say, There are no vitamins in a kiss, but it is a bone builder.

(Rest of chorus members enter by turns and introduce themselves as kittens, etc. then speak the following lines)

Girl Three: A cat can kill you but a little pussy never hurt anyone.

Girl Four: Grandma opened up this cathouse (pause) and she sold eight cats the very first day.

Girl Five: Marriage is like being in the bathtub: after you get used to it, it ain't so hot.

Narrator: And now, ladies and gentlemen, a commercial for Grandma's Cathouse

(Chorus sings)

> Ta Ra Ra Boom de Aye
> Did you get yours today?
> We get ours every day
> That's how we earn our pay.

(Little Red Riding Hood, the wolf and the chorus line go into a song and dance number, to the tune of Sam the Sham's Little Red Riding Hood. The *wolf sings while the chorus girls dance, then all exit except narrator and stooge, who remain at side of stage, continuing with the commercials as Grandma's bedroom scene is set up)*

Narrator: This part of our show has been brought to you by Orgy Pills. Orgy Pills, the makers of that famous cereal Prostituties. Remember folks, Prostituties don't snap, crackle or pop—they just lay there and bang. And now our alternate sponsor.

Stooge: We'd like to introduce to you this evening a brand new laundry detergent called Fugg. F-U-G-G. If Rinso won't rinse it and Duz won't do it, then Fugg it. And now, back to another alternate sponsor.

Narrator: The show is also sponsored by the makers of the breakfast cereal Grape Nuts. Yes, ladies and gentlemen, this cereal has two ounces of Spanish fly in every ten-ounce carton, of great assistance to some of you who have a problem getting up in the morning, or at noon or night. Remember the famous motto of Grape Nuts: a bowl in the morning gets you a box at night.

Stooge: Double your pleasure, double your fun, shack up with two broads rather than one. And now a word from one of our new sponsors.

Narrator: Hardies shoes, the people who make executive shoes for men. Remember the motto of Hardies Shoes, ladies and gentlemen: the gals really go for the guys with the Hardies on. And now another sponsor.

Stooge: Ladies, have you tried the new improved Duz? New Improved Duz is now one-half chicken fat—it'll make you finger lickin' good all over.

Narrator: And now back to our story of Little Red Riding Hood. The wolf finally reaches Grandma's house. He rushes in and says—but let's see for ourselves. *(Exit narrator and stooge as curtain opens on bedroom scene)*

Wolf: I want a woman.

Grandma: I'm a woman.

Wolf: You're too fat!

Grandma: Oh I am, am I? Why don't you try out a new wrinkle?

Wolf: *(The wolf grabs Grandma, pulls her out of bed, takes a rope, ties her up, throws her in the closet. He puts her bonnet on and gets into bed just as Little Red Riding Hood comes in)*

Red: Hello Grandma, what great big eyes you have! Whoo!

Wolf: Yes, my dear, but I still can't see you.
Red: You can't? Well, can you see my hand?
Wolf: No.
Red: No? Well, can you see my hair?
Wolf: No.
Red: (*Opens up the front of her dress and says*) Can you see this?
Wolf: Yeah, now I can see!
Red: Then I know what your trouble is—you're cockeyed! And Grandma, what a big nose you have. Is that your nose or are you eating a banana?
Wolf: You've heard of nose drops?
Red: Yes.
Wolf: Well, mine did!
Red: And Grandma, what big ears you have, you look like a taxi-cab with both doors open.
Wolf: Don't be mean, child. I play piano by ear, you know.
Red: Yes, and I know an old man who fiddles with his whiskers.
Wolf: But I have a neck like a swan.
Red: Too bad it isn't as white. And Grandma, what a big mouth you have.
Wolf: And an appetite to match, my dear.
Red: And what big teeth you have, Grandma.
Wolf: Yeah, the better to eat you with.
Red: Oh! Oh! Are you going to eat me whole?
Wolf: Oh, no. I'm going to spit that part out.

(*Enter narrator and stooge. They stand at side of stage*)

Narrator: Just then the Wolf leaped out of bed and started to rip off all of Little Red's clothes.
Stooge: And Little Red started to scream.
Narrator: And just then a handsome young woodsman rushed in and grabbed the wolf, felled him with a karate chop, killing the wolf. Then he scooped up Little Red in his arms and they went off together, happy about the whole thing.
Stooge: Yeah, he was happy about the whole, and she was happy about the thing.

(*Curtain*)

This second tale is more contemporary. It could well happen, and I think it has. It could be entitled Home to Daddy or Hasn't Paid Admission, but instead it's called:

Will It Come to This?

CHARACTERS: Husband; wife; announcer's voice over PA system.

Announcer: Women's Liberation is reversing traditional family roles. Some husbands now wait at home in their houses for their wives to come home from work. We take you now to just such a scene.

(Curtain opens on living room. Man in kimono and headscarf is dusting and tidying up the room. The phone rings. He picks up the receiver)

Husband: Oh, hello Oscar. *(Pause)* Yeah, I'm getting fed up working like a beaver. I told Gertrude just today, a man's work is never done. She comes home from that strip joint, the Pink Pussycat where she works, and she's finished for the night. But as for us, what with the housework and looking after the kids, to say nothing of the washing, we never get a minute's peace from morning till night. *(Pause)* Sure, come on over for a midnight snack. I'd like to see you. Gertrude's been unbearable to live with lately, and I'm fed up with it. Oh, I have to go. I can hear her key in the door.

(Hangs up as Gertrude enters, attired in stripper's costume)

Wife: Hi, honey, I'm home!
Husband: How did things go at work tonight?
Wife: Lousy. The same old bump and grind! *(Does a brief bump and grind, then falls into chair and takes off her shoes)*
Husband: Would you like your slippers, dear?
Wife: Naturally. *(Husband fetches slippers and puts them on wife's feet)* I suppose you've had an easy day of it.
Husband: Oh, yeah. You think you've got it bad. You don't know how rough it is here at home. I'm just working and slaving and trying to live on the bare necessities.
Wife: *(Indignantly)* Well, it's the bare necessities *(stands up and slaps her thigh)* that put the food on this table.
Husband: Yeah, well, I'd give the shirt off my back to get out of here and go back to a job.
Wife: Well, I'd like to work someplace where I don't have to take the shirt off my back. You know what happened tonight? Huh? Some lousy creep jumped up on the stage right in the middle of my act!

Husband: No kidding! What did you do?

Wife: Well, I just bumped him off *(demonstrates bump with her hip)*.

Husband: *(After a pause)* Oscar's coming over for a beer and a snack.

Wife: You'll have to put him off. I've been working hard all night, I'm way too tired for visitors.

Husband: You don't have to entertain him, he's not coming to see you.

Wife: You don't seem to realize what a hard night I've had. It's all very well for you, sitting around the house all the time and peace and quiet to do it in.

Husband: Are you kidding? Well, you should've been here tonight!

Wife: Oh? What happened, honey?

Husband: First of all, I washed your B string–

Wife: That's G string!

Husband: Not anymore—it shrunk! Then the dog ate one of your pasties.

Wife: The dog ate one of my pasties? What am I going to do tomorrow night? I need it for my act!

Husband: Don't worry about it. I sewed a sequin on an old checker. *(Laughs)*

Wife: *(Laughs also)* That's funny, all right. Look, we've both had a busy day. I'll just go in the bathroom and change into my nightgown.

Husband: Why go in there? Why don't you just change here?

Wife: *(Getting mad)* You know I can't stand to have anyone watch me undress if they haven't paid admission. *(Madder still)* And another thing, my dear George, you just don't know what work is!

Husband: I've had just about enough of your attitude and bad temper. You go out all night, you have your freedom and you keep all the money. The way you dole it out to me in dribs and drabs is disgusting. I have to look after the home, do all the housework, cook, wash, bring up the children and feed the dog. And what do I get out of it?

Wife: You get kept in a good house.

Husband: I think it's a rotten house, and let me tell you this, you're nothing but a mean, cowardly bully, and I'm not going to take any more of it!

Wife: And what do you think you can do about it?

Husband: *(Stamping his foot)* I'm going home to Daddy! *(Starts to cry)*

Wife: Oh for Pete's sake, stop that snivelling. If you have to cry, go out and cry on the lawn, it can do with some water. Now shut up.
Husband: Is that any way to speak to the father of your children?
Wife: Temper, temper, George.
Husband: I won't shut up and I won't be told what to do or not to do.
Wife: Really, George? I seem to have a recall a certain person promising to love, honour and obey. Anyway, I'm fed up, too. I'm going back down to the Pink Pussycat club! Good night!
Husband: Good night, little mother of five.
Wife: What did you say?
Husband: I said, good night, little mother of five.
Wife: *(Pause)* Good night, little father of three (Exit wife)

(Curtain)

A peek into the burlesque scene in Alberta would not be complete without mentioning Ken Graham's brainchild, *Naughty But Nice*, held every spring at the St. Albert Inn. Ken's show became the lynchpin of the St. Albert Festival of the Arts. Graham, who was also a key employee at the Alberta department of culture, wrote many parts for the show. His professional direction produced a smooth combination of old-style burlesque and a tinge of Benny Hill and Monty Python.

Thom Trofimuk, writing for the local *Gazette* newspaper, ran through the list of skits from one *Naughty But Nice* revue: ". . . homosexual ducks in the Sturgeon Galley, a male burlesque-style strip show, a three-man RCMP Musical Ride with horses and all, and the entire fairy tale of Cinderella performed while the entire cast is hopping."

Another Albertan who ran an excellent burlesque revue was Chet Gilmore of Slave Lake, in connection with that town's annual Riverdaze festivities. Chet and his wife Kathy were veteran *Sorry 'bout That* performers before they moved to Slave Lake. Chet's production of *Sorry 'bout That Too* was the show for you if you wanted a naughty, nasty night of shenanigans, clever asides, innuendo and good old-fashioned slap-your-face humour.

There was never a dull moment in the three-act performances, which was a credit to the skill of the cast and the pace of Chet's direction.

The Slave Lake Musical Theatre Association sponsored and presented the revue, but since they had some reservations about the word burlesque, they originally billed the show as an adult vaudeville musical revue.

HOKUM STUNTS

Uncle George and Auntie Mabel
Fainted at the breakfast table,
Isn't that sufficient warning,
Not to do it in the morning.
Ovaltine has set them right,
Now they do it morn and night.

It would be difficult to trace burlesque skits back to their beginnings. Many of the basic ideas for the material in this book and original versions of skits were handed down from one generation of performers to another, or transmitted by hearsay to the stage. In the old days of vaudeville, burlesque and music hall, very little was written about these acts, possibly because performers preferred to keep their routines as secret as possible to prevent encroachment and imitation, passing them on to trusted fellow actors. In this day and age, that kind of secrecy no longer applies.

In his book Crazy Stunts for Comedy Occasions, the famous magician Harlan Tarbell, creator of the Tarbell Course in Magic, says, "There was a species of comedy acts once commonly known among show people as hokum stunts. While these skits appear on the surface to be of a crazy or senseless nature, deeper analysis shows them to be carefully constructed so as to evoke laughter. Whether a stunt plays one minute or ten minutes, it should contain enough plot to stand by itself and gain the interest of the audience."

Here's one such sketch for three men and three women, just crazy enough to be good.

Dr. Cockenlocker's Sickness Transformer

CHARACTERS: Danny the dummy; Dr. Cockenlocker; nurse; Ferguson the patient; girl; dowager.

SCENE: Front of curtain.

Danny: Here I am with the whole day off and my poor girlfriend, Cuddles the doctor's nurse, has to work. Cheese and crackers, I miss my girlfriend Cuddles. I can't stand to be without her for another minute. I don't care if she *is* working—I'm going to that doctor's office and visit her right now, boy!

(Music as he exits. Curtain opens on doctor's office, in which there are two reclining chairs, like those in a dental office. Both chairs are empty, but Dr. Cockenlocker, a weirdo, is present. There is a panel behind and between the chairs, which is rigged to make electrical noises and sparks on cue when a switch is pulled)

Doctor: *(To audience)* Ah, what a great day in my life. I, Dr. Cockenlocker, have finally perfected my invention, the Cockenlocker Sickness Transformer. Allow me to explain. The sick patient sits in this chair *(indicates one of the chairs)*, I turn on the juice and whatever is wrong with the sicko goes into the dummy in the other chair. And I, Dr. Wilhelm Cockenlocker, invented it. Am I too much, Canada? I'm so precious I'm going to have myself bronzed!

(Enter Cuddles, the well-stacked nurse, who hip-waggles across stage to sounds of rhythmic drumming)

Nurse: You called, Dr. Cockenlocker?
Doctor: Oh, no use talking, nurse. You'd better get your tank filled with Ethyl and get rid of that knock. *(To audience)* Isn't she cute? You wouldn't believe it, but when she was 11 years old she was a boy. *(To nurse)* I have to go out for lunch, nurse. I'm expecting the delivery of a dummy for my new experiment. When the dummy comes, you will put him in that chair *(indicates second chair)*. Remember, I expect the dummy any minute! *(Exits, patting nurse on the bum on way out)*

(Enter Danny, immediately, door hits him in face as doctor leaves)

Nurse: *(Spots him and yells)* Dummy! *(Pause)* Danny! You shouldn't have come to the office. If Dr. Cockenlocker finds anybody here with me, he goes into a purple rage.
Danny: Oh!
Nurse: Oh , yes. *(She physically demonstrates all the following actions)* He punches *(hits Danny who goes, "Ugh")* and he hits and he chokes and he smashes them in the belly.
Danny: *(Doubled up and in a mess)* I'm glad he never caught me. I had to see you, Cuddles. I'm so crazy about you.
Doctor: *(From anteroom offstage)* Hey, I changed my mind. I came back early from lunch. I'm here. I'm back.
Nurse: *(To Danny)* It's the Doctor. Oh, quick, sit in this chair, right here. *(Dummy's chair)* And whatever you do, don't make a sound. *(Pushes Danny into chair)*
Doctor: *(Enters)* Nurse, I'll never go to that cafeteria again. Can you imagine? A cover charge for water—aha! Aha! I see the dummy has arrived. Isn't that wonderful. *(Looks dummy over)* This is a disgrace! This is an outrage! They've sent me damaged merchandise. Look at that face—it's melancholy—it's got a head like a melon and a face like a collie. *(Anteroom bell rings)* Ha, it's a patient. I'll bring him in *(Looks at dummy)* Whew! That's the last time I buy a dummy from a non-union gypsy. Cheap is cheap. *(Exits)*
Danny: *(To nurse)* Well, I'll see you tonight. *(He gets out of chair and embraces her)*
Nurse: Oh, yes.
Doctor: *(From anteroom)* Step right into the office, sir.
Nurse: Quick, quick, back in the chair! *(Danny gets back into chair)* And don't move a muscle.
Doctor: Come right in, sir. *(Doctor enters with patient)* Your name is Mr. *(looking at chart)* Fergoosin *(emphasis on goosin)*?
Ferguson: That's *Ferguson*!
Doctor: Meet my nurse.
Nurse: Pleased to meet you, Mr. Fergoosin *(Nurse exits to sound of drums as she waggles away)*
Ferguson: I think I'm going to have to send your nurse back to my shop.
Doctor: To the shop?
Ferguson: Yes, she has a little hitch in her get-along.

Doctor: Well, Mr. Fergoosin, we're very busy. What seems to be the trouble?

Ferguson: Every once in a while when I get to talkin', hahahaha-haha (*sounds like a nutty rooster in the middle of the sentence*)

Doctor: I'm sorry, I wasn't listening. What was it?

Ferguson: Well, I have a speech impediment and every once in a while when I'm talking, it comes out hahahahaha.

Doctor: Oh, this is serious. You are suffering from linguinia of the esophagus.

Ferguson: Linguinia of the esophagus?

Doctor: Oh, it's a very rare ailment. If left unchecked it could spread to your minestrone. But have no fear, Mr. Fergoosin. Dr. Cockenlocker's Sickness Transformer will cure you. You will sit in this chair (*indicates empty chair*) and whatever is wrong with you will go into that dummy.

Ferguson: (*Looking over dummy as he sits*) I don't think that dummy can take much more.

Doctor: I have no time for nonsense. Nurse, you will adjust this cord to the patient's knee and I will plug in the dummy. (*Nurse walks over during his instructions to sound of drums*) The dummy is plugged in and (*pause as he looks at dummy again*) Yes, cheap is cheap. All right, I will now turn on the transformer and whatever is wrong with Mr. Fergoosin will go into the dummy. Ah-so! (*Turns on machine, which emits noise and flashing light*) I will now release the patient.

Ferguson: (*Steps out of chair and says in a beautiful baritone*) Why this is wonderful. My speech impediment is gone. Doctor, you're wonderful, you're the most wonderful doctor in the world.

Doctor: Years of practice and self-denial, my good man. (*Doorbell in anteroom office rings*)

Dummy: Ahahahaha.

Doctor: Another patient. Let me show you the way out, Mr. Fergoosin. You do have your cheque book with you, don't you?

Ferguson: Yes.

Doctor: Fine. (*Ferguson and doctor exit*)

Danny: I'm going to get out of here while I still can, hahahahaha.

Nurse: What did you say?

Danny: I said, I want to get out of here while I still can, hahahaha. Oh, this is terrible. I've got that man's speech impediment. How did I get into this mess, hahahahaha?

Doctor: (*From anteroom*) All right. Yes, I am Dr. Cockenlocker. Won't you step into my office.

Danny: Hahahahaha (*trying to get away but has to get back into chair*)

Doctor: Right this way, come with me. (*Enters with girl*) May I say, you are one of the loveliest patients I have ever met.

Girl: Oh, thank you. (*As she walks in, drums go*)

Doctor: (*Looks around and watches her behind*) Seems to be a lot of that going around these days. Now tell me what's the matter.

Girl: Well, you see, I'm a soprano from La Scala.

Doctor: Oh, I've eaten there many times.

Girl: No, no, no. I sing. I'm a mezzo-soprano from La Scala.

Doctor: Mezzo? From La Scala? What is your trouble, madam?

Girl: Well, this year they have too many sopranos, and if I don't lower my voice, I'll lose my job. Oh, Doctor, can you help me?

Doctor: You bet your Sweet Aïda I can help you. Oh, you've come to the right place, beautiful lady. Nurse, put the beautiful lady in the chair. (*Nurse crosses to the sound of drums*) Oh, I love your rhythm, nurse. Now, I'll plug in the dummy and I will (*looks at dummy again*) Oh, yes, cheap is cheap. One lowering of voice operation coming up. I will now make with the magic machine. (*Turns it on to loud sounds and lights*)

(*Girl gets out of chair, offstage baritone voice speaks the lines she lip-synchs as she thanks doctor, doctor ushers her out*)

Danny: Oh, I can't take any more, hahahahaha. I'm going to get a lawyer and (*at this point he breaks into a soprano aria*)

Nurse: I think your mouth broke.

Danny: I'm a soprano. Oh, Cuddles, hahahahaha.

Doctor: (*From anteroom*) All right, if you'll just come into my office.

Nurse: (*To Danny*) Quick, quick, back in the chair.

Danny: Hahahahaha (*in soprano voice*).

Doctor: (*Enters with dowager*) Come right in. Now tell me, what seems to be the trouble?

Woman: Oh, goodness me, it's not my problem, it's my dog's She's about to have puppies.

Danny: (*Leaping out of dummy's chair and bolting for the door*) Oh, no you don't hahahahaha (*in soprano voice as he runs out*)

(*Curtain*)

Here's another creation of Hank Henry and Bill Willard, one which used to satisfy the constant demand for comedy.

Border Town Saloon

CHARACTERS: Black Pedro. He's the top banana, a hokey Mexican macho guy dressed in black bell-bottom trousers, open black embroidered shirt with black sombrero tied loosely with string under his neck. The prospector is small in contrast to big tough Pedro. The prospector is dressed in tattered jeans, a shirt that's seen plenty of wear, a neckerchief, an old, sweat-stained, mangled Western hat and a gimmicked fur coat, along with a pack on his back that looks heavy. Straight man: He wears a business suit with white shirt and tie, sort of a natty dresser. The flock: five girls dressed in long Mother Hubbards, wearing bonnets and carrying tambourines. One of the flock, the drum girl, carries a bass drum. The bartender wears an open white shirt with the sleeves rolled up, dark trousers and a white apron. A tough-talking guy. Extras: four males dressed as Mexicans in white with sombreros, barefoot. Able to sing El Rancho Grande. Señorita: she's Pedro's mate, very sexy, dressed in long, swirling embroidered skirt with revealing blouse.

PROPS: Tambourines, two big bass drums, bottles for the bar, two tables with four chairs each, 'coon coat, toy pistols for Pedro with starter's pistols offstage.
SCENE: Open in one in front of street drop painted to resemble a town near the border of Mexico. Flock of five girls dressed in Hubbards, carrying tambourines, march across stage to recite as march music plays, then fades to drumbeat in tempo to the recitation.

Flock: *(Chant in Unison):*
Reform, reform, we'll reform the world
Reform, reform, our banner is unfurled
Reform, reform, cast away your sin
Reform, reform, and let the light come in.

Drum girl: *(Steps forward to recite)*
My past was wicked and depraved,

I drank the demon rum,
Now I'm pure and I am saved,
I beat this god-damn *(boom, boom in cadence with the syllables)* drum!

(Rest of flock gives her a double-take as she says god-damn)

Drum girl: *(Speaking)* Sistern, sistern, there's work to be done. We must go at once to the Border Town Saloon.
Flock: The Border Town Saloon!
Drum girl: Yes, sistern, the Border Town Saloon. I heard tell they sell whiskey there.
Flock: Whiskey!
Drum Girl: Yes, whiskey. And I heard tell they have wild parties there.
Flock: Wild parties!
Drum girl: Ah, yes indeed. And I heard tell they have men there.
Flock: MEN!
Drum girl: Yes, men that need saving.
One of the flock: Save one for me!
Flock: *(Exits right, marching off with drum girl beating her goddamn drum, all shouting in unison)* Reform, reform, we'll reform the world Reform, reform, our banner is unfurled, etc.

(As flock exits, street drop goes up to reveal barroom set. The bar is up left and two sets of tables and chairs are above centre and right. Enter prospector, followed by straight man)

Prosp: Wait a minute, wait a minute. When I went to work for you, you told me I'd be working like a dog. But now you've got me working like a mule. *(Imitates mule's hee-haw)*
Straight: Hey, you got talent. Stop complaining. Just think about when we strike it rich. I can see it now—us digging and striking the mother lode. Eureka! We found it, THE MOTHER LODE!
Prosp: I quit. I'm not carrying any mother's load.
Straight: Now, you don't see what I mean. Imagine digging up tons of precious minerals, oodles of ore.
Prosp: To hell with the oodles. I want gold or nothing.
Straight: That's what you'll get—nothing. *(Prospector gives straight a dirty look, a little threatening)* Heh, heh, I'm only kidding. Come on, let's have a drink. Hey Bartender. *(Pounds on bar)*

(Enter four Mexican males singing El Rancho Grande, followed by the señorita, who hip-swings over to far table, sits and crosses her legs showing a bit of thigh. While quartet is singing, bartender ambles behind bar)

Barkeep: *(At finish of song)* Hey, you bums sing pretty good. What'll it be, boys?
Prosp: *(Takes off his fur coat, throws it on floor, wipes his feet on it and says)* Lassie Go Home. *(At this point a stagehand pulls the coat across stage into the wings by means of a monofilament string that was previously hooked inside the coat, its length trailing unseen across the stage)*

Straight: *(To barkeep)* I'll have a straight milk.
Prosp: My God, milk! I always get mixed up with drunkards.

(Enter flock from right, beating drum and tambourines, chanting Reform, reform, etc.)

Barkeep: Who are you and what in hell are you doin' here?

Drum girl: I am a member of the Dry Society for the Prevention of Intoxication and the Propagation of Non-Alcoholic Beverages *(This is the cue for the orchestra to launch into the tune Dry Society as drumgirl sings the lyrics solo)*

> *We're the Dry Society*
> *With our axe we'll set you free*
> *Beat upon that drum*
> *Down with Demon Rum*
> *Smash that glass and follow me*
> *Pour that whiskey down the drain*
> *Liquor, it will rot your brain*
> *If your nerves get all frayed*
> *Just drink milk or lemonade*
> *We're the Dry Society!*

Drum girl: *(Speaking)* We in the Dry Society are a compatible lot. We believe in spreading the joys of sober living. You men who are sitting here tonight smoking cigarettes, with a woman in one hand and a drink in the other, you believe you are enjoying yourselves. Tell me, are you really happy? Or will you wake up on the morrow, just another face on the barroom floor? What makes a good woman bad? Liquor! And what makes a poor mother's heart sad? Liquor! And what makes a good man bad?

Entire cast: *(Yelling)* WOMEN!

(Cue for music again, all sing Dry Society, except for last three lines, which are soloed by drum girl, then all repeated the final line, We're the Dry Society!!!)

Barkeep: *(When tune finishes)* Hey, you broads, what'll ya have?
Drum girl: We came in for a revival.
Barkeep: We ain't got no revival. But we got the best tequila on the border.
Drum girl: Tequila? What's Tequila?
Barkeep: Why, that's rattlesnake juice, gals. One drink and the mind leaves the body. Second drink and you're looking for a place to lay the body.
Drum girl: Lay the body. Sounds awful exciting, doesn't it, girls?
Girl One: Wow! Yeah, man. Lay the body.
Girl Two: I mean, like, get down, yeah, yeah. *(Does a brief boogie step, catches herself and straightens up, looking quite prim)*
Drum Girl: I think we'd better try some. It's our duty. If we don't, then we'll never know how to reform depraved people, will we? *(She indicates the prospector and the straight man, then points to the Mexican quartet, who have by now moved alongside the señorita, trying to get some action. The señorita ignores them)*

(Bartender pours the drinks into shot glasses. The flock goes up to the bar with the drum girl, discarding the drum and tambourines on the bar. The flock picks up glasses, turns around in unison and downs the drinks. The bartender pours another shot and the flock repeats the action. They move down front for the dance—except for drum girl—discarding Mother Hubbards to reveal sexy black and pink corsets with garter belts and black stockings and high heeled pumps—all of which the Mother Hubbards have heretofore concealed. They dance to a raunchy show tune. As the dance ends, each girl winds up on the lap of a quartet member. The prospector slouches over to the señorita's table and starts smooching with her. The straight man has remained up back, leaning on the bar and watching everything)

Barkeep: *(To prospector)* Hey you, do you know what you're doing?

Prosp: No, but I'm finding out damn fast.

Barkeep: Listen, you bum, lay off that stuff. We don't allow no fooling around below the Rio Grande.

Prosp: Rio Grande? I haven't even reached the Mississippi yet.

Barkeep: Don't say I didn't warn you. That dame belongs to Black Pedro.

Prosp: Black Pedro? Who's he?

Barkeep: Why, he's just the toughest hombre since Marlon Brando. He don't like nobody fooling around with his woman.

(Gunshots offstage. Flock screams, picks up Mother Hubbards, tambourines and drum and runs off, left. Quartet follows with hands cupped as if playing with the girls' bottoms. In roars Black Pedro from right, stalks across stage firing pistols. Out-of-sync shots continue offstage)

Prosp: How about buying a drink?

Pedro: Okay, you bum. *(To barkeep)* Pour him my favourite.

Prosp: What's your favourite?

Pedro: Cheap gin, Spanish Fly and Seven-Up.

Prosp: What do you call it?

Pedro: Upjohn ! *(Barkeep pretends to pour a drink from a bottle into an opaque container)*

Prosp: *(Smells drink and makes face)* It smells terrible!

Pedro: *(Pulls his six-shooter and points it at prospector)* Take a drink or I'll drill you.

Prosp: *(Sips from the glass, which is filled with small white beans, and the prospector has to get about 40 in his mouth for the next sight gag. Holds the beans in the pouches of his cheeks like a squirrel. Pretends to splutter)* Ugh! Ugh! That stuff's awful. Tastes like a specimen.

Pedro: I know, but whose? *(Pedro hands six-shooter to the prospector)* Now you hold the gun on me and I'll take a drink. *(Pedro pretends to drink)* Force me to take a horrible drink, will you? I have a feeling you're in the wrong place—you should be attending a funeral.

Prosp: Whose?

Pedro: Yours *(Pedro delivers a pulled punch to prospector's jaw. Prospector reels from the blow, staggers around and then spits our some teeth, which are actually beans. He comes stage front holding his jaw and keeps spitting beans as long as it gets laughs, ending by spitting them into the band, who get up and hit them back with table tennis paddles)*

Prosp: *(To audience)* This man is impossibly stupid. I need him like I need a second belly button. *(To Pedro)* You're a pretty tough guy, eh, Pedro?

Pedro: Yeah, I'm rough.

Prosp: If you're so rough and tough, you should be fighting bulls, not me.

Pedro: It's nothing to fight *el toro*. Just tell me what to do.

Prosp: Okay, the first thing you do is go into the arena. The band's playing, the crowd's cheering.

Pedro: Why are they cheering?

Prosp: They came to see you gored to death.

Pedro: Who's gored to death?

Prosp: *(Indicates audience)* I think they are! No—you're gored to death.

Pedro: Why should I be gored to death?

Prosp: Because it's their pleasure.

Pedro: Okay, if it's their pleasure, I'll be gored to death. But just once.

Prosp: All right. Now, you're standing in the middle of the arena. The crowds are cheering, the band's playing. So you take off your hat and you bow to the left, then you bow to the right. *(Illustrates bowing)* Then you look up and see the president of your country and his lady sitting in the royal box.

Pedro: Viva El Presidente, viva la Primera Dama, que viva yo!

Prosp: Now you get down on one knee and throw kisses at the first lady's box.

Pedro: *(Skulls)* Ahhhh. I throw kisses at her box. Why do I do that?

Prosp: It's an old Spanish custom.

Pedro: No wonder they have revolutions in Spain. What about the Presidente? He'll come down and beat the shhh—poopoo out of me.

Prosp: Naw, El Presidente likes to have you throw kisses at his lady's box. In fact, if el Presidente could get down to the arena, he would throw kisses at her box himself. But El Presidente can no more get down into the arena than you can get into his lady's box

Pedro: I knew there was a catch to it. Why can't I get into her box?

Prosp: In the first place, there are three or four guards walking in and out at all times.

Pedro: *(Whistles)* That's some bo-o-o-o-x.

Prosp: In the second place, there are three or four other guards on motorcycles, and one of them whizzes in and out of the box every once in a while.

Pedro: What the hell is that, a garage?

Prosp: No. It's the royal box. Now you're ready to fight the bull.

Pedro: After that, I'm ready to fight anything.

Prosp: You're in the middle of the arena. They let the bull in. He rushes at you fast and looks at you.

Pedro: I look back at him.

Prosp: The bull gets mad.

Pedro: I get mad, too.

Prosp: The bull comes at you. Faster and faster. Closer and closer. He has fire in his eyes. What do you do?

Pedro: Spit in his eye to put out the fire.

Prosp: NO!

Pedro: I grab the bull by the tail, swing him over my head and *bam!*—right up into the royal box.

Prosp: No.

Pedro: I can see why. There's no more room in there.

Straight: *(Moves down centre from bar)* Hey Pedro, as a bullfighter, you're a stinker.

Pedro: Stinker? What is a stinker?

Straight: Why, señor, a stinker in our country means a big man. It's a great honour to be a stinker.

Pedro: Gracias. I am a big stinker. I am the biggest stinker in the world.

Prosp: And your brother is a big stinker, too.

Pedro: *Sí*, but I'm a bigger stinker than my brother.

Straight: And furthermore, your horse is really a stinker.

Pedro: Sí señor. My horse is really a fine stinker, but I stink bigger than my horse.

Prosp: Whew! Do you ever stink! *(Holds nose and waves off stink)*

Pedro: Gracias, gracias. You like my girl? She stinker, too.

Señorita: *(Ambles over to join Pedro and men)* You see, Black Pedro is a big man on the border. He's not so bad on the inside, either.

Prosp: So, your boyfriend's a bad man to fool with?

Senorita: *Sí*.

Straight: *(To Pedro)* You shoot a lot of people. What do they do?

Pedro: Sue.

Straight: You have a brother?

Pedro: *Sí*.

Straight: What's his name?

Pedro: Cy.

Straight: *(To señorita)* What's your name?

Senorita: Say.

Straight: Say?

Señorita: That's short for senorita. Señorita Conchita Lolita Bonita Rita Schwartz.

Prosp: Senorita Conchita Lolita Bonita Rita Schwartz. I see.

Senorita: No, say.

Straight: What do you do for a living?

Senorita: Sew.

Prosp: Sew? *(Looking her up and down)*

Senorita: *Sí.* I sew. So what?

Prosp: That's just what I was going to ask.

Pedro: *(To prospector)* I saw what you were trying to do with my señorita, both of you. *(Grabs prospector and straight man)* And now you're going to get it. *(Starts shaking them)*

(Enter flock, beating that god-damn drum as they march on from left, dressed in Mother Hubbards once more. They form a diagonal line confronting the other people, who step back to form an opposite diagonal)

Drum girl: *(Gives a vicious whack on her drum)* Shame on you. *(To Pedro, who reacts a little scared of this strange enemy)* You big bully.

Flock: *(Each girl yells an epithet)* You brute, you coward, you stinker, you bad boy.

Señorita: These girls are right, Black Pedro. You are a very bad man and I am leaving you.

Pedro: Leaving me? But where will you go?

Señorita: I'm going to join the flock.

Drum girl: And I'm getting the flock out of here.

(Drum girl starts beating the god-damn drum as flock forms a line and walks off, with señorita bringing up the rear)

Señorita: *(Just before she leaves the stage, turns and faces Pedro. She bumps)* This is for you. *(Bumps again)* That is for you. *(Bumps, turns and bends over, flipping up her skirt)* and that is for your pa-pa! *(Holds pose for Pedro's next line before exiting)*

Pedro: Hey, look—the royal box!

Quartet: *(Runs on with quartet leader addressing Pedro)* Black Pedro, repent before it is too late. Glory be. We are born again. Hallelujah! We have all been saved by the flock. And, brother Black Pedro, we are no longer afraid of you, so there. *(They all stick out their tongues at Pedro and exit after flock and señorita)*

Straight: Well, Black Pedro, I guess that should deflate your ego.
Pedro: My who-go?
Prosp: Your ego, jerk.
Pedro: Ego, she go. Now I go. But you haven't seen the last of Black Pedro. *(He exits left)*

(Flock and señorita, now garbed in Mother Hubbard and bonnet with tambourine, return to stage and form a line across. They're joined by prospector and straight man. Drum girl starts to beat her god-damn drum when offstage is heard the sound of a booming bass drum. Pedro comes on from left, beating the drum. He takes centre stage, surrounded by cast. In time with his rhythm, they all shout)

    Reform, reform, we'll reform the world
    Reform, reform, our banner is unfurled
    Reform, reform, cast away your sin
    Reform, reform let the light shine in...
    Reform, reform, no more Demon rum
    Reform, reform. . .

Pedro: I'll beat this GOD-DAMN *(boom boom)* DRUM!

(Curtain)

Hal Sisson

The Dry Society

The Dry Society

Liqu-or it will rot your brain. If you'r nerves get all frayed just drink

milk or le-mon-ade. We're the Dry So-si-e-ty

PLAYERS RISQUE THEIR ALL

Procrastination is a crime,
It leads to certain sorrow,
But I can finish this at any time,
I think I'll start tomorrow.

I didn't invent this compilation of burlesque skits and sketches; instead, I collected them over a long period of time, wherever they could be found. You can treat them as an homage to the Peace Players and burlesque in general, plain old entertainment or raw material for your own burlesque revue.

In the words of that old gag master, Billy Glason, there are no old gags—only people who have already heard them. Every gag is new to the person who hears it for the first time, and the audience enjoys knowing what's coming. You can take any gag and apply it to any situation, person or period with a mere twist of a word or by changing the character. A single line can be used in a monologue or as a double gag. You can tell it about a man or a woman, or even about yourself. If you're playing for conservatives, you can tell a gag about the liberals, or vice versa. And keep in mind that a gag may not appear to be funny on paper, but in its proper place and with the proper delivery, it will hit its mark.

I've appeared in most of the foregoing skits and had a great time doing so. I think I was a good producer, getting the revues mounted on the stage and performing the multiple administrative tasks necessary to do so. Not a good director, however, and the first thing a producer should do is line up a competent director. That's not always easy, because directing is a very special talent, as is choreography, musical directing and stage managing. Although it's unlikely, it's a big plus if you can get a director who's also an able stage manager. Acts must move smoothly and quickly in front of the curtain or on the full stage, with no lulls or breaks in the laughs or action.

As a final chapter to this opus, please indulge me while I include a stand-up comedy routine I used in various ways while appearing in some thirty-five revues. Stand-up keeps changing over the decades. Nowadays the style is to take alleged personal experience, or a specific subject matter and poke fun at it. Three or four decades ago, the style was a series of jokes punctuated by one-liners. Here are some of them in a routine called

The Old Fart

CHARACTER: Old fart, dressed appropriately, comes onstage from wings, front curtain. He's sweeping the floor with a push broom and is ostensibly oblivious to the audience. There is a bench centre stage. Sees audience as if for the first time—does double take. He's a little shaky, maybe slightly tipsy.

"Hello, folks (*pause*) I don't know you well enough to call you ladies and gentlemen.

"Look, if anyone asks you, just tell them you haven't seen me. You see, I just recently escaped from the Resthaven Home for Old Farts. Dwart Farquhart is the name and old fart is the game. Down at the old folks' home they regard me as being A.W.O.L.—that's After Women or Liquor.

It's also a military term. Yes, I was once in Her Majesty's armed services myself, although you wouldn't know it to look at me now. I didn't get a commission—I was on a straight salary. I was stronger in those days. Why, a small muscle in my eye could pick up a full-grown girl. . . But I once was in the toughest outfit of them all: the Navel Air Force (*pause, then to skeptics*) Don't scoff. I know some of you men likely think you were in tougher outfits than the Navel Air Force. But if you've ever tried to force air through a navel, you'll know what I'm talking about.

"I wouldn't say I had a distinguished military career, except for one thing I'm proud of, and that is that I wrote the unofficial Royal Canadian Air Force song. Not Off We Go into the Wild Blue Yonder. No, I wrote the unofficial song: Button Up Your Overcoat and Fly!

"And then I wrote—specially for Churchill at the height of the blitz—Don't Worry Winston, the Wright Brothers Couldn't Get It Up the First Time, Either. . . Not a big hit back then *(pause)* and apparently not one now, either.

"I don't like the songs of today. I hate that rock 'n' roll stuff and all those decibels. In the old days of the big bands they had lots of good songs. Oldies but goldies. Maybe you remember some of them, like: Don't Go Near the Hydrant, Nellie, the Firemen will Hose You for Sure. Remember that one? No? Or how about Take Me Behind the Rock Pile, Honey, I Get a Little Boulder There. Bend Down Baby and Touch Your Toes and I'll Show You Where the Wild Goose Goes. *(Gyrates and sings)* Wild goose, wild goose, which is best. . . Ooooh, I think I hurt myself.

"Then they had fake song titles that featured someone's daughter: She Was Only a Fisherman's Daughter, But When She Saw My Rod She Reeled, or She Was Only a Banker's Daughter, and She'd Only Open Her Drawers for Cash, or He Took Out His Cashier, But She Turned Out to be a Teller.

"I know, I know, some of you think I'm just a dirty old man. But let me ask you this: of what use is a clean old man? Ask any older woman in the audience, she'll tell you they're no use.

"I'd like to do an old piece *(to woman in audience)* no offence, ma'am. But here's a song I learned at Sophie Tucker's knee—not a pretty sight, ladies and gentlemen. I'll sing it for you if you like—even if you don't like. *(Again ostensibly to woman in audience)* I know this act smells, lady. I'm closer to it than you are. . . I travel a lot—with this act, I have to.

"Did you hear about the 65-year-old flasher? He was going to retire, but then he decided to stick it out for one more year. . . You know why they spell sex s-e-x, don't you? Because no one ever learned to spell *(goes into a series of hip gyrations and mouth noises)*.

"Ladies and gentlemen, you've been more than kind. I thank you very humbly and most sincerely. I'm somewhat overwhelmed by your warmth and your charity. It's most comforting, for as you get on in years, you have to do the best you can with what you've got. I haven't got much, ma'am, but I hang onto it with both hands.

"Where was I? Oh yeah, the song! Well, this is an authentic British music hall song. It's so old, I don't think anyone here will ever have heard it before.

> Don't cry, dear daddy,
> Why are you sad today?
> Is it because dear Mother,
> Has left you and gone away?
> As the tears rolled down me trousers,
> I said to my daughter (pause) Jack!
> I'm crying because your mother has gone (pause),
> And I'm frightened she might come back!

"You know, those song title jokes from the Thirties were funny. And they remind me of what Confucius, that famous old Chinese philosopher, once said when he saw the nun fall down on top of the court jester: "This is virgin on the ridiculous!"

"Some of you probably remember those 'Confucius say' jokes—that was another form of humour in the old days. Confucius say man who drive car with automatic transmission is shiftless bastard. . . Confucius say woman who goes to man's apartment for midnight snack usually only get tit-bit. . . Confucius say woman is like automobile. On a really cold morning when you really need it—it won't turn over!

"Enough of that nonsense. Let's be serious for a moment (pause). That's long enough! I picked up a copy of the Peace River *Record Gazette (pulls it out of side pocket of robe)* to find out what's going on in town. Great newspaper, lots of information. *(Pretends to read)*

"Here's an item from the business page. A Peace River businessman sitting in the Aces and Eights bar complained to the bartender about the terrible state of the economy. He said, 'I'm in the furniture business and I could lose my ass.' A girl sitting down the bar piped up and said, 'Look buster, I'm in the ass business and I could lose my furniture!'

"Here's another local item, about the town council. They're always good for a laugh. They're planning to spend 50,000 dollars to build a downtown urinal! *(Pause, looks up at the audience)* What's the matter with them? Why don't they go whole hog, spend 100,000 and build an arsenal?

"Say, where's a woman's yet? *(Moves forward and stares down at audience)* Can any of you ladies tell me where is a woman's yet? How did I get this old and not find that out? *(To particular woman in audience)* Look, if it's embarrassing, maybe you could just point! The reason I'm asking is there's a headline here that says, Gun fight in Grande Prairie! Woman shot three times, bullets are in her yet!

"Here's an interesting item. The mayor of Edmonton is taking positive action against hookers. Swears he's going to drive all the prostitutes out of town. *(Looks up)* Well, he really must mean it! I saw him driving three of them down Jasper Avenue last Saturday night.

"Let's see what they've got in the entertainment section. Ah, here's an item about vintage recordings. There's one with I Wanna Hold Your Hand on the front side and I Wonder Who's Kissing Her Now on the back side. . . Well, as long as they're not kissing her yet! . . . Although I hear they do that in Montreal.

"I only got one quarrel with the *Gazette*, and that's where they put their classified and personal advertisements in the paper. I speak from personal experience. Yeah, I put an ad in there. Real tasteful, too! It said, 'Elderly gent wishes to meet with well-stacked Chinese broad for picnics and outings' and I added my phone number. I stood in the phone booth outside the Travellers Hotel—that's where I was staying at the time, outside the Travellers Hotel—and I waited and I waited, but the phone didn't ring. Then I bought a paper and checked it. Do you know what they'd gone and done to me? They'd gone and put my ad under Used Equipment for Rent! *(Puts newspaper back in pocket)*

"Would you call that responsible journalism? I wouldn't. *(Pretends to see woman leaving)* Please ma'am, don't go just yet! I'm coming to the best part—the finish. . . I realize you can't say much for my talent, but my courage demands respect. . . So, as the captain said to the maids on the *Titanic* when they hit that iceberg: 'Let's make use of the time we've got left.' So let's see the rest of the *Sorry 'bout That* burlesque revue. *(Adds while exiting)* And like I told you, if anyone asks, just tell them you haven't seen me."

That could be the end, but sometimes I'd add or subtract. A mean average optimum time for stand-up is ten to twelve minutes. You pick and choose your material with the aim of creating a laugh or smile every twenty seconds, or build up to a much larger laugh reaction from the audience. So sometimes I'd throw in one or more of the following:

"Well, I may as well stop foolin' around and start my act. . . I guess all the prudes are gone by now. . . This is not my regular act —my regular act stinks.

"I hope this show has been a success for you and brings you happiness. Just remember, success is getting what you want, and happiness is liking what you get!

"It's not only an honour for me to be here tonight—it's a goddam inconvenience. . . So as soon as this show's over, I hope you just get out of here fast so I can clean this place up. . . I know you think I'm just an old fart and don't know nothin', but I got a cigar butt and I got a couple of bucks in my pocket and I can sit in the park and read my paper—except when it's too cold. Like this spring. It was so cold in the park, I had to throw a bucket of hot water on two hookers to get them off a lamp post."

"Here's a sad item in the paper. Youth killed on motorcycle. He was crossing High Level bridge when a van approached. The aerial on the truck was broken and sticking out from the side of the van, and the jagged end of the aerial pierced the youth right through the chest. He was dead on arrival at the hospital. The Edmonton Journal reported that he died of vanaerial disease.

"Here's another one: Archaeologist finds skull of woman, two million years old. *(Pause)* I wonder how he knew it was a woman? *(Another pause, reads on)* Ah, yes—the jaws were open!

"The Court News section's interesting: Court awards girl $100,000 for broken heart in a breach of promise suit. Her sister got $5,000 for a hip broken in an accident. *(Pause)* Well, that proves only one thing—never break a girl's heart. Kick her in the ass, it's cheaper.

"How about this letter to our local advice columnist? 'Dear Nan Glanders: I'm worried about the problem of overpopulation. Why don't young women realize they could have fewer babies by fooling around with older men, who have usually been fixed so they can't get anyone in trouble? Signed: Sixty and Sterile but Able and Available.'

"Here's a story about a breeder who crossed a dog with a hen and got a poodle who cocked his own doodle. . . I always thought you got pooched eggs!

"The RCMP have successfully crossed a balloon with a red light and got a brothelizer. And I understand they've crossed a donkey and an onion. Usually you get an onion with long ears, but occasionally when everything goes just right, you get a piece of ass which is so great it makes you cry. . . Then there was the man who crossed an elephant with an Axminster rug and got a big thick pile on his carpet.

"There's so much that can happen to your body with age. The memory goes—oh, you forget things. I can admit that in mine own instance, my memory of late has become extremely bad. Only last night I was getting into bed when my lovely young adorable wife turned to me and said, 'Dwart, you've had it! And I couldn't remember whether I had or not. . . There are many among you here tonight who might agree that age may sometimes be an advantage. And to apply the old cliché perhaps, there's many a good tune played on an old fiddle. But as you get on in years, you'll find that your organs begin to leak. *(Pause)* I've had enough of this laughing. When you've achieved a state of silence—may I continue speaking to the more intelligent ones? The rest of you are a pack of drunken oafs.

"What's that you say? No, I'm not a senile old fart. I know that sex is not good for one *(pause)* but it's all right for two. . . I remember this one girl. She was so frigid that every time she uncrossed her legs the furnace cut in!. . . I knew this farm boy in the air force who came from Mossbank, Saskatchewan. He was trying to date this girl, but she said she only went out with city boys because farm hands were too rough!

"This guy was dumb. He was so dumb, he nearly froze to death in front of an Alaskan whorehouse, waiting for the red light to change. . . He said he used to sow his wild oats every Saturday night and then go to Church Parade on Sunday and pray for a crop failure.

"I met a religious girl in Victoria once, who wore black garters above the knee—in memory of those who had gone beyond. . . I have to tell you that the girls of my day weren't really like the girls of today. All girls are nice, especially present company. But gentlemen, I beg to inform you that you're besotted by hussies in this city. Be careful, you could be attacked. . . I had an experience this very day. I was in a local drinking tavern. By chance I'd gone there to meet a sick friend. This place is locally known as the Pelvis, because it's such a low joint. And I was having this drink they're serving now to travellers, called Spantran. It's quite good. It's half Spanish Fly and half tranquilizer. Two glasses of that and you go out looking for it. But if you don't find it, you could care less. . . I thought I'd found it when I perceived this fair young maiden. Believe me, gentlemen, when I say that her beauty was so stunning it commanded me to speak. I said, 'Ma'am, at your service. My name is Dwart Farquhart.' She replied, 'Oh, hello there, my name is Shirley Timex!' 'Is it, ma'am?' I said. 'Curious name, Shirley Timex. You aren't by chance related to the famous people who make the twenty-dollar watch?' She said, 'The name's the same, the price is right. But mine's a different movement!' *(Goes into a circular bump and grind)*

"Yes, the names girls go by in these modern times. I met another girl the other day. Said her name was Chas Titty. . . a work of art was Chas Titty. Told me she'd been voted Miss Soft Drink—I think because she'd go out with any man from Seven-Up. . . I just called her Chas for short, because her second name is quite a mouthful.

"One gal had on some designer jeans which were so tight she looked like she'd been poured into them, or maybe melted into them. I asked her, 'How in the world would you go about getting into a pair of pants like that?' She said, 'Well, you could start by buying me a drink!' *(Breaks into song)*

You can tell that she isn't my mother,
Cause my mother's 89,
And you can tell she isn't my sister,
Cause I wouldn't show my sister such a helluva good time
And you can tell that she isn't my sweetheart,
Cause my sweetheart's too refined,
Then who is she?
It's easy to see
She's just a personal friend of mine.
Just an innocent kid,
Doesn't know what she did,
Just a personal friend of mine!

"Thank God today there are cosmetic aids to help the older man render himself a little more attractive to members of the opposite sex. There are things now which darken a man's hair, brighten his eyes, whiten his teeth *(pause)* and lift his *(gives a little jump, whistle)* and away we go! They even have perfume. Of course we men don't call it perfume, we call it aftershave or smack-on.

But you really have to be careful where you smack it on. . . I don't know what they put in that stuff, but *(high-pitched voice and motion of smacking it on genitals)* by God, that smarts! If ever you meet a man who smells nice but is limping along, you'll know what happened—he has literally chased the jockey out of his shorts.

"They've given these colognes masculine-sounding names, like Hud, Old Spice, Tabac and Two Days in a Hot Saddle. That's a good one but a little strong—you can smell it at fifty paces.

"They have a new spray deodorant now, derived from women's perfume, which they simply call Shhhhh *(Expels air into mike)* which when pronounced backwards is *(sucking sound into mike, sniffing in through nose and mouth).* When you spray it on, it makes you invisible. It doesn't kill the odour, but everybody wonders where in hell the smell's coming from.

"I want to thank you again for being such a patient and good audience. If I've offended anyone here tonight, believe me, I've just tried to do my bit in aiding and abetting the sexual revolution. And thank you again for trying to understand what the hell I've been talking about.

"I used to be a fake lascivious old fart when putting on this act —now I am one. *(Ends with last verse of Shaving Cream)*

And now folks, my story is ended,
I think it is time I should quit,
If any of you feel offended,
Stick your head in a barrel of
SHAVING CREAM,
Be nice and clean,
Shave every day and you'll always look keen!

(Curtain)

Here's a chance to print one of the best reviews the Peace Players ever received during two decades of performing in northern Alberta, penned by Keith Ashwell of the *Edmonton Journal*, in the July 16, 1981 edition.

Players in a raunchy romp

There's a bumper crop of corn at Theatre 3 and everybody who sees this show is going to enjoy harvesting it with these marvellous Peace Players.

I laughed last night the way I used to laugh at Skegness Pier, and then at the Peterborough Embassy and then on dear old Auntie BBC, before she put on her wrist-cutter knickers and said a relieved farewell to such naughty comedians as Max Miller, Max Wall, Arthur English and Jewell & Warris.

How I remember. Imagine explaining to a director of a theatre board the point of a TWA joke that does the coffee, me or tea routine as succinctly as you could imagine.

The show is nothing less than a raunchy romp through the best of the sexy skits in showbiz.

This is a confident, multi-talented troupe. The acting is quick and slick and the variety of sit-coms and blackouts—from soft sleaze to "oh no! they got away with that one!"—so, so varied and yet so disarmingly delivered that if you feel a fit of prudery coming on, you have one minute to get out of the theatre or three hours to overcome it, with the greatest of pleasure.

Well, thank God for some honest base humour. The show touches all (unmentionable) bases. Even the dance numbers, superbly performed by the Synergy Chorus Line, are full of pulsing-pelvis innuendos.

Julian Packer is an excellent clown-faced MC. Bill Seaman is old enough to be decently seedy. Hal Sisson is seasoned enough to be a perfect drunken heckler or a lewd old wino. And Jim Robertshaw, who more customarily plays it straight at Alberta Culture, does some risque routines with hardly controlled lust.

The show begins with a really naughty Count Dracula skit. It ends with an hilarious sight-gag chorus.

In between are the best and the worst of Playboy's jokes and cartoons and if you can't laugh at them, emigrate to the Peace country until this company leaves Edmonton grimacing again.

—30—

One final bit before I turn the spotlight over to other voices in the next chapter. This may make no nevermind to many readers, except as a theatrical success story in a typical western Canadian town, namely Peace River, Alberta. In the Fifties, prior to the official founding of Peace Players, several productions began to appear in the town, the earliest ones promoted by the ski club and the Anglican Church's Chi Rho Club. The shows took place in Athabasca Hall, the only venue in town with a stage. There was a stage in one of the local schools, but it was literally useless because of school board policy to utilize it as an auxiliary classroom; the janitor controlled it, you couldn't in any way mar the hardwood floor and outside user taxpayer groups were not welcome.

Athabasca Hall, a fine addition to the town, was part of a complex that had been donated in the Dirty Thirties by an anonymous English philanthropist, who did the same for several other western Canadian communities. It had a hardwood floor—very suitable for dances—the size of a basketball court, a proscenium arch stage of reasonable proportions, a green room and a lighting booth over the entrance foyer, suitable for the projection of movies. The basement housed a large banquet room and a kitchen, which produced many fowl suppers—and that isn't a mis-spelling.

Those early shows were followed by productions of *Twelve Foot Davis Nites*, from 1958 to '60. As I mentioned earlier, Twelve Foot Davis, though short in stature, got his name from mining a previously undetected twelve foot wide claim during British Columbia's Cariboo Gold Rush in the 1860s. Having sold his claim for a small fortune, Davis later became an independent fur trader along the Peace River, in competition with the Hudson's Bay Company. If you gaze up at the beautiful high river valley banks above the town of Peace River, you'll see the grave of Twelve Foot Davis who, at his own request, was buried there with his feet pointing downhill so he could piss all over the old Hudson's Bay trading post.

These Nites featured an evening of gambling with funny money and a vaudeville-type revue produced by myself with the aid of others of a like mind, and sponsored by the hard-working, community-minded Kinsmen Club of Peace River. We erected a stage at one end of the old downtown wooden hockey arena. There may still be some wooden nickels kicking around from this event. At one of the last performances, one of the town's arsonists made a weak and unsuccessful attempt to burn down the arena. At the time this was not felt to be a reflection on the quality of the theatrical performances, but in retrospect this has to be considered as a motive.

Without Athabasca Hall, theatre could not have thrived in town. In 1971-72 the hall was enlarged, front and back, with funds from the federal Winter Work program. The town council, the Anglican Church, the Kinsmen and Rotary clubs and many private donors supported the project. The town and the Synod of the Anglican diocese of Athabasca, who owned the property, entered into a lease arrangement, with a sub-lease to Peace Players. This exceedingly favourable arrangement is still in effect today. The Anglican Church has made a great contribution to the town by providing the only adequate theatre facility from 1935 on, one that has formed an integral part of the cultural and recreational life of Peace River.

A good deal of credit is also due to the Alberta department of culture, whose policies and grant system have done so much to encourage drama and theatre outside the major centres of Calgary and Edmonton. Peace Players was officially organized in 1967 as a Canadian Centennial Project. Until then, theatre had operated sporadically and not too well. Mainly because Peace River did not have an official town idiot in those days, and everyone had to take turns. If you thought it was your turn, you reported for duty at the town office and told them your plans.

The new theatre group experimented with many productions that worked exceedingly well, like *Guys and Dolls*, *Oliver*, *Li'l Abner*, *Finian's Rainbow* and *Fiddler on the Roof*, all under the direction of Don Weaver. Julian Packer, Pearl Baldwin, Jim Robertshaw, Bill Pobuda and many others directed a long list of other productions.

Some things didn't work out, of course, which is only natural. We tried to get Brigitte Bardot and her brother Guillaume for a one-night stand, but failed. Then there was the time we brought in an eight-piece band from Castor, Alberta, who called themselves the Castor Eight. We even tried to get Raquel Welch to perform The Hunchfront of Notre Dame, but she left us flat and holding the bag.

The Peace Players' first-ever effort and the show that provided the financial backbone of the club was *Sorry 'bout That*. I knew it would work from my comedy stints in the RCAF and at the University of Saskatchewan. If you're selling sex and booze, you can't miss. I'm the first to admit the success of the show would have been impossible without the assistance of an ever-changing group of directors, actors, choreographers, chorus girls, costume mistresses, make-up artists and the administrative and technical personnel. See the next chapter for as full a list of Peace Players as I could compile.

I understand via the grapevine that the Peace Players are contemplating *Sorry 'bout That: The Second Generation,* under the direction of Chris Black. In addition, Jill Cairns has been producing mini-versions of *Sorry 'bout That* as well as other burlesque entertainment for various social functions in northern Alberta and Edmonton.

OTHER VOICES

Friends may come and friends may go,
And friends may peter out, you know;
But we'll be friends through thick or thin,
Peter out or peter in!

Fran Dowie—One of the Greats of Theatre in BC

by Diane Farnsworth,
Vancouver scriptwriter
and filmmaker

Fran Dowie (right) and cast at the Theatre Royal in Barkerville, BC.

Fran Dowie was born on September 15, 1920 to a Vancouver vaudeville actor, Francis Oliver Dowie the second, and the singer Violet Payne Fleming. Fran was preceded by several generations of Dowies in the entertainment business.

Fran's grandfather, Francis Oliver the first, performed in the first minstrel show, *The Old Black Stockings*, on a London stage, then moved to Canada in 1890, where he appeared as the top comedian with *Mez Merry Mascotts* in 1918. Francis the second appeared in *The Old Black Stockings* with his father, then later performed in *Dumb Bells* and became known as the rubber-faced comedian.

Fran's parents took up residence in Vancouver's Kerrisdale district, where young Fran and his brother Fredrick attended St. Ann's Academy. Violet Fleming avoided the scandal of being in show business by maintaining a normal home life for her children, believing the old saying of the period, which held that an actress was a girl who was no better than she should be.

Young Fran's first taste of show business came by accident when his father was doing a show at the Seaman's Institute in 1927. After noticing the seven-year-old in tow, several sailors requested that the lad sing a song. The following day, *Vancouver News-Herald* columnist Bob Bouchett wrote: "Last night I saw a group of performers and amongst them was a 7-year-old boy who held the audience in the palm of his hand. His name was Francis Dowie."

During the Great Depression Francis Sr. toured overseas, and on his return, he built a living marionette theatre for young Fran.

"My father saw this type of marionette in France and was so impressed he came back and built one," Fran later recalled.

The marionette theatre consisted of a wooden frame and a black velvet curtain with several holes cut out where Fran's head could poke through and rest on a hand-carved puppet body.

Several years later at the ripe age of twelve, Fran appeared on a grander stage, at Vancouver's Orpheum Theatre. Like his performance at the Seaman's Institute, Fran's debut was completely unplanned. When Francis senior explained to manager Frank Newman that his partner Slim was too inebriated to go on, Newman pointed out that they had booked a double act, not a single. It was Newman who suggested that young Fran perform, saying, "What about the boy? Young Frankie's great. Put him on!"

Reproduced here is Fran's first skit with his father, performed at the Orpheum Theatre in 1932. While Francis Dowie senior played a comic song on the piano, young Fran strolled in.

Young Fran: Excuse me, sir, is this the place?
Francis Senior: Is this the place?
YF: A fellow outside said you need a partner.
FS: A partner? What can you do?

YF: I can sing, dance and pull a little joke.
FS: Oh, you can, can you?
YF: Incidentally, do you have a little 'older?
FS: A little 'older?
YF: Yeah.
FS: What kind of 'older?
YF: A cigarette 'older.
FS: A cigarette 'older for you?
(Fran nods)
FS: How old are you?
YF: I'm 12.
FS: What does a little boy like you want a cigarette 'older for?
YF: Mommy says I can smoke when I get a little older.

Francis Dowie Sr. had no other option, as he was booked for 26 weeks with two shows a night. It was decided on that day that young Fran would perform the full circuit with his father. Shortly thereafter, the living marionettes were incorporated in the Francis and Frankie Show.

"There were five acts of vaudeville, a short, a cartoon and a movie twice a day and there were 26 famous theatres," says Fran.

Violet sewed Frankie an Eaton suit for the act, but insisted that he continue with his studies, so Fran would come home from school, take a nap, then get on the interurban bus with his father to go to the various theatres. When Fran graduated from high school, his very astute teacher, Sister Mary Ethalin, told him, "Your art is what you will depend on in life because you're terrible at mathematics and grammar."

In the early 1940s, Fran joined the Royal Canadian Air Force and was stationed in Trenton, England. Fran was interested in flying, but because he was a strong swimmer, he was assigned to instruct swimming.

"They lost more pilots in the English Channel when they crashed, because they couldn't swim," says Fran.

In Fran's spare time he began to put on shows, which impressed the officers and evolved into the occasional paid performance at the officers' club. The US military decided to recruit performers for military shows and the Canadians, not to be outdone, started recruiting performers for a Canadian army show, then later a Royal Canadian Air Force show. Fran was recommended by a wing commander, sent to Ottawa to audition and hired as a full-time entertainer. In 1943,

Fran and a group of professional entertainers from the RCAF created *The Black Out Show of 1943*. They worked full time at writing and performing their own songs and routines. It was during this time that Edna Mae Bond caught Fran's eye. Edna (Candy Kane) was a dancer, musician and singer in the show. Fran and Edna were married on September 16, 1943.

Several years and two children later, Fran was back in Vancouver and feeling restless, as fewer and fewer opportunities to perform presented themselves.

His mother Violet used to advise Fran, "When people ask, don't say you're an actor. Say you're an artist, because show business is a hobby, not a profession!" Francis Sr. disagreed with his wife and told Fran, "Why are you here dabbling around like this? Go to England and if you're any good you'll hit it, and if you're not, come back and run a chicken farm."

Recalling his father's suggestion, Fran phoned an old air force buddy in London who had become an entertainment agent. The friend assured Fran that if he was as funny as he had been in the air force, he could book him.

In 1948, Fran and Edna sold their home and car, packed up their children, Susie and Sandy, and headed for England without looking back. The week they arrived, Fran was booked as a headliner with the Cyril Stapleton Orchestra and later billed as Fran Dowie the Atomic Comic. For twelve years the Dowies toured Europe. In addition to performing, Fran wrote skits and gags and Edna composed music and designed costumes.

In 1960, Fran and Edna returned to Vancouver with Susie, Sandy and their younger children, Sally and Christie. The Dowies performed on a few television programs such as the *Circle Seven Ranch* show with Evan Kemp. During this time, WAC Bennett was developing rural British Columbia and had decided to restore the gold rush town of Barkerville. As a result, the Dowies received a call from Gordon Hilker that changed the course of their lives. After two years of playing mostly legion halls, an opportunity that lasted for nearly twenty years manifested itself: creating an authentic vaudeville show for Barkerville.

In the 19th century, Barkerville's fire hall used to double as a theatre. The town was on the touring circuit, and English and American celebrities like Oscar Wilde and Mark Twain often performed there.

Fran says that when fire broke out in Barkerville in 1868, "They were too busy watching shows to notice that the town was burning to the ground!"

A trunk full of scripts from the period turned up when the foundation for the new theatre was being laid, and Fran rewrote one of the plays, called *Diamond in the Rough*. He cut it down to twenty-five minutes from its original two and a half hours. From 1963 to 1965, Edna helped write the Theatre Royal shows and designed the costumes. Then in 1966, Edna and Fran parted ways and were divorced.

Fran later hired, then married, comedienne Louise Glennie, who put her energy into the project by thoroughly researching the Cariboo gold rush era, making sure the costumes, language and history were authentic. Fran and Louise continued to put on the Barkerville show during the summer, hiring and training hundreds of young performers as well as working with seasoned entertainers like Fran's father and brother (who had changed his name to Taller O'Shea) along with Sid Williams, Leo Prescott, Norman Long, Ross Ladlee and Linda Campbell, to name a few. The Dowie children also joined the cast on several occasions. Tourists from all over the world visited Barkerville and took in the vaudeville show.

In 1967, Fran discovered the talent of singer-comedienne Gillian Campbell and sent his newfound protégée to perform as Klondike Kate at the Palace Grand in Dawson City, then brought her back to Barkerville in 1968.

In the late Seventies, Fran met Jim Henson and Frank Oz while teaching a puppetry workshop for the Puppeteers of America at Columbia University in Washington, DC.

"Jim Henson was in the second row taking my class!" Fran marvelled.

After the workshop, Henson invited Fran for lunch at the cafeteria and offered him a job on his next movie, Muppets Go Hollywood, which Fran worked on in 1979. As time went on, Fran became even more involved with puppetry, building string, mouth, life-size, finger and hand puppets and working with various materials for parades, puppet shows and television shows. Each puppet he built exuded a unique personality. Over the years, Fran also created numerous props for television programs such as The X-Files, The Crow and Scottie's Tissues.

Like his father, Fran incorporated his talent of puppetry in his vaudeville act, as well as the annual Santa Claus event he and Louise performed on Granville Island through the 1980s and '90s. After Louise's death, Gillian Campbell played Mrs. Claus with Fran at Santa's Workshop at Lonsdale Quay in North Vancouver. Numerous write-ups and television spots resulted, referring to Fran as "the real Santa Claus".

In the mid-90s, Fran received a phone call from Norman Young, announcing that he had been selected for the BC Hall of Fame and would have his name etched into a sidewalk star on Granville Street across from the Orpheum Theatre.

"He told me my star would be in front of McDonald's where the rubby-dubs throw up," Fran recalls.

Fran's photograph hangs on the wall of the Orpheum Theatre along with other local pioneers of the arts who were chosen for the BC Hall of Fame.

Fran's craft of puppetry and performance has rubbed off on his daughters Susie and Christie, who continue to perform and create beautiful puppets and props for stage and television.

Fran, who has entertained audiences around the world since 1932, is an authentic vaudevillian, designated a BC Legend by the White Spot restaurant chain. He has trained scores of youngsters over the years, who are now some of Vancouver's most successful theatre and film performers, agents and producers.

Now retired, 85-year-old Fran is a member of the Society for the Preservation of Vaudeville, which his daughter Susie Francis founded in 2001. The society performs up to 20 vaudeville shows annually. Many of the routines and songs are "Fran Originals". The society raises money for the Vaudevillians' Bursary Fund for eligible students enrolled in the Performing Arts program at Douglas College (www.thevaudevillians.com).

The Early Years of Victoria's Smile Show

by Verna Smith (formerly Moore)

In the summer of 1948, I received a call from a gentleman by the name of Jerry Gosley. He asked to come and see me about starting up a variety show. Jerry had seen a picture in the local newspaper of me and my then husband doing a balancing/acrobatic act in

Victoria's Athletic Park, and he thought I might be a suitable person with whom to team up.

My husband and I had toured on an American vaudeville circuit in the early 1940s and had the good luck to work with the Will Mastin Trio and Sammy Davis Jr. Sammy would get the show together and act as emcee for the productions. I learned a lot from him about producing and directing a show.

Jerry Gosley had started the *Smile Show* while stationed with the RCAF at the air force training base at Patricia Bay during World War II. He

Jerry Gosley (left) & Verna Moore at officers' mess in Korea during 1952 **Smile Show** *tour.*

told me he wanted to revive the show now that he had immigrated to Victoria from England. We agreed to keep the same name for the show.

After much discussion, we came up with a group of eight local artists and a four-piece band. We were able to practice in the Britannia Branch hall of the Canadian Legion, then on Blanshard Street, and after many rehearsals and professionalizing the show, we picked a date for our first performance at the same legion hall.

Jerry, being a printer, made the promotional flyers. We mixed up some flour and water and ran a glue-dipped paintbrush over the flyers, posting them up on all the telephone poles we could find in the Victoria area. We invited Audrey St. Denys Johnson to review the show for the local daily newspaper.

On opening night, the hall was packed. Our first show was a great success and Audrey gave us a wonderful write-up in the paper. Then the offers started to come in, and we performed for the various branches of the armed services and other legion branches, as well as at local hospitals, seniors' homes, prisons and nightclubs.

We soon received a call from Washington State to "entertain the boys" at Fort Lewis army camp outside Seattle, where the GIs just loved British humour. The Korean War was on, and as we were walking across the airfield to catch our plane home, I suggested to Jerry that we go to Korea. Jerry exclaimed, "Are you crazy?" "No," I replied. "They had entertainers in World War II and they'll need them again." I urged him to contact the liaison officer at Pat Bay Air Base and find out where we should apply. Jerry did, and it was with none other than General George Pearkes, the minister of national defence.

We planned to take eight entertainers and do one-and-a-half-hour shows. The reply came back that eight was too many, so we suggested four entertainers, and this arrangement was accepted. We were offered a five-and-a-half-week tour of Japan and Korea and given officer status. We represented the Canadian Legion and wore the standard blue jacket with gray trousers or skirt, complete with legion patches and Canada epaulets.

The *Smile Show* consisted of Jerry, myself, singer Irene Henderson and Al Denoni playing the movable piano—the accordion. We travelled 12,000 miles and presented 90 shows to an estimated 15,000 British Commonwealth and American troops. Our largest show played to an audience of 1,100 Canadian troops.

We received a royal welcome on our return, and our first performance at home consisted of a three-night engagement at the old York Theatre (now the McPherson Playhouse). We followed up with many shows on the mainland and all around Vancouver Island, mostly at legion halls. We then began running yearly, long-running summer season shows, first at the Langham Court Theatre, then later at the newly renovated McPherson. The *Smile Show* proved to be a wonderfully popular tourist attraction as well as a favourite with local audiences, and it ran for some thirty years. I left the show in the later Fifties or early Sixties, while Jerry carried on with the help of many great performers, such as Bill and Sylvia Hosie and their whole family, Bebe Eversfield and a host of others.

In 1992, shortly before Jerry passed away, the four members of the Korea tour held a forty-year reunion at Jerry's house.

Vaudeville and My Part in its History

by Woody Woodland

Jack Benny started as a violinist in the pit of the Waukegan Theatre in Illinois. I started as a trombonist in the pit of the Casino Theatre in Toronto. From 1956-59, we played four one-hour shows a day for six days a week of pure vaudeville.

Well, pure except for the exotic dancers, who stopped at nothing. Many a fluttering piece of lingerie wafted into the orchestra pit. Once an errant garter momentarily dangled on the extended slide of my trombone! Needless to say, my performance was temporarily suspended.

No amount of money could possibly buy the experience I gained, and it was instrumental in my development as a musician and comedian. I heard some of the best, mediocre comics of a fading era. If I'd known it was an era, I would have paid more attention.

"Doctor, Doctor, I broke my leg in three places. He told me to stay away from those places." "My dog could read. He saw a sign, it said Wet Paint. . . so he did." Not brilliant material, but when used in the right sequence and with the right timing—irresistible.

Howard "Woody" Woodland, musician and vaudevillian extraordinaire.

The musical and comedic material of the vaudeville era didn't disperse into the ether with the advent of the electronic era. Some of the best skits and jokes continued to enjoy success, but with the new technology, it was curtains for vaudeville itself.

I was fortunate. At beautiful Butchart Gardens in Victoria, British Columbia, I had a new international audience for every show. All I had to do was make happy people happier. To build my act, I used some of the material I'd heard from the Casino Theatre orchestra pit, along with much of the music.

From trapeze acts to tap dancers, bicycles to budgie birds, they had all passed within a few metres of my head, which was at eye level with the casino's stage. One unicycling chimp took offence to my head and menacingly raised his cycle and approached, intending to maim the trombone player. I promptly retreated to safety, under the stage. What did the conductor do? He bought me a hard hat.

At Butchart Gardens, I used my Australian heritage to good advantage. In an act straight out of vaudeville, I was costumed in boots and a bush hat with cork hanging around the brim (to keep away the flies) and a didgeridoo in hand, setting the scene for patter such as: "My Uncle George has a kangaroo farm in Sydney, Australia. . . he's makin' beer from the hops. He's passed on—he died drinkin' shellac. . . but he had a marvellous finish. He travelled all over the world. He went to Paris. He saw the Eiffel Tower. He didn't know what Eiffel meant 'til he looked up at the pigeons."

Butchart Gardens was a bastion of vaudeville from 1969-1991, with a very successful mix of production numbers, skits, vocalists and orchestra numbers. I provided the continuity by appearing in my aforesaid costume. A murmur would ripple through the audience (or was it a groan?) as I appeared stage right then ambled across the stage delivering one-liners in an Aussie accent: "The doctor went to see a chap in hospital in Sydney, Australia. He said, 'Did you come in here to die?' And the chap said, 'No, I came in here yesterdie.'"

My musical experience gave me the opportunity to play a succession of different instruments in a six-minute spot. Once I played a set of tuned tin cans attached to a toilet bowl. The tune, of course, was the Can Can. After this novelty part, I would solo on my principal instruments, the trumpet and trombone.

A vaudeville career is a lifetime of joy, if you have the right venue, happy people, no hecklers and a beautiful stage. In the wonderful setting of Butchart Gardens, no performer could have had it better.

Think Well of Burlesque

by Don Weaver

The establishment of a little theatre drama club is a must in any community. Hal and Doreen Sisson provided the encouragement to motivate a group of us to act, and in 1967, our club launched its inaugural season with the musical *Guys and Dolls* and a burlesque revue aptly named *Sorry 'bout That*. The revue proved so successful, we produced a new show for twenty consecutive years and I directed sixteen of them.

Don Weaver, director of **Sorry 'bout That** *for most of its history.*

Sorry 'bout That allowed us to produce our own musicals and plays and to bring in three professional theatrical groups a year. It seemed northern Alberta, of all places, was ripe for the production of risqué burlesque shows during the Sixties, Seventies and into the '80s. We didn't worry much about political correctness and we presented the same type of material one might see in Las Vegas, L.A. or New York, minus the topless action. My wife Margot would read the scripts and groan that they were terrible, but then when they were presented on stage, she'd join the rest of the audience in falling off her seat laughing. Timing and expression is everything in this type of humour, and the show played to capacity crowds from all over Alberta.

I recall a few growing pains with the first revue, in that the Catholic Women's League decided to occupy the first two rows. These seats were mysteriously empty after the first act.

Sorry 'bout That was a mix of one-liners, skits, songs, beautiful chorus girls, blackouts and abundant burlesque humour. It was a relatively easy show to mount because it was segmented, had a small cast of up to twenty and featured outrageous costumes and a minimum of props and sets. Over the years we were blessed with many very talented individuals in every aspect of theatre, who somehow made their way to our community.

Typically we mounted the revue in six to eight weeks. The script segments lent themselves to the players separating into groups with their own rehearsal times, and often locations, leaving Sundays for intense rehearsals with the entire cast.

A band always made for a better production, but the show could be put on with just piano and drum accompaniment. The drums were essential to punch the one-liners and emphasize the movements of the actors, especially the ladies.

The key to directing the revue, after the skits had been set, lay in pulling all components into one coordinated, polished, slick production during the last two weeks of rehearsal.

How I Learned to Bump and Grind at Fifteen

by Lindy Sisson, Executive and Artistic Director of the
Vancouver International Children's Festival

Growing up in a small town provides few opportunities to try new things, so when one comes along you learn to dive in and take advantage of it. When I was nine and a dance teacher came to town, my world changed forever.

Judy Calvert was married to a Mountie in High Prairie and for nearly four years I took ballet lessons from her in Peace River. In 1972, when I was twelve, they let me take the big kids' jazz class, and this is where I heard the Beatles for the first time. Peace River's radio station, CKYL (aka squeaky YL) only played country music. Thank heavens my parents were into jazz and big band. My first taste of rock and roll was a little late, but very sweet. All good things come to an end, however, and Judy's husband got transferred and that was the end of the dance school.

While Judy was in town, she also worked with the Peace Players on their musicals and on *Sorry 'bout That*. I learned a lot from her, not just because of her love of dance and her ability to inspire the kids she taught, but because of her attitude to life, which showed in her work. I remember one number she did called Loving You Has Made Me Bananas. Judy had had excellent classical training in Toronto but she was not egotistical about herself or her work, which enabled her to capture the humour of lyrics like, Oh, your red scarf matches your eyes. From her I understood that the chorus line of *Sorry 'bout That* was an extension of the humourous skits it was centred on, and that the numbers worked much better if you didn't take them or yourself too seriously.

This didn't mean I didn't work hard at the job when I was given the responsibility of creating dances for a burlesque revue at the tender age of sixteen due, to Judy Calvert's departure. No one else was willing to try, and since I was the daughter of the producer and one of the actresses, *Sorry 'bout That*

Lindy Sisson in reprise of Joel Gray's role in **Cabaret.**

became a family endeavour. Dad had not only collected comedy skits, he also had lots of ideas for dance numbers. At first I went with these, but later came up with my own ideas. Generally speaking, the classic number from *Chicago* truly applies: you gotta have a gimmick or theme to work with.

The weird part was that I was so much younger than the collection of teachers, mothers or housewives that auditioned and got into the chorus. Overall they were great to me, and they realized that age didn't matter. I had a lot to offer and they had a lot to learn.

The composition of the chorus line was very interesting, as the experience and appearance of the chorines varied greatly. The trick was to create dances that were visually theatrical, with the steps being just hard enough not to be boring, while not making anyone look clumsy. We weren't the Rockettes, nor Vegas show girls, but we presented some really fun dances that added variety to the steady diet of jokes in the revue. Over the years *Sorry 'bout That* developed a core group of pretty good dancers, while others came and went annually.

I was too young to be in the chorus line myself at first, and later, when I was allowed to be on stage, the director tried to bar me from the cast party, as I was not yet of drinking age! All work and no play didn't seem fair to me so I just had to go anyway. To prepare me for public performance among these older women, my mom decided that something had to be done about my stick legs. One of my nicknames was Lindy Long Ankles. So she ordered me calf pads, hip pads and a push-up bra from the Frederick's of Hollywood catalogue. Thinking back on this makes me shake my head and laugh, but it did add to my confidence and make me blend in—otherwise I would have been a dancing twig!

What we found worked best in the revue was a combination of older gems with some more popular musical numbers. The key was to create dances that make the dancers look good. They had to feel comfortable about what they were doing, so we needed to find a balance between the style of the dance we were trying to create and the dancer's ability level. A lot has changed since the Seventies and early Eighties as far as how sexy a dance can be. I would say that our dances were suggestive, but didn't use outright striptease moves. There was indeed bump and grind but nothing similar to the dance scenes from the movie Flashdance.

To give you an idea of the type of music we used, here's a run-down of a few of the dances we did. Some of them had gimmicks like the use of black light in 'Taint no Sin to Take off Your skin and Dance Around in Your Bones, where the girls wore black body suits which had glowing skeletons painted on the back and bikinis on the front. For Peter Gunn, I remember us wearing short trench coats and popping out of big onstage boxes which we rotated to spell out Sorry 'bout That. In Me and My Shadow, the artful placement of lights created shadows. One of my favourites was Cell Block Tango, where the cell bars were made from black stretch elastic so the chorus could easily move in and out of jail.

Other numbers I choreographed included: King of the Road,

Cherry Blossom Lane, In the Mood, All that Jazz, Pink Panther, Mean to Me, Sweet Georgia Brown, Puttin' on the Ritz and something called Bananas. I particularly enjoyed choreographing a reverse strip for my Dad, where he started off practically starkers (in nude underwear) and ended up dressed as a cop who proceeded to arrest the audience for watching an indecent act!

One of my fondest memories of Athabasca Hall, where we performed, was the costume room. It was chock full of all kinds of crazy outfits that were used by different groups and raided for Halloween. I remember watching a high school production with my mother, when she suddenly remarked, "Oh, I wondered where my fur stole had gotten to!"

We had different costume mistresses and seamstresses over the years, but by far my favourite was Lady Anne Gunning, if just for her sheer eccentricity. She was a little old British lady with a heart of gold, who smelled of her beloved farm. One time she made these body suits that zipped up the front, and right before I was to go onstage, the zipper re-opened and would not zip up. So she sewed me in—which made for an interesting costume change afterwards!

Another personal costume faux pas was the night I left my tap shoes at home, but didn't notice until one of the breaks in the show. Luckily I could run home to get them, as the hall was only three blocks from our house. In those days, no one in Peace River locked their doors, following the example of the famous independent fur trader, Twelve Foot Davis, who never locked his cabin door, as legend had it. On this occasion, though, we had a houseguest from the city, who had locked the door while she took a bath. Remembering how my brother Ted used to sneak in and out at night, I climbed in through his bedroom window where the woman was staying—just as she walked in. She totally freaked out as I ran past and said, "I just need my tap shoes and you locked the door and didn't answer my knocks. Don't you know never to lock your door?" The only time I remember actually having to lock the door was when the local newspaper, the *Record Gazette,* announced we were going on holidays. How clever of them to let everyone in town know.

The chorus usually consisted of six to eight girls, depending on the interest that year. We never had men, so one year I opened the show as Joel Gray singing Wilkommen from *Cabaret.* I had a lot of fun, but my mom was nervous as hell because of my age. Another year we had a wonderful actress in the show named Pearl

Baldwin, and I asked her if she'd do a Marlene Dietrich number called Honeysuckle Rose, and she agreed. I rounded up a group of four guys to be her German guard and had them enter from the rear of the hall and proceed through the crowd to the stage. It was a big hit with both the men and the women in the audience.

Sometimes we'd take the show on the road, and on one occasion, Grande Cache hired Peace Players to perform. We couldn't get any other women to go that far, so I ended up as a solo chorus line, tap dancing on a boxing ring—in front of an arena filled with drinking men. I had never been so nervous before a performance and wondered if this was really such a good idea. But the main comics needed time to change between acts, and I was encouraged to feel that everything would work out fine. Thankfully the lighting technician was a close friend who said to me, "Just look out and pretend you're dancing for me and never mind the rest of them." That really helped.

I also got to choreograph the Peace Players' musicals such as Peter Pan, in which I also appeared as Tiger Lily. This gave me a taste for musicals and later on in my twenties, I would go on to work with ELOPE, the Edmonton Light Opera, and with South Pacific and Company. After high school, I attended the University of Alberta, where I got a Bachelor of Arts in Drama and Anthropology. I also joined the dance group Orchesis, which began my interest in modern dance as well as jazz, which up to then had been my passion. After graduation I went to Grant MacEwan College for a year and studied dance full time—a dream come true. Then I obtained a grant to study musical theatre choreography in New York and spent two summers in Manhattan, which was quite an incredible experience. I almost got to take classes with my idol Ann Reinking, but she was called away on a project while I was there. While in New York I was able to see a great many musicals, but I have to say the best dancing I saw was in the advanced jazz classes, which I would watch before or after my intermediate ones. There was phenomenal talent in those classes, but unfortunately, it remained mostly unseen.

After I left for university, Laura Gloor, one of the girls from the *Sorry 'bout That* chorus line took over the choreography. Carol Meyers, the tap dance teacher in town, would often work with them as well. After two years, they decided to fly me in on weekends to work with the chorus again. I did this from 1981-83, and I also taught an adult jazz class whenever I was in town. Other *Sorry 'bout That* choreographers included Sheila Phimester, Susan Marshall and Wilma Watson.

My parents were proud of my progression and ability as a dancer and dance maker, and I was grateful for the opportunity, one that I would never have had if I'd grown up in the big city. My dad found out about an award for choreography and wanted to have me recognized for my contributions, so he nominated me for what I later found out was the Chalmer's Award. The jury must have been pretty amused at this application, featuring old-time jazz dance and musicals by such a youngster, as the Chalmer's is an incredibly prestigious award whose recipients are seasoned modern dance and ballet choreographers.

My career in choreography wasn't award-winning, but it has been incredibly interesting and personally rewarding. The greatest recognition I got was being asked to create a piece for the Women in the Arts Festival in Edmonton, and having one of my works chosen to be featured at the Calgary Olympics University Arts Festival. The last theatre choreography work I did was when I was hugely pregnant with my first child twelve years ago. A director friend of mine was doing a gay theatre work called *Party*, and asked me to choreograph the finale. We'd worked together before on some staged readings and musicals and he knew most of my previous work included humourous elements and was always funky, so he thought I was indeed the best person for the job. I figured I had nothing to lose and a lot of wild rehearsals to gain—providing quite the juxtaposition to my pending motherhood.

I had started choreographing small town non-dancing women in a comedy burlesque revue, and now I brought the house down with a finale in which naked men performed jumping jacks, in a theatre piece about a group of gay men playing a party game akin to Spin the Bottle! What a fun ride "my brilliant choreography career" has been.

Song, But Not Dance Man

by Claude Campbell

My involvement in burlesque turned out to be a very rewarding experience. *Sorry 'bout That* had a successful launch as part of our community celebration of Canada's Centennial year. I started out with the revue as part of a male quartet. The audience was more enthusiastic, even raucous, than people attending the church and community choirs and light musicals I'd participated in before.

I had some initial misgivings, as I thought burlesque was a thing largely of the past, due mainly to what I saw as the puritan element that felt some things in life should not be exploited on stage. In 1944 London, while in the RCAF, I attended a town hall show, which had evolved from burlesque. The authorities shut down the show shortly after, because the star's monologues were deemed to have exceeded the limits for that kind of public discourse.

Claude Campbell of "You'll Get Used to It" fame.

So where does burlesque really stand? The Oxford English dictionary offers some help with its definition, quoted in part here: "imitating derisively; mock serious; derisive imitation; caricature; travesty." Webster's defines the word as: "to make ridiculous by means of take-off; comically misrepresented; and (not so kindly) coarse or ridiculous caricature."

Our show combined straightforward entertainment and burlesque material that satirized and parodied experiences regarded by a certain segment of society as too sensitive or personal to submit to public view. I believe that as long as the subject matter deals with true-life experience, all mocking and caricature short of callous exploitation is acceptable.

One day Hal handed me the musical score for You'll Get Used To It. This was a solo number requiring absolute immobility and an extremely slow, deadpan delivery. My interest was immediately aroused as I recalled attending the Canadian *Meet the Navy* show in London 29 years earlier. John Pratt of Montreal was performing the same song, which had propelled him to stardom. The trick, as Pratt so ably demonstrated, was to mock the glory and prestige of the navy, while appearing to innocently extol it. It was more of an act than a song.

We changed the words to make the show the target, and opening night is still vivid in my memory. In pitch black, I felt my way around the closed curtain to the front of the stage and stood motionless, struggling to keep my knees from shaking, as the spotlight hit me. My costume followed Pratt's example of oversized coveralls that added poignancy to the sad-sack character. At first there was silence, then a growing rumble of laughter as I finally gave the pre-arranged signal to my wife in the orchestra pit and she struck the first notes on the piano, timing the rest of her accompaniment perfectly to allow for the pauses when the audience response was too loud for me to proceed.

Two year later, Hal handed me another script entitled Rapid Robert Rides Again. It was political satire loaded with situation comedy and one-liners, a take-off on Robert Stanfield, the leader of the Conservative opposition in Parliament, often referred to as the best prime minister Canada never had. This show coincided with a northern development conference in our town, expected to draw many government and business leaders. Hal, with his usual business acumen, hoped to sell out one night of the show to these groups. He did, and we played to an audience full of people who might have been strange to the burlesque milieu and perhaps thought themselves more sophisticated in the ways of the theatrical world. The consensus was that they enjoyed it as thoroughly as any other group, and I am satisfied with my own happy memories.

Forgive me if I take advantage of this rare opportunity to tout some successful experience in the distant past. I rejoined the Sorry 'bout That cast to play Edmonton during Klondike Days, where I reprised my role in You'll Get Used to It. The Edmonton Journal critic said near the end of his review, "Claude Campbell is the star of the evening for playing a sort of cadaverous Buster Keaton and assuring us 'we'll get used to it.'" The Bulletin critic's concluding remarks were, "And the man who sings You'll Get Used to It. . . with despairing insufficiency is terrific."

The number of people like myself who have had similar experiences illustrates the value of small theatre groups like the Peace Players in community life.

Running the Gamut

by Julian Packer

"Sorry 'bout that," Hal said, tears in his eyes. Well, he would, wouldn't he? He'd just turned down a somewhat too sober and sombre Englishman for a part in his show. Couldn't play a drunk, you see. A humbling moment. Hal was choked; so was I. It was 1968 and Hal needed curvaceous chorus girls and doddering drunks. I failed on both counts.

But the following spring, Hal mentioned that this somewhat sober and sombre fellow might be capable of performing the part of Ben in the Peace Players' provincial One-Act Festival entry, which was entitled, *The Dumb Waiter*. I did perform, and I won the Best Actor award. So Hal, tearfully, asked me to join the cast of *Sorry 'bout That*, a show that went on to entertain northern Alberta audiences for many years.

There followed a brief interlude. My wife Sue (who had successfully auditioned for the chorus line) and I returned to the UK in 1970, and by 1975 we were proud parents. Hal, at the time doing a stint on the school board in Peace River, phoned out of the blue to say there was a teaching job in town that might be of interest to me.

We came back, and it turned out that the Peace Players were short of chorus girls. It was Sue he needed, but he was willing

(From left) Sue and Julian Packer. Both acted in and Julian directed a number of Sorry 'bout That *skits.*

to take the baggage, too. He paired me with a real actor, Mike Arnold, in a play called *Babel Rap*, which was highly successful at the one-act festival, but thanks to Mike's brilliance, we got invited to perform for Alberta Culture events, too. So what can we learn from this? Hal has a great eye for chorus girls and he knows where to put the baggage.

Being in *Sorry 'bout That* was akin to doing the clubs or rep theatre in England. You learned to survive or you gave up, or if you had no sense of how useless you really were, you carried on regardless. You learned to judge the mood of an audience, learned resiliency when they just didn't get it and wouldn't laugh and you learned how to get off the stage quickly when the need arose. It was a very good training ground, especially for farce. Not bad for musical theatre, either, but definitely not for the classics.

We did try Julius Caesar, actually. Very good for humility, especially if you were the director. Julius had never been so badly
mauled, and that was only what the actors did to it. I wouldn't say
the audience disliked it, but they clapped just to prove that there
was still life in the theatre.

But we did have our moments. Walter Kaasa, head of the
Alberta Department of Culture, in a weak moment for which he
probably never forgave himself, was asked by yours truly (in
Edmonton at the time, trying to learn some choreography) what
part he'd really like to play. "Dracula," came the reply. So do
Dracula the Peace Players did, and fangs for the memory, Walter.

We had another pro join us for that production: George Palmer,
an extraordinary set designer who built to an eighth of an inch. He
was a perfectionist from whom we learned much, including ways
of diverting his attention away from slight mistakes, such as a window not built to his exact specifications. This was in 1979. If he'd
noticed, the window would have had to be rebuilt, even though
we were only hours away from opening. Hal had an actor stand in
front of it every time George made an inspection. Thanks, George.
Thanks, Walter. Great times.

Hal Sisson knew from previous experience what a small-town
audience would appreciate. Others like me took time to realize
that people who worked hard for their money wanted above all to
relax into laughter and be entertained when they came to a theatre.
They appreciated what purists might scoffingly term commercial
theatre: farce, musicals, comedy, satire, local humour, dance and
physical action (which is probably what Shakespeare's productions were like in Elizabethan times) and they became pretty dis-
cerning over the years.

Today's small-town audiences are quite well-travelled, and it's
not unusual to hear local shows compared with the same works
presented in Los Angeles, Toronto or London. Even if we couldn't
compete technically, there's a lot that can be said for enthusiasm,
good delivery, great timing and the kind of punch that burlesque
skits teach actors to give.

Being so far from large centres, the Peace Players became quite
adventurous in adapting, mixing, localizing, cutting and otherwise
tweaking plays to make them fit the local appetite and expose local
performing talent. Giving enthusiastic amateurs, be they dancers,
musicians or wannabe technicians, the opportunity to take part in
a competent production makes individuals and the community

healthier. There are limits, though. We once put a really off-key singer into a parrot costume to drown the singer's voice.

Sometimes institutional theatre frowned, but we still improvised. When Samuel French refused to allow us to turn a BBC play into a musical, we simply wrote our own script and paid the royalties for the music we used. Confidence about this sort of thing began with an analysis of *Sorry 'bout That* scripts—choosing some and rejecting others. Hal was a master at blending one script with another. It made for vibrant theatre, and as a director, few things gave me greater pleasure than someone saying, "I like what you did with. . . " or "That bit was yours, wasn't it?" Or after a recent production, "Who would have thought that you could use Monty Python with Abba and tap dancing and call the whole thing Ray Coone!"

Hal's *Sorry 'bout That* was a great teacher. The skits and sketches have been well-travelled, well-adapted and well-used. A rendition of If I Should Ever Lose My Job performed for an Anglican synod, the Cinderella Bounce re-written as The Parable of the Good Samaritan and Jokes and Kapes performed at I don't know how many bonspiels.

And what fun we had! Peter Pan stuck in mid-flight through a window, Mrs. Markham's door flying off its hinges and an actress who fell off the stage onto the flautist's flute, while singing Why Don't We Do This More Often? Then of course that evergreen *Sorry 'bout That* actor Bill Pobuda who, while playing a drunk, missed the steps as he came down into the audience and carried on as if it was rehearsed. How did he do that as he smiled through his tears? You're right, Hal, I could never have played a drunk.

I See London, I See France

by Jill Cairns

There is a popular myth regarding females, women, girls, broads, dames—call us what you like—who are involved in burlesque chorus lines, that the terms burlesque and chorus line are synonymous with stripping.

I'm really thankful I didn't know that at the beginning when Hal Sisson asked me, "How would you like to sign up for an exercise class that involves dancing?" The next thing I knew, I was on centre stage, scantily clad, in front of an applauding audience.

I thought I kind of had a handle on the roots of burlesque,

although I'd never been exposed to it. And I did realize that the ladies were scantily clad on most occasions. And I believed that feathers, fans and balloons were incorporated in their onstage activities. But burlesque dancers didn't actually strip, did they?

To me, the best part of burlesque dancing is that it leaves something to the imagination. After due consideration and the passage of a number of years, my participation still never ceases to amaze

me. Being part of *Sorry 'bout That* is one of the best things I've ever done. Who'd a thunk it? Not me, that's for sure.

I'm sure everyone has totally forgotten my debut on opening night in November 1983—except me and John Marshall. He took great delight in telling me that I did indeed look as terrified as I felt! Thankfully, he didn't tell me that until about three seasons had passed.

I don't know who recruited Sheila Phimester to choreograph, but I'm damn glad someone did, as it worked brilliantly in the tradition of some mighty fine chorus lines over the years.

Jill Cairns, **Sorry 'bout That** *producer, chorus line dancer.*

I feel very fortunate to have been involved, and to still be involved, in the Peace Players. Never in a million years would I have guessed I'd be doing live theatre. In the city, I would never have had the opportunity to learn so many aspects of theatre from so many talented folks. I would recommend the experience to anyone. In fact, my daughter Megan took her first steps at a dance rehearsal.

What the Hey!

by Bill Pobuda

Coming from cities like Calgary and Edmonton, it was quite a culture shock to find myself in the small town of Peace River in 1974. I adapted the best I could, considering I had very little choice.

In the fall of 1975 I heard about the Peace Players, and, as they say, the rest was history. In the Peace Players I found a bunch of like-minded people who were ready to experiment with drama to the fullest. I first got involved in regular plays. The next year I asked to be part of the show called *Sorry 'bout That* and it was an experience I shall never forget.

First of all, Peace River appeared to be a rather staid community, very connected to its churches. Athabasca Hall, where the Peace Players held their performances, was an Anglican Church Hall. In later years it would be taken over by the Town of Peace River. I feel that *Sorry 'bout That* was a big reason for the change.

I could not believe that a drama group could get away with the material that we used in *Sorry 'bout That*, but I soon realized that whatever the outward standards of a community might be, when it came to this show they seemed to evaporate into thin air. Today, I often think the popularity of the show was due to the connection between audience and actors in this genre. The revue ran for an unprecedented twenty years and was the longest-running burlesque show in western Canada. The content was the responsibility of Hal Sisson, who, at his own expense and on his own time, gathered together some of the finest burlesque material available.

Bill Pobuda, **Sorry 'bout That** *actor and director.*

The actors were amateurs, but they put their heart and soul into every performance. Because of this, the audience responded to them in a way that was like magic. The material was in some parts politically incorrect and anti-feminist, and in others just plain zany and stupid. But then that's burlesque. And when the actors and the audience got their chemistry going, look out.

Sorry 'bout That was the backbone of the Peace Players, its ace in the hole. The drama group flourished in the 70s and 80s and added thousands of dollars worth of equipment, supplies and improvements to Athabasca Hall, to make the Peace Players one of the most successful amateur theatre groups in Alberta.

I have to speak of the many talented people that made *Sorry 'bout That* possible. It seemed that every year, somebody new would appear in the community and want to get involved. There have been many teachers, doctors, lawyers, judges and other professional and trades people, independent business people, housewives and radio personalities. You would wonder how all these different types could get along in the close confines of the theatre setting. But once rehearsal started, we all became a family and there was only one purpose—to put on the best possible show. With so many diverse interests, we were bound to get into some hilarious situations, both on and off stage.

The show was staged in the early winter, and in Peace River that could mean temperatures as low as thirty below. On such cold days, Hal wore his buffalo hide coat and matching fur hat. We were always having trouble with some area of bureaucracy because the hall was old and some considered it a potential fire trap. So the fire inspector would show up to make sure we were running a safe operation—which was always a matter of opinion. We usually packed 230 people into the hall, which was officially rated for only 180. They were packed in tight, and smoking and drinking, so the inspectors had some concerns—maybe that someone would drop a cigarette on the hardwood floor and the building would burn to the ground before anybody noticed.

One evening, a new fire inspector, stationed 120 miles away in Grande Prairie, showed up to inspect the empty hall and wanted to close us down because he felt there weren't enough exits. This was about two weeks before our show was to go on and of course about ninety percent of our tickets had already been sold. Hal approached the bureaucrat with his usual decorum.

"Let's dispense with the bullshit," he said, "and get right to the crux of the matter. Do you know what I do?"

"No, I don't," replied the fire inspector.

"I'm a lawyer in this town, as well as a Peace Player, and you can't just come in here and unilaterally state we're closed down. You'll need a court order for that, so let's see it."

As the fire inspector had recently suffered at the hands of a member of the legal profession during a nasty divorce settlement, hearing that Hal was a shyster only added fuel to the fire.

"No, I don't. I'm the fire inspector and I was brought up North from Edmonton to create safety in all these old northern town buildings."

"From the big city, eh? And what's wrong with this one?" Hal asked. "It's been safe for about thirty-five years or more."

"There's a funnel effect on this side entrance—this larger set of swinging doors funnels toward a smaller door and could cause a people jam."

"For God's sake, less than five years ago your department gave their official okay to this entrance when this part of the building was renovated. They okayed the plans, they can't backtrack on that."

"I don't care. That was then, this is now and I say it isn't proper."

"Well, your department was either wrong then or you're wrong now. So let's go to court and find out which."

They were starting to circle one another, and I knew Hal was starting to lose his cool when he asked the inspector to accompany him into the can so he could stuff his head into the toilet and flush it. At this point I stepped between them to prevent what seemed to be impending bloodshed in the woodshed. I re-established a calmer atmosphere and the inspector left in a huff, swearing we hadn't heard the last of him. I can't recall we ever heard any more about the alleged problem and we went on with the show.

It's a known fact that where there's one bureaucrat, many more are lurking in the wings. This situation was no exception. On the first night of the revue, the liquor inspector showed up and wanted to know where the hot food was that the club was required to have, in order to comply with the liquor permit we needed for each show. Prior to this, it had been the Peace Players' practice to order Kentucky Fried Chicken for those who wanted food—and those orders were supplied with alacrity by the grateful business owner, who might even have been a Peace Player.

The liquor inspector was not impressed. He said that from then on, hot cooked food would have to be readily available on the premises. Now that's a horse's patoot of another colour. The audience likely wouldn't miss the food, but they did expect booze to be served at this burlesque revue, and we needed the liquor licence to get it. With everything else that went on with the production in every part of the hall, how were we going to manage a temporary restaurant as well? At the time we were using the kitchen for the chorus girls' dressing room.

Of course the show must go on. With Hal's ingenuity and knowledge of the law, he came up with a foolproof plan, together with an attitude of: first things first and deal with any consequences later in court—which gives you a second chance to win.

On the first night of the performance, he came storming into the basement of the hall in his buffalo robe with a microwave oven packed under his arm. From his pocket he pulled out a pre-cooked hamburger which he had bought at a local convenience store. He indicated to the bar manager, the beer and booze slingers, the actors and the stagehands that if the liquor inspector showed up and wanted hot food, we were to turn on this microwave and serve him a hot hamburger.

The liquor inspector was smart enough to stay away till the final performance of the show about two weeks later, and he asked for hot food. We madly searched high and low, but we couldn't find the burger to put in the microwave. It was later discovered that one of the actors had at some time eaten it—which was maybe a good thing, because, being a two-week-old burger, it was lucky that the liquor inspector didn't eat it. The show wasn't closed down because of the incident because it was over, but the hot food problem remained. So what to do?

A year or two previously, the Alberta minister of culture, Horst Schmidt, (no, he didn't have a sister called Carlotta) had attended *Sorry 'bout That* with a large group of Japanese officials on a business tour of the province. When they later sent Horst a letter of thanks, they stated that the event they had most enjoyed was their evening in Peace River at the burlesque show. I'm presuming it was because they saw the natives in their natural habitat and were treated as merely part of the scene themselves.

Using this as an example, Hal went to the top and argued the case for a more reasonable approach to the Alberta liquor laws as they applied to theatres such as ours. Why did the Peace Players have to apply every time we wanted to have such amenities, and be granted them as a favour? He was successful and was thereby instrumental in getting liquor laws changed for all drama groups in rural Alberta.

I spent approximately twenty-five years acting, directing and participating in all aspects of *Sorry 'bout That*, and I must say it was a most enjoyable time in my life. For anyone considering putting on a burlesque show, I can't think of a better type of entertainment to involve actors and encourage audiences to just sit back and have a roaring good time.

Peace Players Through the Years

The Peace Players who have appeared in *Sorry 'bout That* are listed in alphabetical order below.

Gordon Abar, Darcy Anderson, Maureen Anderson, Shirley Anderson, Julia Angus, Rick Angus, Anne Arnold, Ginny Arnold, Mike Arnold, Ron Arnold, Anita Arsenault.

Terry Baay, Gerald Baldwin, Pearl Baldwin, Lorraine Ball, Bob Ballantyne, Lee Barkley, Debbie Barnes, Linda Barvir, Jayne Bates, Lynn Bates, Gail Baxendale, Jill Beane, Mike Begg, Jack Belez, Robert Belzile, Myles (Boe) Bennett, Chuck Benson, Sharon Bergeron, Norris Bick, Sheena Billingham, Sue Billingsley, Donna Bjelke, Chris Black, Bev Blakely, Lee Blakely, Lynn Blakely, Terry Blakely, David Blench, Judy Blench, Roxanne Blench, Dennis Blondeau, Edna Bondar, Brenda Bourgaize, Colleen Breker, Kevin Breker, Annette Broatch, Andre Brodeur, Gil Brodeur, John Brotman, Pat Brown, Terry Brown, Dee Browne, Judith Browne, Ralph Bruger, Len Brulotte, Marie Brulotte, Jan Buchinski, Carol Bunnah, Susan Burdeyney, Ken Burkholder, George Byers.

Coralie Cairns, Jill Cairns, Judy Calvert, Lynn Calvert, Brian Cambridge, Chris Cambridge, Malcolm "Ming} Cambridge, Paul Cambridge, Theresa Cambridge, Annabelle Cameron, Claude Campbell, Jean Campbell, Colleen Canning, Susan Canning, Dan Carefoot, Lee Carson, Ron Carson, Kay Carter, Joe Cartier, Phil Cartier, George Caspar, Judy Chambers, Janice Champagne, Phyllis Chodak, Fred Churchman, Chris Ciona, Jim Clark, Pete Connelly, Ken Cook, Cheryl Cooney, Emmett Coughlan, Greg Corcoran, Joan Corcoran, Michelle Corcoran, Barney Cote, Pete Czuy.

Mike Dalton, Evan Dearden, Jennie Dearmer, Debbie Dechant, Suzanne Dempsey, Terry Dodsworth, Coreen Doel, Ian Donahoe, Danielle Douchet, Wenda Douchet, Shirley Douglas, Diane Drummond, Jim Drummond, Dawna Duffy, Rita Duggal, Marcie Dumontier, Gaylene Dyck.

Roger Elder, Sue Ellis, Ray Estetvelot, Dave Eustace, David Evans, Todd Evelyn.

Cathy Farly, Liz Ferris, Sue Fisher, Kevin Fitzpatrick, Jim Fletcher, Orren Ford, Phyllis Ford, Edna Fortier, Deborah Foster, Graham Foster,

Louis Fraser, Carol Freeland,Halyna Freeland, EllenFriedl, Fred
Friedmeyer, Pierrette Friedmeyer.

Jean Gadica, Ken Gall, Wilma Gamble, Betty Gardiner,
Elizabeth Gardner, Sharon Gardner, Rosi Gerochti, Irene Gervais,
Don Gibson, Scotty Gilliland, Chet Gilmore, Kathi Gilmore, Laura
Gloor, Deanna Gorman, Peter Goyeau, Carolyn Grant, Myrna
Grimm, Sheldon Grimm, Sharon Groff, Pauline Guenette, Mabel
Gullion, Shirley Gunning, Lady Ann Gunning.

Glen Haley, Gordon Haley, Andre Hall, Daryl Halstead, Rudolph
Hampel, Vi Hansen, Doreen Hapner, Jenny Hardacre, Garry Harrington,
Lester Harris, Manfred Harter, Elvira Hartwick, Ron Hartwick,
Betty Harvey, Anne Harvie, Dale Hawkey, Suzanne Hawthorn, Ron
Henderson, Louise Herbert, Maureen Herbert, Vicki Hibbard,
Grant Hicks, Marg Hicks, Fred Hiebert, Inez Hildeman, Anne
Hodgkinson, John Hokanson, Rene Hokanson, Robert Hokanson,
Kathie Holt, Jim Hood, Marilyn Hood, Barb Hornbeck,Ken
Horneland, Barry Horner, Keith Howard, June Hughes, George
Humphries, John Hurley, Rosemary Hurley, Arlene Huybregts,
Larry Hyrniuk, Randy Hyrniuk.

Brian Imray, Jen Imray (Gray), Malcolm Imray. Don Jackshaw,
Sylvia James, Lorraine Jegard, Maurice Jegard, Daisy Johnson, Evan
Johnson, Grant Johnson, Lew Johnson, Mona Johnson, Myrna
johnson, Alan Johnston, Hugh Johnston,Ken Jordan.

Ron Kapicki, Barbara Kell, Doug Kinch, Lynn King, Denise Kit,
James Klassen, John Klaus, Lindsay Klyich, Mary Kneil, Cathy
Knight, Wayne Kozak, Enid Krahn, Diane Kubanek.

Jo Laboucane, Clare Lachambre, Julie Lacoursiere, Gertrude

Hal Sisson (fifth from left) and an early **Sorry 'bout That** *cast and
crew, with Don Weaver at front and centre.*

Lambrecht, Hugh Lamont, Keith Langille, Carmen Lavoie, Doris Lavoie, Gerald Lawrence, Pat Leahy, Joyce Lebreque, Phyllis Lehner, Bob Leszczynski, Doris Lockwood, Neill Lorenz, Doreen Logan, Stan Logan, Bev Lowe, Larry Lynch, Faye Lund.

Terry Machan, Harry Maddison, Jeannie Maddison, Alisen Maddox, Ken Maddox, Darryl Mahan, Christine Mailloux, Anne Mandlsohn, Jim Mann, John Mann, Sue Manyluk, Brenda Marean, Steve Marean, John Marshall, Susan Marshall, Bob Martin, Neil Martin, Rob Martin, Jan Masurik, Linda Mawer, Marianne Maykut, Sybil McCandles, Jean McCoy, Bob McDowell, Arlie McGuire, Alice McIlroy, Rick McIntosh, Gerry McKay, Theresa McKelvie, Irene McKeown, Hilda McLaughlin, Lucy McLeod, Scott McNabb, Judy McNally, Tim McRory, Bernard Methot, Ed Mills, Elaine Mills, Margot Milner, Kay Mitchell, Peter Moir, Larry Moore, Steve Moreside, Roger Morgan, Adrian Morris, Marlene Morrison, Peggy Morrison, Chris Motz, Ralph Moyle, Rocky Moyle, Barb Mroczek, Mary Muir, Miles Muir, Pearl Muir.

Louise Nagy, Tom Nagy, Don Napier, Anne Neary, Tom Neary, Dot Nergaard, Don Norheim, Vicky Norheim, Alan O'Brien, Trudy Oetzel, Carol Anne Oickle, Karen Old, Eunice Olsen, John O'Mahoney, Marilyn O'Neil, Betty Onyschuk, Peter Onyschuk, Dorothy O'Sullivan.

Julian Packer, Sheila Packer, Sue Packer, Don Palmer, Val Palmer, Frank Palotas, Glenna Papp, Heather Parenteau, Gary Parks, Stan Parks, Donna Paul, Marie Paul, Dale Payment, Jack Peacock, Pat Peacock, Bob Pekrul, Gordon Pelchat, Linda Pelchat, Elaine Petluck, Will Petluck, Lorne Pettifor, Andrea Phimester,

Peace Players (from left) Jim Robertshaw, Lindy Sisson and Phil Prato in rehearsal for the finale of If I Should Ever Lose My Job, a routine the Peace Players learned from Jerry Gosley.

Graydon Phimester, Laachlan Phimester, Sheila Phimester, Ida Picca, Joyce Pinckney, John Piocyk, Marvin Pipke, Darlene Plastow, Jill Plazier, Bill Pobuda, Phil Prato, Hino Prignets, Celeste Pryde, John Pryde.

Rich Rafferty, Ann Marie Rasmussen, Janet Rathwell, Ira Redwood, Erika Richards, Bob Richardson, Patty Richardson, Carol Riley, Jim Robertshaw, Penny Robertshaw, Bill Robertson, Carol Roch, Neville Rogne, Ann Rognvaldson, Dwayne Rowe, Lynda Rusinek.

Cinde Sand, Ed Scarlett, Darlene Schell, Sheila Schell, Sandy Schroh, Barb Schultz, Sheila Schultz, Janice Scott, Larry Scott, Bill Seaman, Joanne Seaman, Pam Seaman, Ron Seward, Cindy Shaw, Terry Sheasgreen, Bill Sheets, Doug Sherris, Mel Sherris, Janice Shields, Tom Shields, Gary Shilliday, Dave Shima, Norma Shwartz, Len Simon, Doreen Sisson, Hal Sisson, Lindy Sisson, Ted Sisson, Ernie Skip, June Skip, Rick Skip, Karen Smar, Anita Smith, Elaine Smith, Millie Smith, Ross Smith, Donna Sokoloski, Malcolm Sokoloski, Anne Sorensen, Elvira Sorensen, Gottfried Sprecher, Millie Sproule, Millie Sprowl, Peggy Spychka, Nelda Stainbrook, Murray Steele, Debbie Stephen, Mel Stevenson, Elaine Stewart, Shirley Stewart, Lois Stranahan, Lorne Stranahan, Bert Stromstedt, Sharon Sydorko, Darlis Symmington, Debbie Szmata, Wanda Szmata, Amanda Szpuniarski.

Barb Tagg, Geof Tagg, Liz Tait, Al Teichroab, Lynette Thoma, Dan Thompson, Diana Thompson, Linnell Thompson, Jack Thorpe, Roger Throness, Rita Timushka, Pamela Towers, Dorraine Trytten, Gene Trytten.

Debbie Van de Pol, Rick Van de Pol, Jackie Vann, Dave Van Tamelen, Shelly Van Tamelen, Greg Varrichio, Karen Varrichio, Angela Verriour.

Fred Wagner, Edith Wall, Donnie Walker, Ron Walker, Mike Watson, Wilma Watson, Don Weaver, Edith Weaver, Jim Weaver, Karen Weaver, Margot Weaver, Theresa Weaver, Marion Weber, Teddy Weber, Chris Welligan, Chris Wesolowski, Sharon Wesolowski, Ed Whitenett, Eve Whitmey, Reg Whitten, Ruth Willms, Donna Wilson, Jackie Wittchen, Marie Wityshyn, Tony Wityshyn, Marilyn Wiwcharuk, Margaret Ann Wood, Linda Woodhall.

Carol Yaremko, Phyllis Young, Frank Zaborski, Joann Zaborski.

Hal Sisson costumed as Igor for the sketch
Fangs for the Mammaries.

Hal Sisson

is a reformed lawyer and resident of Victoria, British Columbia. His eight published books include the perennially popular short story collection *Coots, Codgers and Curmudgeons*, and a trilogy of novels featuring sleuthing seniors Phil Figgwiggin and Mike Fowler. Sisson, who was born in Moose Jaw, Saskatchewan, worked as a reporter for the *Saskatoon Star-Phoenix*, then ran a law practice for 30 years in Alberta's Peace River region. His goal is "to write more fiction before bucket-kicking time." Readers can visit Hal's website at www.halsisson.ca.

LaVergne, TN USA
21 August 2009
155479LV00002B/65/A